THE
Parents
GUIDE
TO THE
BEST
FAMILY
VIDEOS

THE Parents GUIDE TO THE BEST FAMILY VIDEOS

**Great Movies
for Parents and
Kids to Share**

Patricia S. McCormick
and Steve Cohen

St. Martin's Griffin 🙌 New York

TO JACOB, MATT, MEAGHAN, AND PETER

with the wish for many years of happy movie watching!

ISBN 1-58238-054-6

First Edition: November 1999

10   9   8   7   6   5   4   3   2   1

CONTENTS

INTRODUCTION

Why We Wrote This Book

We love movies. Our kids love movies. And we love watching movies with our kids—sometimes. Unfortunately, over the past five years or so there have been too many instances where the joint movie-watching experience has been a drag. And there were too many more times when we, as parents, grimaced, argued about, or just plain disapproved of the films that our kids wanted to watch. Going to the movies and renting videos was becoming a battlefield of competing tastes and values.

It all came to a head about four years ago when a new film was about to open, and Patty's then sixth-grade daughter, Meaghan, and her friends were burning up the phone lines talking about it—what they would wear, which theater they'd go to, who would sit with whom.

Patty wasn't exactly privy to these conversations, but she just knew something exciting was afoot. Then came the day: Meaghan announced that she and *every single girl* in her sixth-grade class were going to the Friday 6:30 P.M. showing of *Leprechaun*.

Patty took a look at the advertisement for *Leprechaun*—which consisted of the word "Leprechaun," a picture from the movie, and, in the lower left-hand corner, the letter "R." She immediately—much too hastily, she now realizes—said, "No! This is surely not a movie for eleven-year-olds."

The next scene at their home was like something out of a Greek tragedy, complete with wailing, gnashing of teeth, rending of garments.

Meaghan all but threw herself at her mother's feet, imploring her to let her go or she would be the *only* girl left out of this momentous occasion: "Everybody's going! Everybody!"

Later, Patty did what Meaghan first dared her to do and then begged her not to: Patty called someone else's mother. It turned out that the mother of the girl organizing the event (the first girl in the class to get her ears pierced, the first girl to get her own phone line, etc.) knew nothing about the plans. When Patty told the girl's mother the title, she thought it was a St. Patrick's Day fairy tale. But once the mother heard it was rated R, she said she had no intention of letting her daughter go.

Patty didn't call anyone else, she just decided to see what would happen. The next day, the girl with the pierced ears and the private phone line came in and blithely said she wasn't allowed to go. A couple of other kids then admitted they couldn't go either and the great *Leprechaun* expedition died a natural death. By the way, this film—this do-or-die film, this film that was so momentous at the time—was so bad, it closed within a week and wasn't even available at the video store when we recently checked.

Steve's sons, being slightly younger, hadn't pushed to see *Leprechaun,* but the scene was repeated in his house too many times to count, with some of the more vocal experiences involving *The Rock, Con Air,* and most recently *Saving Private Ryan.* It was this last film that reinforced the reasons we decided to write this book. Because even when a film is acclaimed or important or brilliantly made, it still might not be appropriate for children of certain ages or for your family's sensibilities.

In a sense, we wrote this book for ourselves and for our friends, our relatives, and, most important, our kids. Not surprisingly, once we began compiling a list of favorites (ours and others'), it became obvious that we were doing something else: we were helping parents become better consumers of films—not critics (we don't consider ourselves critics either) or film aficionados, but *choosers* of movies and videos. We hope parents will feel more knowledgeable and confident about making film choices and better able to explain those choices to their kids with the help of *The* Parents *Guide to Family Videos.* Both parents and children will be able to share and enjoy the marvelous experience of film.

But Why Should Anyone Trust Our Taste?

This book is intended as a "best of" list of movies on video. And any list of "bests" is, by definition, subjective. So who are *we* that we should be telling you what is great, mediocre, too violent, or too scary? We're probably pretty much like most other parents except that we've probably watched many more movies. (Patty has been writing about movies for the *New York Times* and *Parents* magazine for years; Steve, a bona fide movie aficionado, sees several a week when he's not at his job at Scholastic Inc.) Between us, we screened more than 500 films to come up with the 250 we recommend in this book.

Our kids—three boys and a girl between us, ranging in age from seven to fifteen—are, of course, perfect children. (Did we really say that? Sorry.) They're great kids and probably pretty typical in their likes and dislikes.

This means that our experiences have been pretty typical as well. We've watched classics, the latest popular hits, and junk. We've liked some movies in each category and, sometimes surprisingly, disliked others. We think our tastes are pretty mainstream. But to ensure that we didn't lose perspective, we listened to lots of other people. We checked out their suggestions, listened to their children, and sometimes reconsidered our own reviews. One thing became clear: everybody has strong opinions about movies!

So we made a decision early on: this list of best movies is our personal opinion. (And sometimes we have disagreed with each other!) You undoubtedly will agree with some of our personal favorites and disagree with others. What we hope you'll conclude is that overall, as parents, we're pretty much in sync with other parents. We're not at either extreme: we're not overly permissive or prissy. We're neither elitists nor couch potatoes who will watch anything. We are, we hope, fair.

As you check out our reviews and compare them to your own preferences, you'll come to appreciate our (unintended) biases. You'll understand, then, when to agree completely with our recommendations and when to rely on your own tastes. Our goal is to become your principle source of movie advice. To achieve that, we have to earn your trust. We appreciate your giving us that chance.

How to Use This Book

As you will see, this book is organized into two main sections:

➤ An alphabetical listing of some 250 movies on video. (We say *some* because a few listings mention sequels, related titles, or collections. The total number of reviews depends on how you choose to count.)

➤ Several Top 10 lists.

Each review has three main components in addition to the basic factual data about a film:

➤ A short write-up that summarizes the plot and gives a bit of insight about the stars, the music, the directors, and other pertinent aspects of the film.

➤ An at-a-glance assessment of the amount of sex or nudity, violence, inappropriate language, and suspense/fear factor.

➤ An age-by-age rating of the film using a scale of zero to four stars.

Whether you choose to use the alphabetical listings of the movies or to peruse the Top 10 lists is up to you. You can also decide whether you want to plow through our recommendations from A to Z or category by category. You may decide you like a particular star or a special director, and then view everything that person has made. Movies are a very personal medium. This book is designed to help you decide what is right for you.

Please Let Us Know What You Think

We want to hear from you. We want to know when you agree with our recommendations and when you disagree. We encourage you to keep a record of your own ratings and favorites and to let us know about them. If we've left out a movie that you think should be included, please tell us. We don't promise to include it in the next edition, but we do promise to consider it! Please E-mail us at Moviesp@aol.com.

Thank you in advance for your feedback.

Some Thoughts on Becoming a Better Movie Consumer

Let's start by discussing an issue that we've already touched on—a lesson we learned the hard way: you can't judge a movie by its title. OK, *The Texas Chain Saw Massacre* isn't exactly a subtle title. But who would have thought a movie called *Leprechaun* was a film about a green, four-foot-tall slasher?

Adding to this confusion for parents is that movie studios tell us less and less than they used to. Old films came with a neat little synopsis: "A heartwarming tale about a boy, a dog, and a stranger." Nowadays movies are given the briefest, most inscrutable, sometimes misleading titles. Today, a movie about a boy, a dog, and a stranger is just as likely to be a tale of kidnapping, drug-running, and animal experimentation.

Newspaper advertisements for movies often contain little more than reviewers' blurbs. And all too often these reviewers aren't legitimate reviewers at all, but rather "blurb producers"—individuals subsidized by the studios, whose principle function is to produce quotable sound bites for the studios' advertising needs. If you've never personally read the publication (or heard of the station) that the reviewer represents, then you should assume that the so-called reviewer is really a blurb-producer. And then discount the review. In fact, it is almost safe to assume that the movie is such a stinker that no legitimate reviewer said a decent word about it.

Another problem in choosing movies is the surprise plot twists you'll encounter in kids' films. The best-known example is probably *My Girl*. It starred Macaulay Culkin at the height of his *Home Alone* popularity. Unfortunately, three-quarters of the way through the film, he dies. Or consider *Contact*, an alien movie that turns out to be a three-hour meditation on the existence of God and our place in the universe. Read everything you can find out about the plot or about surprises it holds.

A Primer on Ratings

No one needs to tell you about all the flatulence jokes and other bits of bad-taste humor you'll find in kids' movies. You've already heard them and cringed. Nor do you need to be reminded about the gratuitous profanity you've heard—first at the movie and later repeated by your preschooler. What is the norm?

More than a few times, as we were about to view films, we were confused by the PG or PG-13 ratings the movies had received. The story line certainly didn't justify these "older kids" ratings. When we checked with the producers to find out why, they told us (off the record) that they threw in a little profanity just so a film didn't get a G rating, which is the kiss of death as far as the discerning elementary school viewer is concerned.

So what do the ratings really mean? The Motion Picture Association of America (MPAA) developed its rating board in the 1960s in response to threats of government intervention at a time when films first began exploring controversial story lines involving nudity, profanity, and violence. Today, this board—a full-time group whose only real qualification is that they are parents—considers issues such as theme, language, nudity, sensuality, drug abuse, and other issues in making its determinations. The board is nominally independent, though it is financed by the film industry.

Here, in a thumbnail sketch, are the board's rating criteria:

G: General Audiences. All ages allowed. This film is certified as containing nothing offensive to the board, but it is not a certificate of approval, nor does it signify a children's film. Violence must be at a minimum; no nudity, sex, or drug use is shown.

PG: Parental Guidance Suggested. Some material may not be suitable for children. This label plainly states that some material may be unsuitable for children. There may be some profanity, some violence, even brief nudity. There can be no drug use in a PG film. But the MPAA reminds parents that this designation represents "a warning."

PG-13: Parents Strongly Cautioned. Some material may be inappropriate for children under 13. Note the use of the words "strongly cautioned." The MPAA in its official description of the rating system urges parents to "be very careful" about such films. These films include violence, profanity, and nudity (but if the nudity is of a sexual nature, the film may win an R rating). Any drug use in a film will automatically trigger a PG-13 rating. Repeated use of harsher, sexually oriented expletives automatically triggers an R rating, as will any use of such words in a sexual context.

R: Restricted. Under 17 requires accompanying parent or adult guardian. These films definitely contain adult material: "hard language, tough violence, nudity with sexual encounters or drug use." Enforcement of this restriction, however, varies from theater to theater.

NC-17: No one under 17 admitted. The board gives this label to films it believes most parents would consider "patently too adult." It does not necessarily mean "obscene or pornographic," which are legal terms.

Violence and Kids' Films

While we have little respect for producers who gratuitously throw in a bit of profanity, we're really down on a specific kind of violence that has been developed just for children. It's the *Home Alone* school of violence: violence so cartoonish, it's clearly over the top. And yet it is so realistic looking that, thanks to makeup and special effects, it seems utterly convincing: the actors—real people, not cartoon drawings—look like they have really gotten hurt.

Personally, we find this kind of "humor" sadistic. More important, researchers have determined that this type of violence is confusing to young children who are told not to use physical force to solve problems. Similarly, this kid-movie violence can be damaging to older children who have seen so many paint cans and barbells fall on people's heads that they become inured to it.

Studies show that children who see violent films, from slapstick violence to the kind involving an AK-47, are less empathetic to the suffering of others, more aggressive, more reactive and defensive when they're in a tough spot. These studies found that children who see an abundance of violent films suffer from increased fears and night terrors, and have more concerns over their personal safety than kids who don't watch this violence. Finally, children who watch violent films can develop a callousness toward violence that leads to what researchers call "stimulus addiction": they need to see increasingly scary movies in order to get the same jolt.

Kids love and deserve films where the grown-ups are outwitted, proved wrong, or brought down a peg. Children don't often get that kind of gratification in real life. No wonder it's such a staple and satisfying element of good children's entertainment and literature. But it seems like no children's film is complete nowadays without the grown-ups getting a comeuppance that in real life would require a trip to the hospital.

The "Other People" Issue

You can be as careful as you like about what your child sees, but you are only one of a number of people who have a great deal of influence over what he or she views.

Other kids are the most potent influences on what your child will want to see. There will always be some child who will tell your child about how he is allowed to go to any movie he wants. Such a child may boast about or act out favorite scenes from the last R-rated movie he saw, insinuating that your child is a nerd, a geek, or a baby if you don't allow him or her to see *Men in Black* or *The Big Lebowski*.

Then, of course, there are the parents of these other children. Parents who, for philosophical or less lofty reasons, don't have the same standards or tastes that you have. Parents who, as also happened to Patty's daughter during that very eventful sixth-grade year, will invite your child to a birthday party and show her an R-rated video or movie without asking you, the parent, how you feel about it.

Then there are strangers—ticket clerks and theater managers and video store clerks—who will sell a ticket or rent an R-rated movie to a child who can barely see over the counter, even though the MPAA clearly states that R-rated movies are off limits to children under 17 unless accompanied by an adult.

There *are* theater and video clerks who enforce the ratings. But there are also people in line who will "help out," offering to buy tickets for underage kids turned away at the box office, and then accompany them into the theater.

And finally there are baby-sitters. Make sure your baby-sitter knows your standards. And, while we're at it, make sure your video store knows your policy; you can easily put an electronic block on the movies you do not want your child to rent.

Don't get us wrong. We love the movies. We think films are the most vibrant and powerful art form in this country today. We've seen plenty of R-rated movies that we think are wonderful, and which, *after* we've screened them, we have practically insisted that our teenagers see. But that is parental discretion, not peers or strangers making decisions for our children.

Some Age-by-Age Suggestions

We're going to share some information, gleaned from educators and psychologists, about how children develop, and how they deal with different types of information and stimuli. We hope this will make it easier for you to make decisions about what movies are right for your child.

Obviously, our recommendations are highly subjective. They have to do with content, with tone, with the kind of humor, the vocabulary, how visual the film is, even with its length. But we also based our decisions on developmental data and psychological theory about how children at various ages process what they see on screen and why they want to see what they want to see. You probably know or sense these things intuitively. The following information provides the information you need to back up your intuition and common sense.

TODDLERS

➤ Toddlers are drawn to the bright, quick-moving onscreen images but often can make little sense of what they see. They are, however, wonderful mimics and often love to copy the actions, songs, and words of the characters they see on screen. According to Amy Jordon, senior researcher at the University of Pennsylvania, they find it especially comforting to watch favorite videos over and over again, achieving a sense of mastery from the videos, and developing language skills and behavioral clues from what they see on TV.

➤ The latest research about TV viewing by very young children shows that they can also be easily overstimulated, even bewildered, by the quick-moving images. We recommend very little video viewing for toddlers—who, developmental psychologists say, learn best from a hands-on exploration of the world around them. Short, quiet, slow-moving videos made especially for this age group can be a fun part of your toddler's learning and entertainment but should not occupy much of his or her time. For this reason, we recommend very few, carefully chosen videos for this age group.

PRESCHOOLERS

➤ Research shows that children between the ages of two and five, even up through six, can't always differentiate between fantasy and reality. They fully expect the Power Rangers to be able to come over for a play date or to be able to go to Sesame Street. The more it looks real, the more it seems real. This is especially true when the program involves live actors.

➤ Kids this age can't understand screen devices such as thought bubbles, wavy lines or spirals to indicate dream sequence, or pages of a calendar flipping. Not until they're five or older will they understand that the character went into an imaginary world. Even then, Jordon says, they won't get it unless the device has a visual and auditory component. They need a clear signal, a statement, that this is a dream, a flashback, a fantasy.

➤ Preschoolers need visual cues—clear, unambiguous cues—to understand a story's motive. They love visual humor but will be bored if most of the story turns on verbal jokes or if there are a lot of talky scenes.

➤ They are perceptually bound, which means it's hard for them to pay attention to two competing themes. So they "centrate"—they fixate on one theme, which is usually the most compelling aspect of the action. They pay attention to action, not story. If a story contains some violence and then a resolution or a moral, chances are they'll only remember the violence. Resolution is lost on them because they have been attending to action. (Our advice: if you see that your child is beginning to be scared, don't wait to leave the theater or turn off the video, hoping that once they see the resolution, they'll understand the conflict. They won't remember the resolution; they'll only remember the conflict.)

➤ They respond to appearances. A scary-looking good guy, like a half-animal superhero, is more scary than a nice-looking bad guy according to JoAnn Cantor, professor of communication arts at the University of Wisconsin. For example, E.T. is scary. The Incredible Hulk is scary.

➤ Preschoolers may empathize with animals more than with humans. You may wonder why your child relates to the pet in the story more than to the humans or has a strong fearful or sad reaction to animals in danger. Your child is often relating to the animal's small, powerless status—a condition like her own. But it's not something she can yet articulate.

AGES 7 TO 8

For ages seven to eight, much of the above remains true, but to a lesser degree. Children this age still retain more of the action than the moral and they still empathize with animals. They understand the difference between fantasy and reality, and, says Jordon, they intuitively come to know that there are three types of television shows:

1. What exists, what actually happened: such as the news, or game shows with real kids.
2. What could be real but is not: *Boy Meets World, Party of Five.*
3. What could never be: *Alix Mack, Sesame Street.*

➤ Children in this age group are able to make inferences and understand cause and effect, action and consequence. But they can't carry information in their heads for very long. For instance, if the villain's bad deed is separated too much from the consequences, children won't make the cause-and-effect connection. Similarly, if punishment is delayed too long by a lot of other action, kids will mainly remember the action. Punishment that is delayed for too long will be lost on them. Even though children this age are not so perceptually bound as preschoolers, they recall the action—the violence—more than the resolution.

➤ At this age, kids are just beginning to appreciate the perspective of others. So they may still have difficulty understanding the motives of other characters. We're not talking about one-dimensional bad guy characters in cartoons; we're referring to more complex characters, like an otherwise-nice father who rages when he's drunk. At this age, children need your help sorting through this sort of subtlety after the film is over.

➤ Even though they are ripe for what is called family entertainment— the Disney shows that scared them before, sweet movies like *Mouse Hunt* or *The Borrowers*—it is at this age that children start asking to see adult fare. And why not? Much of the advertising is designed to attract them.

➤ In some ways, children of this age are in a Golden Age. They have the cognitive abilities to appreciate more complex stories and the emotional development to respond to them with empathy, humor, understanding. That's the good news. The bad news is that this era doesn't last long, largely because of the dual pressures of advertising and peer influences. How you decide which adult shows you let them see is very much a matter of personal taste: what your own family's hot buttons are; how ready you and your child are to discuss issues like loss, divorce, death; and societal issues such as drug and alcohol use, corruption, dishonesty. In the reviews contained in this book, we have attempted to identify these issues: a fire, the disappearance of a pet, a grandparent with Alzheimer's disease. We have erred on the conservative side in our recommendations because film is such a powerful medium and children this age are still so impressionable.

8 TO 11/OLDER CHILDREN

➤ Children this age have mastered the medium, know all the devices and techniques, can follow story lines capably and maybe even poke holes in the director's logic.

➤ This is the age when children's interest in TV viewing hits a peak. After this age, their interest in television does not usually increase; academics, sports, and independent socializing take over. It's at this time that their interest in adult fare also peaks. They wouldn't be caught dead watching a kid's show; you have to drag them to G movies.

➤ They want to see movies about kids and divorce, or peer pressure, or adventure, or belonging because these are the issues they're struggling with. They want to see kidlike adults—especially alien fighters—because it arouses their own basic survival impulses. They want to see someone else up against the odds, and they like to be taken right to the edge of scary and survival.

➤ Despite their blasé exterior, two things really frighten them, according to Cantor, author of *Mommy, I'm Scared:* sexual assault and the occult or the paranormal. That's because they're beginning to understand that sexual assault is a real threat in their lives. In regard to the paranormal, there is enough ambiguity in this culture concerning aliens and demons. These supernatural forces become like the witches and ghosts of preschool—nobody quite knows for sure that they're not real.

➤ Most kids this age report having nightmares about movies they have seen, and more than half of them say that their bad dreams and fears were caused by seeing a movie they didn't really want to see (at a slumber party, for example); or by happening to see a film they weren't prepared for. Often, they won't talk about these fears because they don't want to seem babyish or to have their viewing limited.

PRETEENS AND TEENS

➤ Preteens and teenagers understand virtually everything you do (sometimes more), about visual devices, special effects, pop culture language, and the irony of popular humor.

➤ They may act as if they are not upset by seeing violent images or embarrassed by sexual content, and may be reluctant to talk it over with you. (Remember how uncomfortable you felt talking about sex with your mom?) They *are* processing the information, often with friends. It's important to remember that adolescence is a process of defining an identity independent of and outside of the family. Films play a role in self-definition.

➤ They may crave movies as a way of understanding social behavior and sexual mores but may be even more confused by what they see. Still, a provocative movie can be better than a dry "body book." A movie can provide context, story line, and neutral ground for discussing sexual behavior.

➤ This is the age when your child's efforts to get you to let them see older fare hits a peak, peer pressure is the strongest, and their creativity in sneaking into movies and renting videos also peaks.

➤ At this age we tend to be more liberal about films that address provocative social topics, less liberal about films with a lot of sexual content, and even less liberal about films with a lot of violence. That's just our personal bias. We made our decisions based on the intensity of violence, how explicit the sex is, whether each of these is integral to the drama or tacked on for excitement value, and how relevant the story is to our children's lives. Teens and preteens are soon going to be making choices about their own sexual behavior and coming up with their own code of conduct. Movies, even those that present negative role models, help kids decide what that code will be.

➤ Our credo: have faith in your teenagers' reactions to what they see. They are probably becoming savvy, discerning viewers and will find messages, stereotypes, and underlying values in what they see. Give your children credit. Most kids do think about the messages the movies send, provided there is a little downtime afterward. Approach a discussion with the assumption that your child has the intelligence—and exposure to the values you cherish—to be a savvy viewer.

Strategies

Here are some strategies (including the use of this book) to help you become a better consumer of movies and videos.

➤ Read everything you can: newspaper and magazine reviews, the special for-kids reviews by the *New York Times*, Web sites such as *Parents* magazine on-line, and *Parent Soup*.

➤ Say no. If you think a film is going to give your child nightmares, don't hesitate to say no. Although they might not be able to articulate this feeling, children often need and want you to set limits and say no on their behalf. Recommend something else. Stick by your guns.

➤ Say "No, not now. We'll see it on video." This response, offers hope and a face-saving excuse to offer to friends. As you know, images on a large screen in a darkened theater full of strangers can be far more frightening than the same images seen in the comfort of your living room.

➤ Keep a list of acceptable movies handy in your wallet or in your bag when you go to the video store. Be prepared.

If your child sees or wants to see a movie you consider violent, too sexually revealing, in bad taste—or if your child is prone to nightmares—here's what to do:

➤ With preschoolers, leave the theater or turn off the TV immediately. As we said earlier, don't wait for the show to end so they can see what you hope will be the happy ending. Preschoolers will only remember the scary stuff. Hug them, hold them, distract them. Talking it over will probably not do a lot of good. Raising it later is usually fruitless and can send the unintended signal you consider it a big deal, that you're upset about it too, which may only inflame their fears. If your child raises the subject, or it repeatedly comes out in their play—a sign that they are trying to master their fears—then you need to help them understand the difference between fantasy and reality.

➤ Middle school children *can* talk it through. They can exercise logic to show how unlikely it is that a bad thing will happen to them, and can understand that it's just a show. Talk about the actors, the effects, etc.

➤ The next time your children are tempted to see something you consider inappropriate, Cantor suggests that you remind them how it felt to be scared. They may choose not to watch it if they know it will upset them.

➤ Prepare your children for content. If a film involves a mother's death, a divorce, or a pet who is killed, tell them in advance.

➤ Don't belittle their fears. Go along with whatever rituals make them feel safe.

➤ With older children, you will have to make decisions on a case-by-case basis. You may see movies and watch TV shows you'd rather not view, and listen to and show real interest in song lyrics your teens and preteens like. This is the age where a lot of parents abdicate their rights to go to the movies with their children. Our feeling is that your child still needs you. He or she will be better able to handle a movie or a concept he's going to be exposed to anyhow if you're there to talk it over. And, contrary to popular opinion, our experience is that our kids don't mind saying to friends, "I can go with you; but my mother (or father) wants to see it with me."

Conclusion

We would like to leave you with two thoughts:

You have every right to limit what your child sees, no matter what pressure is brought to bear on you. Your children expect you to exercise your judgment, and they will feel adrift if you don't. They may be angry with you in the short run when you do, but a) they expect you to say no sometimes, and b) they will know you care. Whatever you decide—if you lay down blanket prohibitions or if you remove all restrictions, neither of which we recommend—your children want you to care. The best way to show that you do care is to talk about what they see in an open-ended way where there is no right or wrong answer. If you can do this (debate a film without moralizing), you will gain valuable insight into how your children think and who they are—and they will, too.

Which leads to the second thought:

This whole journey, from your child's first theater experience to her first date at the movies, is a process in which she develops a sense of her own emotional reaction to films. All kids have different sensibilities, different tastes, and different needs when it comes to their entertainment choices. Some kids can't take even the smallest amount of suffering by animals, even when they're teenagers; some can't get enough adventure stories, while others find them terrifying; some are undone by anything about death.

When your child is little, watch carefully to see what her individual fears and tastes are. As your child gets a little older, your role starts to change. Your job becomes helping your child develop self-knowledge about her emotional reactions. The most important thing you can do, along with exercising your judgment as a parent, is to listen to your child's responses to movies. Your job is to help her come up with a sense of herself as a moviegoer, a sense of herself that will give her the wherewithal to say, "I don't like horror films," or, "I'm uncomfortable with nudity (or swearing or whatever)." This is an identity that will change over time, naturally.

We have children with utterly different tastes in movies. This makes Friday night video rentals more difficult than you can imagine.

Meaghan, who is almost sixteen, likes everything except action films—dramas, scary movies, and adventure films, you name it. At eleven, she was desperate to see *Jurassic Park*. Patty resisted at first because *she* didn't want to see it. But she finally went—and spent much of the movie with her head buried in Meaghan's shoulder. It was Meaghan who kept reminding her mother that it was just a movie.

Matt, on the other hand, has no tolerance for scary movies. He refused to see *Jurassic Park*, wouldn't rent it, wouldn't go near it when it was aired on TV. "I don't want to see it" was all he would say. He hated *Lassie*—he actually punched Patty in the leg while the PR person at the screening was trying to get her reaction. Matt knows himself well enough to know that that film, and any film where animals or kids are in danger, will bother him. Patty doesn't take him to screenings anymore and she actually recommends films for other eight-year-olds that she wouldn't recommend for Matt.

What we're saying is that you know best. If, after gathering information, you think a film isn't right for your child, it probably isn't. Period. There may be a tempest at first—there may even be wailing and gnashing of teeth—but, like the infamous *Leprechaun* debate four years ago, it will fade into memory.

MOVIE REVIEWS

Abbott and Costello Meet Frankenstein (G)

1948 Comedy
Directed by Charles Barton
Starring Bud Abbott, Lou Costello, Bela Lugosi, Lon Chaney, Jr.

In what many fans consider their best movie ever, Abbott and Costello play a pair of baggage clerks who stumble upon crates containing live cargo: Count Dracula and Frankenstein. Of course, it's Lou who opens the crates, insisting to the dubious Bud that something fishy is going on. Kids will love being let in on the joke as the count repeatedly creeps up to Lou, only to disappear as soon as Bud arrives on the scene. The plot thickens as Dracula tries to borrow Lou's brain for his friend, Frankenstein. This movie has all of the old-fashioned thrills that have been so badly copied in the cartoons: revolving doors, secret passages, and magic potions. Kids will be laughing from the opening scene; they'll love the nonsense, the slapstick, and the silly verbal jokes. You will, too.

SEX OR NUDITY—None. Although Lou gets a swooner of a kiss from his suspiciously pretty "fiancée."

VIOLENCE—None.

LANGUAGE—None.

FEAR FACTOR (SUSPENSE)—Minimal. Even young kids will know this is a send-up of a scary movie.

AGE 0–2		No way.
AGE 3–4	★★	No harm done.
AGE 5–6	★★★★	Right on. A great Halloween rental.
AGE 7–10	★★★★	Ditto. They may complain it's a little tame compared with current cinema fare, but don't be fooled: they'll love it.
AGE 11–12	★★★	*Scream* it's not. But it's a classic, must-see for movie connoisseurs.
AGE 13+	★★★	Ditto.
ADULT	★★★	Good clean fun with great cameos by Lugosi and Chaney.

SUGGESTED AGES—5–12

Absent-Minded Professor, The (No Rating)
1961 Comedy
Directed by Robert Stevenson
Starring Fred MacMurray, Keenan Wynn

The original Disney version of this film is a classic that still holds up, despite the relatively prehistoric special effects. It was originally shot in black and white, but a colorized version is available. Fred MacMurray is the absent-minded professor who accidentally discovers an anti-gravity substance that he dubs flying rubber, i.e., *flubber*. Keenan Wynn is wonderful as the businessman who actually believes MacMurray and tries to steal the substance. In short, a blast from the past.

Compared to the recent version starring Robin Williams, this is refreshing in its innocence and the absence of product placement. This older version is a much better choice.

SEX OR NUDITY—None.

VIOLENCE—None.

LANGUAGE—None.

FEAR FACTOR (SUSPENSE)—None.

AGE 0–2		They're still too young.
AGE 3–4	★★	They can handle flubber.
AGE 5–6	★★★	Prime candidates.
AGE 7–10	★★	They'll see themselves as a bit too mature for this, but will still enjoy it.
AGE 11–12	★★	They really are getting a bit too old.
AGE 13+	★★	Ditto.
ADULT	★★	Enjoy the innocence.

SUGGESTED AGES—3–11

Ace Ventura: Pet Detective (PG-13)

1994 Comedy
Directed by Tom Shadyac
Starring Jim Carrey, Sean Young, Dan Marino

When the Miami Dolphins find their mascot, Snowflake, is missing they hire local pet detective Ace Ventura to track him down. That, with additional kidnapping of quarterback Dan Marino, is the entire plot of this joyously adolescent comedy. If you like the physical comedy of Jerry Lewis or Steve Martin, you and your kids will like the rubber-faced gags and hyperactive humor. We did, in spite of ourselves. There is plenty—maybe too much—scatological and lewd humor, too, just the kind of thing that appeals to the pre-adolescent in us all.

SEX OR NUDITY—Some. The ending involves a gender-bending surprise and a glimpse of lacy underwear; the film opens with Ace receiving a sexual favor from a grateful client. Little kids won't know what's going on (hopefully).

VIOLENCE—Some. A kidnapping and a very fake-looking fight scene with cartoonish brutality.

LANGUAGE—Minimal. There is enough to warrant a PG-13 rating.

FEAR FACTOR (SUSPENSE)—Minimal. It's difficult to get worked up over a kidnapped dolphin.

AGE 0–2		Too young; may even find Carrey's behavior troubling.
AGE 3–4	★	OK to watch if this film is the older sibling's choice, but it's not really for kids this age.
AGE 5–6	★★	Same.
AGE 7–10	★★★	Bingo. They'll love the gross humor.
AGE 11–12	★★★	Ditto.
AGE 13+	★★	They may be getting too self-consciously mature.
ADULT	★★★	Really depends on your gross-out quotient. Carrey's debut film made a fan out of us, even though we tried to resist.

SUGGESTED AGES—7–99

Ace Ventura: When Nature Calls (PG-13)
1995 Comedy
Directed by Steve Oedekerk
Starring Jim Carrey

There is only one reason for anyone to see this movie, and that is Jim Carrey. But that is reason enough for adults and kids alike. It's not his funniest film, but it is plenty funny. In this second of his pet detective films, Carrey's elastic face and rubber limbs are constantly in motion as he is hired to find and rescue a white bat. Unless he can find the kidnapped bat in time, two African tribes will go to war. The plot is ridiculous, the characters silly stereotypes, and the humor largely scatological. In other words, it is the perfect Jim Carrey vehicle.

SEX OR NUDITY—None, though if children are particularly perceptive in this area, parents may have to explain what a virgin is and what Jim Carrey is doing alone under his blanket.
VIOLENCE—Some. One fight scene that is slapstick funny.
LANGUAGE—Some. One curse word.
FEAR FACTOR (SUSPENSE)—Some. With Jim Carrey?

AGE 0–2		No way.
AGE 3–4		Still no way.
AGE 5–6	★★	Enough slapstick to hold their interest.
AGE 7–10	★★★	They'll love it.
AGE 11–12	★★	They'll enjoy it, but know it is not Jim Carrey's best.
AGE 13+	★★	Ditto.
ADULT	★★	There are worse ways to spend 105 minutes.

SUGGESTED AGES—5–99

Adam's Rib (No Rating)
1949 Comedy
Directed by George Cukor
Starring Spencer Tracy, Katharine Hepburn, Judy Holliday, Tom Ewell

Tracy and Hepburn starred together in nine comedies, many of which are considered classics. This one may be the best of them all. Tracy and Hepburn play a married couple who are both lawyers. They wind up on opposite sides of a high-profile case in which Holliday is hysterical—and hysterically funny—as the defendant. She is on trial for trying to murder the lover of her philandering husband. This is both a courtroom battle and a battle between the sexes. Most of all, it is an exceptional treat!

SEX OR NUDITY—Minimal. Lots of talk—witty, fast, and intelligent—but nothing to worry about.
VIOLENCE—None.
LANGUAGE—None.
FEAR FACTOR (SUSPENSE)—Minimal. The issue of justifiable homicide is at the core of the trial.

AGE 0–2		No way.
AGE 3–4		Still no way.
AGE 5–6		Ditto.
AGE 7–10	★★★	Great, but only for the oldest kids.
AGE 11–12	★★★★	They'll appreciate the wit and the chemistry.
AGE 13+	★★★★	They'll love it!
ADULT	★★★★	A classic.

SUGGESTED AGES—10–99

Addams Family, The (PG-13)

1991 Comedy
Directed by Barry Sonnenfeld
Starring Raul Julia, Anjelica Huston, Christopher Lloyd

Who better to represent America's favorite strange family than these wonderful actors? Their style, wit, and evident pleasure in their roles make this a perfectly silly movie for (almost) the whole family. Very young children should stay away, both because the sight gags might make them a bit uncomfortable, and because they just won't get the humor. But for older kids and adults, the thin plot is offset by the good-natured, ghoulish humor.

SEX OR NUDITY—None.

VIOLENCE—Minimal. Cartoons have more violence.

LANGUAGE—None.

FEAR FACTOR (SUSPENSE)—Minimal. Some children may worry that the ghoulish lawyer may actually get away with his scheme to defraud the, uh, ghouls.

AGE 0–2		No way.
AGE 3–4	★	They won't get it, but the costumes and make-up are entertaining.
AGE 5–6	★★	They'll start to appreciate the humor.
AGE 7–10	★★★	Perfect.
AGE 11–12	★★★	They'll appreciate the more subtle humor as well.
AGE 13+	★★★	Still not too old.
ADULT	★★	Much better than the television show.

SUGGESTED AGES—5–99

Addams Family Values (PG-13)

1993 Comedy
Directed by Barry Sonnenfeld
Starring Raul Julia, Anjelica Huston, Christopher Lloyd, Christina Ricci, Joan Cusack

In this sequel to the earlier Addams Family film, a scheming Joan Cusack marries Uncle Fester for his fortune. At the same time, a new member of the family is introduced—baby Pubert—which results in Wednesday (Christina Ricci) being sent off to summer camp, where she exacts her revenge. It is actually quite funny.

SEX OR NUDITY—None.

VIOLENCE—Minimal. A few ghoulish pranks, but nothing to be concerned about.

LANGUAGE—None.

FEAR FACTOR (SUSPENSE)—Some. Joan Cusack *is* trying to bump off Uncle Fester.

AGE 0–2		No way.
AGE 3–4	★	They're still a bit young.
AGE 5–6	★★	They'll appreciate some of it, but little of the subtlety.
AGE 7–10	★★★	Meat and potatoes, or at least fries.
AGE 11–12	★★★	Watch them empathize with the deliciously nasty Ricci.
AGE 13+	★★★	Ditto.
ADULT	★★	Try not to laugh aloud too much.

SUGGESTED AGES—5–15

Adventures of Milo and Otis, The (G)

1989 Animal
Directed by Masanori Hata
Starring the voice of Dudley Moore

A sweet shaggy-dog story about the travels of a kitten named Milo and his unlikely friend, a puppy named Otis. The adventure begins when Milo is accidentally swept down a river in a box and Otis follows, trying to rescue him. Otis chases the box from the shoreline, unable to help Milo. Then Milo encounters a bear cub and Otis saves the day, fighting off the cub and scaring him into a retreat in the woods. As they try to make their way back home, Milo and Otis meet a fox, a snake, baby chicks, and other assorted creatures, but no human beings. The absence of any people, and the comforting presence of an amusing narration by Dudley Moore, is part of the charm of this gentle little adventure story. And this canine/feline road trip ends happily: Milo meets and falls in love with a cat named Joyce; Otis finds love with a pug named Sandra. (By the way, this is a live-action film that used trained animals—no computer-generated images or animatronics. Quaint and utterly convincing.)

SEX OR NUDITY—None. Milo and Otis and their respective mates emerge from a cave after a long winter followed by a litter of kittens and pups, but that's about it.

VIOLENCE—None.

LANGUAGE—None.

FEAR FACTOR (SUSPENSE)—Minimal. Sensitive children may be genuinely worried when Milo goes over a set of gentle rapids and when Otis sets out alone in a snowstorm. Otherwise, it's smooth sailing.

AGE 0–2	★★	May need a lap to sit on during the suspenseful moments.
AGE 3–4	★★★★	Right on target.
AGE 5–6	★★★★	Still young enough to enjoy it.
AGE 7–10	★★	Sadly, they're probably too old to appreciate this film, but may find themselves drawn to the set if younger siblings and parents are watching.

AGE 11–12		No, sorry, they're too old.
AGE 13+		Ditto.
ADULT	★★	A gentle, refreshing adventure. Sweet.

SUGGESTED AGES—2–8

Adventures of Robin Hood, The (No Rating)
1938 Action/Adventure
Directed by Michael Curtiz
Starring Errol Flynn, Olivia de Havilland, Basil Rathbone, Claude Rains

This is the original and still by far the best telling of the Robin Hood tale. Flynn is the classic swashbuckling hero who leads his merry men in battle against the corrupt Prince John (Claude Rains), and ultimately wins over Maid Marion (Olivia de Havilland). Plenty of dueling, wall-climbing, castles, and great scenery. The action is exciting and tame by today's standards, and the only moment that may disturb young children is when Flynn crashes a royal banquet with a deer slung across his shoulders. A must-see!

SEX OR NUDITY—Minimal.
VIOLENCE—Some. This is fighting of the old school: not bloody, but vigorous.
LANGUAGE—Minimal.
FEAR FACTOR (SUSPENSE)—Some. After all, it is an adventure story.

AGE 0–2		No way.
AGE 3–4	★★	They might think it a bit slow compared to contemporary adventures, but have them hang in there.
AGE 5–6	★★★	Terrific entertainment.
AGE 7–10	★★★	Ditto.
AGE 11–12	★★★★	Older kids will really appreciate the quality of the original.
AGE 13+	★★★★	Never too old for this!
ADULT	★★★★	Enjoy!

SUGGESTED AGES—4–99

Adventures of Rocky and Bullwinkle, Vols. 1–12 (No Rating)

1959–61 Animated
Directed by Jay Ward
Starring a moose and a squirrel

Originally made for television, these rather simply crafted cartoons are brilliant parodies of their time. Indeed, watching them now, almost forty years after they were made, they not only put to shame virtually any cartoon made today, it is hard to believe they were made for kids. Yet they never fail to amuse children of almost any age while keeping parents guffawing. How do you describe Rocky J. Squirrel and Bullwinkle Moose? As a classic buddy story? As innocent and buffoon? As treatise on the Cold War? All the above. Along with *Fractured Fairy Tales* and *Dudley Do-Right*, any of the twelve volumes will provide a perfect pick-me-up on a rainy afternoon.

SEX OR NUDITY—Minimal.

VIOLENCE—Minimal. By cartoon standards, almost none.

LANGUAGE—None. Brilliant.

FEAR FACTOR (SUSPENSE)—Minimal. There are villains in this series, but they are hardly scary.

AGE 0–2	★	They won't understand a word of it, but the images are goofy enough to entertain.
AGE 3–4	★★	They won't quite get it, but as cartoons go, this is fine.
AGE 5–6	★★★	They start to get it.
AGE 7–10	★★★★	A terrific cartoon, even if the political references go over their heads.
AGE 11–12	★★★★	Older kids should begin to understand just how brilliant this is.
AGE 13+	★★★★	They'll love it!
ADULT	★★★★	Ditto.

SUGGESTED AGES—2–99

Adventures of Tom and Huck, The (PG)

1995 Action/Adventure
Directed by Peter Hewitt
Starring Jonathan Taylor Thomas, Brad Renfro

This adaptation has what it takes to bring reluctant readers to Mark Twain's classic story: brisk pacing and two appealing teenage stars. You may miss the slow drawl of the original but your kids won't. Here's the story, in case you don't remember it:

Tom Sawyer and Huckleberry Finn, the two biggest mischief makers in Hannibal, Missouri, witness a midnight murder in a graveyard. They take an oath of silence so the killer, the fearsome Injun Joe, doesn't come after them. But when it appears that an innocent man will be hanged for the crime, the boys try to steal a treasure map that will convict the real killer. They lose their canoe, are presumed dead, and witness their own funerals along the way before ending up heroes.

SEX OR NUDITY—None.
VIOLENCE—None.
LANGUAGE—Minimal. Very mild.
FEAR FACTOR (SUSPENSE)—Minimal. Three scenes (a graveyard stabbing, a realistic nightmare where Injun Joe appears to be in Tom's bedroom, and a raft capsizing) are scary, but brief and not overdone.

AGE 0–2		No.
AGE 3–4		Not yet.
AGE 5–6	★★	Some kids this age will find the film scary, but most will have no problem.
AGE 7–10	★★★	Ought to love it, especially if they're "Home Improvement" fans.
AGE 11–12	★★★	Will think it's quaint—a sort-of "Tom and Huck's Excellent Adventure."
AGE 13+	★★	Probably not a good fit.
ADULT	★★★	Sit back and enjoy, and try not to tell your kids it's based on a book you had to read as a kid . . . until it's over.

SUGGESTED AGES—6–12

African Queen, The (No Rating)
1951 Drama
Directed by John Huston
Starring Humphrey Bogart, Katharine Hepburn, Robert Morley

Set in the early days of World War I and beautifully filmed on location in the Congo. Humphrey Bogart won a Best Actor Oscar for his portrayal of a hard-drinking, rough-hewn boat captain. Katharine Hepburn plays a spinster missionary serving with her brother in deepest Africa. When her brother is killed, Bogart offers Hepburn safe passage downriver, away from the Germans. Together they battle the Germans, the elements, and each other. And together they grow, adapt, prevail, and ultimately fall in love. This is a marvelous film!

SEX OR NUDITY—Minimal. Kissing.
VIOLENCE—Minimal. The Germans burn a village, and hit Morley with the butt of a rifle.
LANGUAGE—None.
FEAR FACTOR (SUSPENSE)—Some. They battle the rapids, and, yuck, leeches.

AGE 0–2		No way.
AGE 3–4		Ditto.
AGE 5–6	★	Still a bit young.
AGE 7–10	★★	They'll appreciate the scenery and the adventure.
AGE 11–12	★★★	They'll realize it is more than just a terrific adventure.
AGE 13+	★★★★	They'll love it more.
ADULT	★★★★	You'll love it more.

SUGGESTED AGES—7–99

Age of Innocence, The (PG)
1993 Drama
Directed by Martin Scorsese
Starring Daniel Day-Lewis, Michelle Pfeiffer, Winona Ryder, Miriam Margolyes

An elegant if somewhat slow-moving look at a bygone era and an ill-fated romance. The setting is New York in the 1890s. Newland Archer, a New York blue-blood bachelor, is set to marry May Welland, a pretty if dim girl of impeccable standing. Then he encounters the slightly scandalous Ellen Olenska, a woman who married outside their tight social circle, divorced her husband, and now lives freely, flaunting the conventions of her set. At first it seems that May is going to be a helpless victim to their romance, but she shows unseen wiles in the final scenes, marshaling the strict social code to ensnare her man.

SEX OR NUDITY—Some. The film is erotically charged, but all the action, if you can call it that, takes between characters who are fully cloaked in Victorian garb.
VIOLENCE—None.
LANGUAGE—None.
FEAR FACTOR (SUSPENSE)—None.

AGE 0–2		No.
AGE 3–4		No.
AGE 5–6		No.
AGE 7–10		Probably not, even among the oldest kids in this group.
AGE 11–12	★★★	Let them watch the movie, and then suggest they read the book.
AGE 13+	★★★★	Right on!
ADULT	★★★★	This one's really for you, but your kids can watch along with you.

SUGGESTED AGES—12–99

Airplane! (PG)

1980 Comedy
Directed by Jerry Zucker, Jim Abrahams, David Zucker
Starring Robert Hays, Julie Hagerty, Robert Stack, Lloyd Bridges, Peter Graves, Kareem Abdul-Jabbar, Leslie Nielsen

Entertainment Weekly says this is the funniest movie ever. And while we might quibble with that number one ranking, it is a very funny film. The first of the Zucker brother spoofs—*Hot Shots* and the *Naked Gun* films would come later—it is a take off on *Airport*, countless war flicks, and dozens of other well-known movies, from *Jaws* to *Casablanca*. The problem isn't that it is a bit dated (which it is) or that the movie references will probably be lost on most kids (they will be). The real question is whether it is appropriate for *any* age child. It is filled with sexual innuendo—mild, often hysterical, but very obvious.

SEX OR NUDITY—None, though there are lots of references, and the scene of Julie Hagerty reinflating the autopilot may be the most risqué non-sex scene ever.
VIOLENCE—Virtually none, though there is one silly scene of passengers lining up to pummel an hysterical flyer.
LANGUAGE—None.
FEAR FACTOR (SUSPENSE)—Minimal. Will the plane land safely? What do you think?

AGE 0–2		No way.
AGE 3–4		Still no way.
AGE 5–6	★	Slapstick, but not enough to hold their interest.
AGE 7–10	★★	They'll appreciate the slapstick, but really won't get it.
AGE 11–12	★★★	Not only will they think it is funny, they'll be fascinated by your reactions.
AGE 13+	★★★	Grin and bear the sexual references; they probably already know more than you or they want to admit.
ADULT	★★★	Enjoy, but be prepared to explain a few (off-color) things.

SUGGESTED AGES—6–99

Aladdin (G)

1992 Animated; Comedy
Directed by Ron Clements, John Musker
Starring the voices of Robin Williams, Scott Weinger, Linda Larkin

The plot—a well-worn fairy tale about a princess being forced to marry an evil suitor—is secondary to Robin Williams's star turn as a hyperkinetic genie. This genie, who morphs in and out of character at warp speed, was made for Williams's brand of humor, allowing him to be Elvis Presley one minute and Ed Sullivan the next. Young children may not appreciate all of the genie's imitations, but will be charmed nonetheless. And they'll fall in love with the story's show-stealing sidekicks: a flying carpet that is a fully realized character, and Abu, Aladdin's chattering, co-dependent monkey. The songs in this film are not as strong as those in *Little Mermaid* or *Beauty and the Beast* with the exception of the excellent "Friend Like Me," a fast-paced ballad that allows Williams to show off his dazzling verbal gymnastics.

SEX OR NUDITY—None.
VIOLENCE—Minimal. Only the bloodless, antic Disney variety.
LANGUAGE—None.
FEAR FACTOR (SUSPENSE)—Minimal. The scariest moment is when a cave of treasures morphs into a fearsome face that Aladdin must descend into. There is also a somewhat lengthy period when he is trapped in that cave. Some kids may be troubled by the wild-eyed appearance of the king when he falls under an evil suitor's spell.

AGE 0–2	★	It's not really for kids this young, but if your child is stout-hearted, he or she will be fine.
AGE 3–4	★★★	Could easily become a favorite.
AGE 5–6	★★★★	Ditto.
AGE 7–10	★★★	They'll get a lot more of the verbal jokes, but they're probably too grown-up to go for an animated fairy tale.
AGE 11–12	★★★	Ditto.

AGE 13+   ★   As good as Robin Williams is, it is probably pushing it a bit for this group.

ADULT   ★★★★   There is enough of Williams's brilliance to make up for the thin plot.

SUGGESTED AGES—3–10

Alaska (PG)

1997 Action/Adventure
Directed by Fraser C. Heston
Starring Dirk Benedict, Thora Birch, Vincent Kartheiser, Charlton Heston

Jessie Barnes, age twelve, loves everything about the remote Alaskan fishing village where her family has moved following the death of her mother. Her brother, Sean, fourteen, is bored and miserable and does his best to make Jessie and their father miserable, too. Then their father's small plane crashes in bad weather and the warring siblings must set out to rescue him. At first, they carry their grudge match into the wilderness. But as they encounter treacherous rapids and ruthless poachers—as well as a friendly orphaned baby polar bear—they learn they must put aside their differences if they are to survive.

SEX OR NUDITY—None.
VIOLENCE—Minimal. Poachers shoot at the baby polar bear and he appears to be dead. The plane crash is realistic.
LANGUAGE—None.
FEAR FACTOR (SUSPENSE)—Minimal. The crippled plane teeters on the edge of the mountain for most of the film.

AGE 0—2		No.
AGE 3–4		No. The plane crash scene is too intense for them.
AGE 5–6	★★	May need a lap to sit on but should enjoy it.
AGE 7–10	★★★	Ought to thoroughly enjoy it. May even be nice to their siblings afterward.
AGE 11–12	★★	Maybe.
AGE 13+		No way.
ADULT	★★★	Wholesome if a little predictable.

SUGGESTED AGES—6–12

All Dogs Go to Heaven (G)

1989 Animated
Directed by Don Bluth
Starring the voices of Burt Reynolds, Dom De Luise, Vic Tayback, Loni Anderson

Don't let the title throw you off: this is not a tearjerker about the death of a beloved pet. Well, not exactly. It's about a former career criminal canine, Charlie B. Barkin, who gets rubbed out by an old accomplice and finds himself in heaven. Determined to get revenge, he goes back to earth where he befriends a little girl who has an uncanny knack for picking winners at the racetrack. The friendship between girl and dog is the heart of the story—that, and the short-lived nature of Charlie's return to earth. When it's time for him to go back to heaven, you'll feel your heartstrings being pulled as much for Charlie, who has been redeemed into a good dog, as for Anne-Marie, his bereft little friend. But it may be worth telling yourself (and your children) that Charlie was already dead, right?

SEX OR NUDITY—None.
VIOLENCE—None.
LANGUAGE—None.
FEAR FACTOR (SUSPENSE)—None, really. Death is handled in a matter-of-fact, if wistful, way.

AGE 0–2		Not quite yet.
AGE 3–4	★★	Sure. They have questions about death at this age; here's a movie to help them understand.
AGE 5–6	★★	Ditto.
AGE 7–10	★	Nah, they're too old.
AGE 11–12		Ditto.
AGE 13+		Sorry, double ditto.
ADULT	★★	You'll enjoy the vibrant animation and the quirky character parodies.

SUGGESTED AGES—3–7

Amadeus (PG)

1994 Drama
Directed by Milos Foreman
Starring Tom Hulce, F. Murray Abraham, Elizabeth Berridge, Simon Callow

This Mozart is a far cry from the tortured genius in the dry educational books your children may have read for their research projects. This Mozart, played with exuberance by Tom Hulce, is a bawdy, bad-mannered, goofy genius they can relate to. His story is told by Salieri, the envious court composer who is replaced by Mozart and who, we learn at the outset, may have killed his rival. Herein lies the genius of the film: not only does it give young viewers a courtside seat at history, it does so through the eyes of a man who is cursed to know that he is only good, while his audacious rival is great. The music, of course, is magnificent, an uncannily perfect score to the life of a man who suffered first under an angry, implacable father, and later from his own madness and poverty. Envy, murder, madness: these may not sound like the ingredients for a family film, but believe it or not, this film is funny and tender as well as tragic.

SEX OR NUDITY—Some. The women are saucy, the action suggestive, but never explicit.
VIOLENCE—Minimal. Mild profanity of the eighteenth-century variety.
LANGUAGE—None.
FEAR FACTOR (SUSPENSE)—Some. The final scenes (featuring a nightmarish incarnation of Don Giovanni) may upset some children.

AGE 0–2		No.
AGE 3–4		No.
AGE 5–6		No.
AGE 7–10	★★	Yes, but only for older children in this category.
AGE 11–12	★★★★	Yes, yes, yes. This film poses interesting questions for us mere mortals. It asks us to contem-

plate greatness not from a safe distance, but from a human vantage point.

AGE 13+	★★★★	Perfect for this group.
ADULT	★★★★	*Amadeus* is magnificent, funny, and profoundly sad.

SUGGESTED AGES—10–99

American Graffiti (PG)

1973 Comedy
Directed by George Lucas
Starring Richard Dreyfuss, Ron Howard, Cindy Williams, Harrison Ford

This is the film that not only established director/cowriter George Lucas's career—he went on to make the first *Star Wars* film four years later, and the *Indiana Jones* films after that—but also launched the stars' careers. This is the quintessential coming-of-age flick, with a large cast of appealing characters cruising the streets of a small California town over the course of one night. There is lots of talk about sex, a few mild make-out scenes, one mooning, drinking, and some innocent, 1960s-style pranks. The music is great old rock-and-roll, and the script swings comfortably between comedy and light drama. Because so many people in the cast will be recognizable to kids, and because the angst expressed by the characters rings as true today as it did then, parents and kids will truly enjoy sharing this film.

SEX OR NUDITY—Minimal. Plenty of references to sex, but zip in actuality; pretty much like real life in the early 1960s.
VIOLENCE—Minimal. A fistfight.
LANGUAGE—Minimal. A few curses, but pretty tame.
FEAR FACTOR (SUSPENSE)—Minimal. Do we really worry when Richard Dreyfuss is involuntarily inducted into the neighborhood gang?

AGE 0–2		No way.
AGE 3–4		Ditto.
AGE 5–6	★	Probably won't hold their interest.
AGE 7–10	★★★	Solidly entertaining.
AGE 11–12	★★★★	So this is what it was like in the 1960s; but my parents?
AGE 13+	★★★★	Dead on!
ADULT	★★★★	Relive your youth!

SUGGESTED AGES—7–99

An American in Paris (No Rating)

1951 Musical
Directed by Vincente Minnelli
Starring Gene Kelly, Leslie Caron, Oscar Levant, Nina Foch

Set in spectacularly beautiful Paris, and choreographed to a George Gershwin score, this film won a handful of Oscars. The story is pretty flimsy—Kelly plays an aspiring artist torn between poor, lovely, Leslie Caron and rich, lonely Nina Foch. But the dancing is spectacular and the music magnificent.

SEX OR NUDITY—Minimal. Sexy, but nothing more than a kiss.
VIOLENCE—None.
LANGUAGE—None.
FEAR FACTOR (SUSPENSE)—None.

AGE 0–2		Sorry, no.
AGE 3–4	★	The music and dancing may hold their interest for a while.
AGE 5–6	★★	They'll start to get into it.
AGE 7–10	★★★	They'll love it.
AGE 11–12	★★★	Perfect for this group too.
AGE 13+	★★★	Ditto.
ADULT	★★★	You will love it too.

SUGGESTED AGES—4–99

Anne of Green Gables/Anne of Avonlea (No Rating)
1985/1988 Drama
Directed by Kevin Sullivan
Starring Megan Follows, Colleen Dewhurst, Patricia Hamilton

This outstanding pair of videos makes for exceptional family viewing. Based on the beloved books by L. M. Montgomery, *Anne of Green Gables* tells the story of Anne Shirley, an orphan girl who is adopted by an elderly Canadian farm couple. It traces her journey from childhood to the first pangs of romance. *Anne of Avonlea* continues her adventures as a young teacher who finds that the man of her dreams will also break her heart. Anne, one of the all-time spunkiest heroines in literature or movies, takes big chances and makes big mistakes, but always follows her heart. These faithful, made-for-television adaptations get it just right; each episode is touching without being schmaltzy. Plan a marathon video weekend and rent both the original and the sequel (one of those rare second acts that's as good or better than the first).

SEX OR NUDITY—None.
VIOLENCE—None.
LANGUAGE—None.
FEAR FACTOR (SUSPENSE)—None.

AGE 0–2		Save it for when they're older.
AGE 3–4		Ditto.
AGE 5–6	★★★	If your child is a *Little House on the Prairie* fan, he or she will love these films; otherwise, hold off a year.
AGE 7–10	★★★★	A perfect choice for sleepovers or rainy weekends.
AGE 11–12	★★★	Ditto.
AGE 13+	★★★	They may not want to admit it, but they'll love these films, too.
ADULT	★★★★	Lay in plenty of popcorn and tissues.

SUGGESTED AGES—5–12

Annie (PG)

1982 Musical
Directed by John Huston
Starring Aileen Quinn, Albert Finney, Carol Burnett, Bernadette Peters, Ann Reinking

You know the plot: a feisty little orphaned girl is rescued from a barbaric orphanage by a wealthy benefactor. In addition to a fine cast, this version has great songs and good choreography—rare commodities in children's films. Younger kids may need you to supply historical information about the Great Depression, F.D.R., and that sort of thing. And all kids will want to be reassured that orphanages like the one run by the cruel and tipsy Miss Hannigan don't exist anymore.

SEX OR NUDITY—None. It's implied, but never shown.
VIOLENCE—None. Kids will consider the menial labor that Annie and her friend perform cruel and unusual punishment, but it's not violent.
LANGUAGE—None.
FEAR FACTOR (SUSPENSE)—None. Some sadness, but no real scary scenes.

AGE 0–2		Not yet.
AGE 3–4	★★	Just barely old enough to enjoy it.
AGE 5–6	★★★★	Right on.
AGE 7–10	★★★	Older kids will think themselves too mature for this one, but you may be able to talk them into it.
AGE 11–12		Just too juvenile to hold their interest.
AGE 13+		Ditto.
ADULT	★★★	An old-fashioned song-and-dance show for the whole family.

SUGGESTED AGES—4–10

Apollo 13 (PG)

1995 Drama
Directed by Ron Howard
Starring Tom Hanks, Bill Paxton, Kevin Bacon, Gary Sinise, Ed Harris

On the surface, *Apollo 13* is about a jinxed space mission. But, as you and your child will soon deduce, it's really about a lost vision: the collective national belief that the space program was something to be proud of, and its men and women were real-life heroes. With dazzling verisimilitude and a cleanly chiseled plot, *Apollo 13* tells the story of three astronauts who are nearly lost in space when the ship's oxygen tank explodes en route to the moon. An air purifier is jerry-rigged to keep them alive while the ground crew tries to come up with a way to safely land the damaged space capsule. The technology will strike latter-day viewers as quaint, but the resourcefulness and bravery of the crew is awe-inspiring. The beauty of this film is that it avoids sentimentality while at the same time stirring up plenty of emotion.

SEX OR NUDITY—None.
VIOLENCE—None.
LANGUAGE—Minimal. Fairly tame, all-American type of profanity. Nothing your kids haven't already heard.
FEAR FACTOR (SUSPENSE)—Some. This film is loaded with dramatic tension. Kids who are old enough to understand the stakes are old enough to find it riveting, but not exactly frightening.

AGE 0–2		No way.
AGE 3–4		No way.
AGE 5–6	★	Not really right for them; they can watch with older siblings, but may fidget during key moments.
AGE 7–10	★★★★	A-OK.
AGE 11–12	★★★★	Lift off! Just perfect.
AGE 13+	★★★★	Ditto.
ADULT	★★★★	A good, nostalgic yarn.

SUGGESTED AGES—8–99

Are You My Mother? And Two More P.D. Eastmann Classics (No Rating)

1991 Animated

This half-hour-long selection of video shorts is perfect for the smallest viewers. The title story, *Are You My Mother?* features a lost but determined little bird who encounters a lot of surprises in his quest to find his mother. *Go Dog, Go!* shows all shapes, sizes, and breeds of dogs en route to a big, zany, treetop dog party. And *The Best Nest* tells the story of a couple of birds in search of a new home. Bright little songs and clever narration make this easy viewing. And there's plenty of the repetition and alliteration little children love.

SEX OR NUDITY—None.

VIOLENCE—None.

LANGUAGE—None.

FEAR FACTOR (SUSPENSE)—None.

AGE 0–2   ★★★★   A perfect first video. Buy the books too so your child can see the connection between the written story and the visual one.

AGE 3–4   ★★★   Not too old for it.

AGE 5–6   Will rightly think of themselves as too sophisticated for this one.

AGE 7–10   No way.

AGE 11–12   Sorry, no.

AGE 13+   Ditto.

ADULT   ★★★   You may be surprised at how satisfying these stories are.

SUGGESTED AGES—1–4

Austin Powers, International Man of Mystery (PG-13)
1997 Comedy
Directed by Jay Roach
Starring Mike Myers, Elizabeth Hurley, Michael York

Austin Powers, Great Britain's grooviest swinger-spy of the 1960s, is defrosted after a thirty-year deep freeze so that he can stop Dr. Evil's plans for global destruction. But since Dr. Evil also has spent the past thirty years in a cryogenic pod, his schemes are hopelessly dated. The anachronistic, time-challenged arch enemies (both played by Mike Myers) chase each other around Las Vegas, where Powers's crushed velvet bellbottoms and vinyl boots aren't exactly out of style. The best bits involve Powers's effort to seduce his beautiful assistant (Elizabeth Hurley) with politically incorrect come-ons about free love and "shagging." Despite his mod manners, outdated attitudes, and bad teeth, Powers saves the world and wins the affections of his shagadelic sidekick.

SEX OR NUDITY—Some. The filmmakers go to preposterous lengths *not* to show private parts, which will, of course, keep young viewers on the edge of their seats, hoping. There is also a running gag about a penis-enlarger pump and a hot tub seduction scene with the ill-named Alotta Fagina. All of this is more harmless than it sounds.

VIOLENCE—Minimal. All slapstick, cartoonish gimmicks that are clearly just gimmicks.

LANGUAGE—Minimal. Mild and antiquated. But most children will quickly figure out what "shag" and "randy" mean.

FEAR FACTOR (SUSPENSE)—Minimal. The look of the sets is so overtly phony, kids will know this a spoof and that no real danger is imminent.

AGE 0–2		No way.
AGE 3–4		Ditto.
AGE 5–6	★★	Maybe. Much of it will be over their head, but it's still a fun rental.
AGE 7–10	★★★	They can easily follow the save-the-planet plot and the silly retro humor, although some of the James Bond send-ups will be lost on them.

AGE 11–12 ★★★★   The target audience.

AGE 13+   ★★★★   This group will get even more of the retro references and sexual innuendo.

ADULT   ★★★★   You'll laugh in spite of yourself.

SUGGESTED AGES—8–99

Babe (G)

1995 Animal
Directed by Chris Noonan
Starring James Cromwell, Magda Szubanski

This clever, heartwarming movie tells the story of a little piggy who stays home while all the other pigs are trucked off to market. Bereft and motherless, Babe is adopted by a female collie and her litter of pups on the Hoggett farm. Thus begins an identity crisis for Babe, who comes to believe that he is a sheepdog. Thanks to his exquisite good manners and innate leadership abilities, he *is* a pretty good sheepdog. So good, in fact, that Farmer Hoggett enters Babe in the National Sheep Dog Trials. A combination of Jim Henson creations and live, trained animals compose a convincing cast of talking sheep, dogs, cats, and one very goofy duck. A trio of singing mice complete the cast. A rare children's movie. Gentle, inventive, and never condescending.

SEX OR NUDITY—None.
VIOLENCE—None.
LANGUAGE—None.
FEAR FACTOR (SUSPENSE)—Minimal. There is a momentary threat that Babe will be sent to Pig Paradise.

AGE 0–2	★★	Gentle enough for them, even though much of it will be over their heads. They'll love it nonetheless, especially the singing mice.
AGE 3–4	★★★★	You may end up having to buy this tape, your kids will want to watch it so often.
AGE 5–6	★★★★	Happily, they're not too old for this one.
AGE 7–10	★★★	Ditto.
AGE 11–12	★★	Babe has developed a bit of a cult following among this age group, making it a safe rental as long as you pretend it's for their younger siblings.
AGE 13+	★	A stretch.

ADULT   ★★★★   You'll be pleasantly surprised at how entertaining it is.

SUGGESTED AGES—0–99

Baby's Day Out (PG)
1994 Comedy
Directed by Patrick Read Johnson
Starring Joe Mantegna, Joe Pantoliano, Brian Haley

Parents may find the premise of this film—a nine-month-old baby on the loose—a little hard to warm up to. But kids seem to know that this baby is far from helpless. This baby, a veritable Rasputin in rompers, escapes every manner of accident. He crawls out a window, under a speeding truck, and through a construction site—at one point sitting happily on a steel girder as it swings through the air—all the while eluding a pair of kidnappers on his tail. We were biting our nails at first, but once our kids reminded us it was only a movie, we were OK. They found it hysterical. We found it amusing.

SEX OR NUDITY—None.
VIOLENCE—Minimal. The bad guys get their private parts hit, kicked, and set on fire. It looked like it hurt to us. Our kids said we were being silly.
LANGUAGE—Mild.
FEAR FACTOR (SUSPENSE)—Minimal. You'll be in worse shape than your kids.

AGE 0–2		Why give them ideas?
AGE 3–4	★★★	They'll identify with the baby's lust for freedom and they'll love the slapstick.
AGE 5–6	★★★	Will think this is like *Home Alone* in diapers.
AGE 7–10	★★	Still worth a try.
AGE 11–12		Forget about it.
AGE 13+		Ditto.
ADULT	★★	Just keep telling yourself it's only a movie.

SUGGESTED AGES—3–10

Back to the Future (PG)

1985 Fantasy/Science Fiction; Comedy
Directed by Robert Zemeckis
Starring Michael J. Fox, Christopher Lloyd

This isn't a great sci-fi movie, to use the term loosely, but it isn't bad either. What makes it particularly appealing for kids is that they recognize Michael J. Fox from about a million television reruns, and they think they know who Christopher Lloyd is as well. Lloyd plays the wacky inventor who transforms a Delorean sports car into a time travel machine. Fox, his young friend and true believer, uses the transporter (half accidentally) to escape from terrorists pursuing Lloyd. (Their serpentine chase with guns ablazing is as close as the movie ever gets to violence.) Fox is transported to 1955, where he is convinced that he must introduce the mismatched teenage boy and girl who in the present are his parents, or else he will never be born. The high point has to be Fox's taking the stage at a school dance, and breaking into a hard-rock guitar riff. When the audience silently stares, mouths agape, not sure what to make of this new sound, Fox goes with the flow, telling them, "I guess you're not ready for this, but your kids will love it."

There are lots of references to sex, but nothing is actually shown. There is, however, some cursing.

SEX OR NUDITY—Minimal.
VIOLENCE—Minimal. A shootout that precipitates the escape.
LANGUAGE—Some. There's lots of cursing.
FEAR FACTOR (SUSPENSE)—Minimal.

AGE 0–2		No way.
AGE 3–4		Ditto.
AGE 5–6	★	Still too much for all but the oldest kids in this group.
AGE 7–10	★★	Getting there.
AGE 11–12	★★★	Perfect.
AGE 13+	★★★	Ditto.
ADULT	★★	Not bad.

SUGGESTED AGES—6–99

Bad Day at Black Rock (No Rating)

1955 Drama
Directed by John Sturges
Starring Spencer Tracy, Robert Ryan

For years we used the expression, "It's a bad day at black rock." But we had never seen the movie, so we really didn't have any idea just how bad a day it really was! Don't make the same mistake: see the film, but only with older kids; younger children just won't get it.

Spencer Tracy is a mysterious visitor to a small Western town whose collection of nasty residents (Robert Ryan, Ernest Borgnine, Lee Marvin) clearly have something to hide. We, the audience, figure out what that secret is a bit more slowly than does the hero.

It is a film about prejudice and bullies, which makes it a perfect film for kids. There is plenty of dramatic tension, but by today's level of pyrotechnics, younger children might (unfortunately) see it as being a bit slow.

SEX OR NUDITY—None.
VIOLENCE—Some. A fistfight, a shooting, and the use of a Molotov cocktail at the showdown.
LANGUAGE—None.
FEAR FACTOR (SUSPENSE)—A lot. Moderately high.

AGE 0–2		No way.
AGE 3–4		No way.
AGE 5–6	★	Still pushing it for this age group.
AGE 7–10	★★	A great drama, and this group should just start appreciating this film.
AGE 11–12	★★★	Perfect.
AGE 13+	★★★	Ditto.
ADULT	★★★	Great to share with older kids.

SUGGESTED AGES—10–99

Bad News Bears, The (PG)

1976 Sports; Comedy
Directed by Michael Ritchie
Starring Tatum O'Neal, Walter Matthau

This is the first and the best of what has become a kid's film genre: the story of a hard-luck team that goes the distance. The plot: a beer-guzzling has-been of a coach turns a bunch of misfit Little Leaguers into champions. He has some help in the form of a wisecracking pitcher who has a mean fastball and who happens to be a girl. It's hard to say what's most charming about the film: the corps of wonderful child actors who make up the team (especially young Tatum) or the gentle satire in the dialogue. Whatever it is, it's a winning combination.

SEX OR NUDITY—None.

VIOLENCE—None.

LANGUAGE—None. Mild, very mild.

FEAR FACTOR (SUSPENSE)—None.

AGE 0–2		Not quite old enough, but no harm in letting them watch with siblings.
AGE 3–4	★★★	A solid double.
AGE 5–6	★★★★	A home run.
AGE 7–10	★★★★	A grand slam.
AGE 11–12	★★	Probably a little old for this one.
AGE 13+	★★	Ditto.
ADULT	★★★★	As good as it gets.

SUGGESTED AGES—4–12

Band Wagon, The (No Rating)

1953 Musical
Directed by Vincente Minnelli
Starring Fred Astaire, Cyd Charisse, Oscar Levant, Nanette Fabray, Jack Buchanan

Fred Astaire plays a has-been movie star who tries his hand putting on a Broadway play. The story isn't bad, but it is the dancing and songs that are simply superb. "That's Entertainment" came from this film, as did "Shine on Your Shoes" and "Dancing in the Dark." In short, this is marvelous entertainment for all.

SEX OR NUDITY—Minimal. A sexy dance.

VIOLENCE—None.

LANGUAGE—None.

FEAR FACTOR (SUSPENSE)—None.

AGE 0–2		No, sorry.
AGE 3–4		Pushing it.
AGE 5–6	★★	Sure, why not?
AGE 7–10	★★★	They'll enjoy it.
AGE 11–12	★★★	Perfect.
AGE 13+	★★★	Ditto.
ADULT	★★★	Among the best.

SUGGESTED AGES—6–99

Barney's Great Adventure (G)

Fantasy/Science Fiction
Directed by Steve Gomer
Starring Barney, Trevor Morgan, Diana Rice, Kyla Pratt

In his feature film debut, Barney meets a formidable opponent: nine-year-old Cody, tough guy and cynic extraordinaire. Cody is too cool to believe in Barney, despite all 434 pounds of purple plush singing-and-dancing evidence. Still, the indefatigably optimistic dinosaur won't give up. Then Cody discovers a mysterious egg that takes him, his sister, and her friend on a journey through places both real and fantastic. With Barney's smiling encouragement, Cody finally trusts his imagination and the egg yields its secret.

SEX OR NUDITY—None. Are you kidding?

VIOLENCE—None. Not a bit.

LANGUAGE—None. "Oh, man," is as rough as it gets.

FEAR FACTOR (SUSPENSE)—None. Smooth sailing.

AGE 0–2	★★★	No problem, although it is a little longer than the television segments they're used to.
AGE 3–4	★★★	Perfect. The pacing is brisk enough to hold them. There are also a lot of interactive opportunities (sing-alongs and audience participation bits) to keep them from getting restless.
AGE 5–6	★★	No self-respecting elementary school child would admit to liking Barney, but this film actually has a lot of fantasy elements that might appeal to the younger children in this age group.
AGE 7–10		No way.
AGE 11–12		As if.
AGE 13+		Is this punishment?
ADULT	★★	You may be pleasantly surprised.

SUGGESTED AGES—2–7

Bean (PG-13)
Comedy
Directed by Mel Smith
Starring Rowan Atkinson, Peter MacNicol, Pamela Reed

The National Art Gallery in London tries to get rid of Mr. Bean, a dim-witted security guard, by passing him off as an authority on *Whistler's Mother*, which has just been purchased by a Los Angeles museum. Mr. Bean (a British Jim Carrey without all the flatulence jokes) pops a used air-sickness bag on a fellow traveler, leads airport security on a low-speed chase by going the wrong way on a conveyor belt, and loses his watch while trying to stuff a Thanksgiving turkey. This, however, is nothing compared to what he accidentally does to poor *Whistler's Mother*. And *that's* nothing compared to what he does when he tries to repair the damage.

SEX OR NUDITY—Minimal. A fleeting glimpse of a nude poster of Whistler's sister.
VIOLENCE—None.
LANGUAGE—Minimal. Little and relatively tame, although Mr. Bean learns to give the finger at the end of the film, a gesture that is repeated so exuberantly, it is sure to be imitated.
FEAR FACTOR (SUSPENSE)—None. Worriors will be concerned about Bean's fate, but there is never any real danger.

AGE 0–2		Not yet.
AGE 3–4	★	Will enjoy the slapstick, but may be restless between gags.
AGE 5–6	★★	Will find Mr. Bean's antics, especially his efforts to dry his pants on a rotating fan, unspeakably funny.
AGE 7–10	★★★	Ditto.
AGE 11–12	★★★	Only the most hardened skeptics will be able to resist.
AGE 13+	★★★	Be careful they don't become Bean addicts.

ADULT   ★★★   Hilarious if you're in the right mood. Amusing
                                 if you're not.

SUGGESTED AGES—4–99

Beauty and the Beast (G)

1991 Animated
Directed by Gerry Trousdale
Starring the voices of Paige O'Hara, Robby Benson, Richard White, Jerry Orbach, Angela Lansbury

Great family entertainment. The cast is energetic, the songs witty, the story moving. The plot: a young prince is turned into a beast and is destined to remain a beast unless he can find someone to love him. He meets Belle, a feisty farmgirl who storms the castle to find her father, who is imprisoned there. It's not exactly love at first sight for Belle. It takes the earnest musical intervention of an entire cast of household objects (former servants who were caught under the same spell as the prince). There's a climactic fight where the villagers storm the castle and one of Belle's former suitors (the chauvinist Gaston) fiercely battles the kindly beast. But, like many Disney movies, it ends with a wedding.

SEX OR NUDITY—None.
VIOLENCE—A lot. Sensitive children will find the storming of the castle and the final fight scene too much to bear.
LANGUAGE—None.
FEAR FACTOR (SUSPENSE)—A lot. Belle's father appears to be in real danger at least once, and the Beast takes a frightful fall from the castle parapet.

AGE 0–2	★	Not really for them, but they can safely watch with older siblings.
AGE 3–4	★★★	They ought to love this lively remake of an old tale.
AGE 5–6	★★★★	Ditto.
AGE 7–10	★★	Getting a little old for this one.
AGE 11–12	★	A stretch.
AGE 13+		Not likely. (Although it is, at heart, a love story.)
ADULT	★★★★	You'll be charmed.

SUGGESTED AGES—3–10

Beethoven (PG)

1992 Comedy; Animal
Directed by Brian Levant
Starring Charles Grodin, Bonnie Hunt, Dean Jones, Stanley Tucci, Oliver Platt

A surprisingly funny but predictable film about a family that adopts a runaway puppy that grows up to be an enormous slobbering St. Bernard. Charles Grodin is the perfectly cast grumpy father, Dean Jones is cast against type as the corrupt veterinarian, and Stanley Tucci and Oliver Platt are his bumbling assistants who kidnap dogs for Jones's gruesome experiments. As mentioned, the film is predictable—with Beethoven playing matchmaker and saving the day—but it all works quite well. A confession: as fairly new dog owners, we were convulsed with laughter at the new-puppy-at-home scenes. They truly hit home!

SEX OR NUDITY—None.
VIOLENCE—Minimal. Dognapping, bullies picking on the nerdy son. And a crooked vet who hits dogs.
LANGUAGE—Minimal. The perfect real-life child-parent exchange: "That sucks." "Don't say sucks."
FEAR FACTOR (SUSPENSE)—Some. The dognappers are dastardly; a child who can't swim falls into the deep end of a swimming pool.

AGE 0–2		Not quite for them.
AGE 3–4	★	OK. But they're still a bit young.
AGE 5–6	★★★	Perfect.
AGE 7–10	★★★	Ditto.
AGE 11–12	★★	They may pretend to be a bit too old, but they will howl.
AGE 13+	★	These guys really are too old.
ADULT	★★	Surprisingly pleasant.

SUGGESTED AGES—4–9

Ben-Hur (No Rating)
1959 Action/Adventure; Drama
Directed by William Wyler
Starring Charlton Heston, Jack Hawkins, Stephen Boyd, Haya Hara-reet, Sam Jaffe

This film won eleven Academy Awards, which is still the record. If we had a category in this book for epic films, this movie would set the standard for all others. It is grand, it is biblical (in proportions and content) and it is long (almost three hours). But it is well worth the time. It is, of course, the story of Christ, played by Charlton Heston. We've had trouble over the last, say, forty years, accepting him in any other role. Stephen Boyd plays Messala, Ben-Hur's boyhood friend who becomes a staunch Roman and is thus destined to play a key, opposing role in his friend's life. Purists may take issue with depictions and interpretations—we're no judges—but as a film, it is highly entertaining. The chariot race is, of course, a classic; but there is so much more to recommend this film. Make an afternoon or night of it!

SEX OR NUDITY—None.

VIOLENCE—Some. Cruelty and injustice were all too plentiful in those times; but there is nothing too gruesome in the film.

LANGUAGE—None.

FEAR FACTOR (SUSPENSE)—Some. Drama, but no disconcerting suspense. Younger children may find the scenes in the leper colony disturbing.

AGE 0–2		Sorry, no way.
AGE 3–4		Still too young.
AGE 5–6	★★	The spectacle may hold them a bit, but not for three hours.
AGE 7–10	★★★	They should be captivated.
AGE 11–12	★★★★	Ditto.
AGE 13+	★★★★	Perfect.
ADULT	★★★	It will still hold your interest.

SUGGESTED AGES—6–99

Benji (G)

1974 Animal
Directed by Joe Camp
Starring Higgins (the dog), Peter Breck, Deborah Walley, Edgar Buchanan

This classic dog film about a very smart, incredibly cute pooch who rescues two children from kidnappers is *barely* tolerable for adults. Undeniably, kids love it, but the issue for us is whether parents can stand to watch it. The bottom line is that Benji is terrific enough as a dog to overcome the considerable resistance we have to *Benji*, the movie, for adults.

SEX OR NUDITY—None.
VIOLENCE—Some. This is about a kidnapping, which could be disturbing for younger kids. And there is a gun.
LANGUAGE—Minimal. A "shut up" or two.
FEAR FACTOR (SUSPENSE)—Some. Much of the action takes place in a spooky abandoned house. But there is never any question about whether Benji will save the day.

AGE 0–2	★	Pushing it a bit.
AGE 3–4	★★	Perfect.
AGE 5–6	★★	They'll still appreciate the pooch.
AGE 7–10		No way.
AGE 11–12		Not even if they're nostalgic for the pup.
AGE 13+		No way.
ADULT	★	Do it for your kids—once.

SUGGESTED AGES—2–6

Big (PG)

1988 Comedy; Fantasy/Sci-Fi
Directed by Penny Marshall
Starring Tom Hanks, Elizabeth Perkins, Robert Loggia.

When seventh grader Josh Baskin is turned away from a carnival ride because he's too short, he wanders off, alone and frustrated, to a magical fortune-telling machine. He puts in a quarter, wishes to be big, and wakes up the next day as a boy in a man's body. Somehow he ends up at a toy company where his genuine innocence and boyish creativity land him a job in charge of new product development. Kids will love seeing the way he turns his apartment into a giant playground and the way he breaks office protocol with typical seventh-grade horseplay, nose-picking, and general goofing around. But when the pressures of the adult world—including a bona fide office romance—get to be too much, they'll sympathize with his desire to return home.

SEX OR NUDITY—Minimal. Sex on Josh's bunk bed is implied, but not shown.

VIOLENCE—None.

LANGUAGE—Minimal. Mostly the clumsy, inaccurate seventh-grade variety.

FEAR FACTOR (SUSPENSE)—Minimal. The fortune-telling machine is surprisingly menacing for an inanimate object. When Josh can't find it to reverse the spell, sensitive kids may be truly worried for him.

AGE 0–2		No.
AGE 3–4		Not yet.
AGE 5–6	★★	Maybe.
AGE 7–10	★★★★	Right on target.
AGE 11–12	★★★★	Ditto.
AGE 13+	★★★★	A home run.
ADULT	★★★	You'll be charmed, especially by the now-famous scene where Hanks and Loggia play "Chopsticks" on a giant computerized keyboard.

SUGGESTED AGES—5–99

Big Sleep, The (No Rating)

1946 Drama
Directed by Howard Hawks
Starring Humphrey Bogart, Lauren Bacall

Bogart plays Raymond Chandler's hard-boiled private detective, Philip Marlowe. Bacall is a wealthy client, love interest, suspect—or so we think. The plot is so convoluted that even Chandler had trouble figuring out what was going on. But the dialogue is crisp, the acting smooth, the mood evil, and the screen chemistry irresistible. Will kids be able to follow the plot? Nope, but most adults can't either, and that shouldn't keep anyone away.

SEX OR NUDITY—Minimal. Lots of sexual overtones, but no sex or nudity.

VIOLENCE—Some. A few fists, shots, and plenty of menacing characters, but little violence.

LANGUAGE—None. A bit opaque, but nothing offensive.

FEAR FACTOR (SUSPENSE)—Some. A good melodrama, but nothing yucky.

AGE 0–2		No way.
AGE 3–4		Ditto.
AGE 5–6		Still ditto.
AGE 7–10	★★	Older kids will start to appreciate it.
AGE 11–12	★★★	"Pretty cool" is a typical comment.
AGE 13+	★★★	They may actually understand who is doing what as clearly as you do.
ADULT	★★★★	A classic.

SUGGESTED AGES—10–99

Black Beauty (G)
1994 Animal; Drama
Directed by Caroline Thompson
Starring David Thewlis, Andrew Knott

A touching remake of Anna Sewell's 1877 classic, *Black Beauty* tells the story of one horse's odyssey from owner to owner and from peril to peril. Beauty, captive but always loyal to his human owners, relates how it feels to have a bit placed between one's teeth and how terrifying it is to be tethered to the stall during a barn fire. The anthropomorphized Beauty goes from one master more brutish than the next; finally, just when you think he's had it, his luck changes. What saves this from being an ASPCA propaganda tract straight from the horse's mouth is the care spent re-creating the look of old London and the way the horse is developed into a three-dimensional character capable of such observations as, "We don't get to choose the people in our lives. For us, it's all chance."

SEX OR NUDITY—None.
VIOLENCE—Minimal. Viewers will hear the lash of the whip and see a hand poised to strike but will not see the sting. Beauty and the other horses appear injured (one is even shown being carted off to the glue factory), but the effect is never gory.
LANGUAGE—None.
FEAR FACTOR (SUSPENSE)—Minimal. There are several scary scenes including the barn fire, a flooded bridge, and a headlong ride by a drunken groom.

AGE 0–2		No.
AGE 3–4		Not yet.
AGE 5–6	★★	OK, but not for the faint of heart.
AGE 7–10	★★★	If they've never read Sewell's book they will be moved by this heartrending story told from the horse's point of view. If they're already familiar with the book, they'll appreciate it all the more.
AGE 11–12	★★	Maybe.

AGE 13+   ★★   Probably a little too long in the tooth for this one.

ADULT   ★★★   But you're not.

SUGGESTED AGES—5–11

Black Stallion, The (G)

1979 Animal; Drama
Directed by Carroll Ballard
Starring Kelly Reno, Mickey Rooney, Teri Garr, Hoyt Axton

Warning: the first half of this G-rated film contains a very frightening sequence where a young boy and a horse are trapped aboard a burning ship, then thrown overboard. But don't skip it on account of those scenes. *The Black Stallion* is one of the best family movies in recent memory.

Both eleven-year-old Alec and a mysterious black stallion are restless during a Mediterranean crossing—the boy, because his father is gambling with the ship's owners, the horse because he is frightened and mistreated by his owners. They form a tentative bond and then, without warning, a ferocious storm hits and they are both thrown into the sea. The horse somehow manages to save the boy and the two end up on a deserted island, the only survivors of the shipwreck. Idyllic scenes of their island life together—the horse timidly eating from the boy's hand, the two of them splashing in the surf—are among the most exquisitely photographed and moving moments you're likely to see in a family film. But then they're rescued, separated, reunited, and go to live at Alec's home. There, an old horse trainer (Mickey Rooney, in an Oscar-nominated performance) realizes that the horse is fast, very fast. Soon the stallion, known only as "the Black," is in training for a big race and Alec is weighing in with the professional jockeys. The racing scenes, interspersed with flashbacks of the two of them racing on the island beach, are absolutely thrilling despite the predictable ending of the race.

SEX OR NUDITY—None.

VIOLENCE—None.

LANGUAGE—None.

FEAR FACTOR (SUSPENSE)—A lot. As in any good adventure yarn, the heroes face many perils, including a poisonous snake that terrifies both boy and horse. These scenes are undeniably scary, but in an epic, old-fashioned way.

AGE 0–2		Too scary.
AGE 3–4		Still too scary.
AGE 5–6	★★★★	This story of a remarkable friendship is ideal for children this age, even if they have to close their eyes during the scary parts.
AGE 7–10	★★★★	An unforgettable film experience, but don't be surprised if even younger kids climb up on your lap for the first part.
AGE 11–12	★★★	They may resist it at first, but they'll be drawn in and moved too.
AGE 13+	★★★	Ditto.
ADULT	★★★★	A gem that will leave you wishing there were more films like it for yourself and your children.

SUGGESTED AGES—5–99

Borrowers, The (PG)

1977 Comedy; Fantasy/Sci-Fi
Directed by Peter Hewitt
Starring John Goodman, Jim Broadbent, Mark Williams

As pens, paperclips, batteries, Legos, and socks disappear around the Lender house, young Pete begins to suspect something. But it isn't until he catches a four-inch-tall girl, Arietty, that he learns about Borrowers, the legions of tiny people who live under floorboards and rafters, procuring, appropriating, but never "stealing" things from their human hosts. Arietty's father, Pod Clock, borrows the Lenders' dental floss for rappelling wire, her mother borrows a watchband to hold up her skirt, and Arietty herself uses a credit card for her bedroom door. But the Borrowers' cozy lair is threatened—as is the Lenders'—when a greedy banker, Ocious P. Potter, tries to evict both families from the house. With great pluck and inventiveness, the tiny Borrowers triumph. Wildly oversized stage sets, where household items were reproduced at a 14 to 1 scale, are used to show the Borrowers exploring the Lenders' home, and some scenes were shot using computer animation, but the effects are seamless. An all-around winner.

SEX OR NUDITY—None. Not even a teeny, tiny bit.

VIOLENCE—None.

LANGUAGE—None. Not a speck.

FEAR FACTOR (SUSPENSE)—Minimal. There are some scary moments when it looks like one of the Borrowers is about to be sucked up by a vacuum cleaner or drowned in a milk bottle, and there are some scenes when Ocious Potter gets his just desserts. But it is clear from the start of the film that this is good, clean fun where no one really gets hurt

AGE 0–2		Over their heads
AGE 3–4	★★	No problem, but you'd be better off waiting a year or two.
AGE 5–6	★★★★	Just right. This adaptation of Mary Horton's books is so convincing that kids this age will be

looking for Borrowers hanging from the chandelier when they leave the theater.

AGE 7–10 ★★★★ Ditto. Children this age will delight in pointing out the way real-life items are put to use by the Borrowers. (The most observant will see, for instance, that Pod is dressed in a driving glove, that Arietty's dress is made from a shirt cuff, and that the crash helmets are really walnut shells.)

AGE 11–12 ★★★ Even if they are a bit more sophisticated than their younger siblings, children this age will also be caught up in the adventure.

AGE 13+ ★★ Probably a stretch.

ADULT ★★★★ A delight.

SUGGESTED AGES—5–12

Brave Little Toaster, The (G)

1987 Animated
Directed by Jerry Rees
Starring the voices of Jon Lovitz, Timothy E. Day, Deana Oliver

If you can get past the seemingly silly title, you're in for a real treat. This film takes a clunky, implausible premise and a cast of inanimate objects, and, through sheer imaginative alchemy, creates an action-filled and genuinely moving film. Here's the premise: a little boy and his family stop coming to their vacation cottage, leaving the appliances—a toaster, a vacuum cleaner, a blanket, and others—bereft. Kids, especially preschoolers who often endow inanimate objects with real-life characteristics, will have no trouble accepting this concept. And, because the film-makers have done such a good job creating fully developed characters out of these objects, adults will readily follow suit. The film follows the appliances on their quest to find and rescue the little boy, who grows up a bit over the course of the story. A heartwarming testament of the power of loyalty.

SEX OR NUDITY—None.
VIOLENCE—None.
LANGUAGE—None.
FEAR FACTOR (SUSPENSE)—Minimal. Little viewers, and some big ones, will become quite attached to the little toaster and his cohorts. When they appear to be in danger—notably from a metal crusher at a dump—they may be genuinely upset. You can assure them that everyone is safe in the end.

AGE 0–2	★	They're probably too little to understand it and may be frightened by some of the scrapes that the little toaster gets into.
AGE 3–4	★★★★	A real gem. Be sure to watch this one together; sensitive kids will need a lap to sit on.
AGE 5–6	★★★★	Ditto.
AGE 7–10	★★	They probably won't admit to liking something so corny, but they ought to enjoy it nonetheless.

AGE 11–12		Nah. One look at the title and they'll be out the door of the video store.
AGE 13+		No way.
ADULT	★★★★	Our guarantee: Watching this film with your child is time well spent.

SUGGESTED AGES—3–9

Breakfast Club, The (R)

1985 Drama
Directed by John Hughes
Starring Molly Ringwald, Emilio Estevez, Ally Sheedy, Anthony
Michael Hall, Judd Nelson

Well-acted, well-written drama for teens only and parents, if they'll let
you watch it with them. This tightly scripted film shows what happens at
a special all-day session of detention attended by the prom queen, the
jock, the insecure neurotic, the geek, and the tough guy. At first they're
all determined to have nothing to do with one another, but as the day
wears on, the talking starts and they reveal, little by little, how much
they have in common. By the end of the day, some startling revelations
have been shared and the basis for real understanding has begun. Who
knows, though, what will happen on Monday when they see one another
in the hall.

This film earned an R rating, presumably for its language. But it's perfectly appropriate for teens.

SEX OR NUDITY—Minimal. A lot of talk.
VIOLENCE—Minimal. A halfhearted fistfight.
LANGUAGE—A lot. Authentic, but not offensive.
FEAR FACTOR (SUSPENSE)—None.

AGE 0–2		No way.
AGE 3–4		Ditto.
AGE 5–6		Ditto.
AGE 7–10		Ditto.
AGE 11–12	★★★★	They'll like this film's authenticity and respect for teens, and will enjoy figuring out who the characters' real-life counterparts are at their school.
AGE 13+	★★★★	This is their life on film!
ADULT	★★★	Surprisingly endearing. Refreshing, even.

SUGGESTED AGES—12–adult

Breaking Away (PG)

1979 Sports; Drama
Directed by Peter Yates
Starring Dennis Christopher, Dennis Quaid, Daniel Stern, Jackie Earle
Haley, Barbara Barrie, Paul Dooley

Right, this is that nice film about the bike race. Actually, it is more of a
coming-of-age story about four friends who grew up in the college town
environment of Indiana University but who are non-college townies.
(They refer to themselves, and are pejoratively called, "cutters" by the
college kids—for the rock-cutting tradition of the quarry workers who
also live in the town.) It is also a story about dreaming—of different
countries, different lives—and the fear of trying to live those dreams.
This is a lovely movie; gentle, thoughtful, and funny.

SEX OR NUDITY—None.

VIOLENCE—Minimal. A fistfight.

LANGUAGE—None.

FEAR FACTOR (SUSPENSE)—Minimal. From a bicycle race?

AGE 0–2		Sorry, no way.
AGE 3–4		Ditto.
AGE 5–6	★	Still pushing it.
AGE 7–10	★★	A bit soft for the younger kids, but will connect with the nine-year-olds and above.
AGE 11–12	★★★	They may be put off with the slow pace at first, but will like it enormously.
AGE 13+	★★★★	They will be surprised by how much they connect with the characters and by how much they like this film.
ADULT	★★★★	A really nice film to share with slightly older kids. The relationship between the main character and his parents is at the heart of this entertaining, good-natured movie.

SUGGESTED AGES—9–99

Brian's Song (G)

1970 Sports; Drama
Directed by Buzz Kulick
Starring James Caan, Billy Dee Williams, Jack Warden

Based on the true story of Chicago Bears football star Brian Piccolo, who died of cancer, and his best friend, Gale Sayers. This made-for-television movie is a wonderful tearjerker. A contradiction in terms? Not at all! This film is poignant yet witty, and more about life than death. Set in the mid-to-late-1960s, the friendship between Sayers and Piccolo was an improbable one: Piccolo (Caan in one of his earliest and best performances) was white, an extrovert, and a plugger who overcame modest size and average ability. Sayers (Williams) was black, terribly introverted, and a superb natural athlete. In fact, they were the first interracial teammates to room together. Their rivalry and friendship develop throughout the film, and Piccolo's death, while demanding a full box of Kleenex, is more inspiring than depressing. Don't be put off by the thought of having to discuss death with your children. This is a lovely film.

SEX OR NUDITY—None.

VIOLENCE—None. Even though this is about football.

LANGUAGE—Some. One "a—" and two important scenes involving the use of the N-word.

FEAR FACTOR (SUSPENSE)—Some. There really isn't any question whether Piccolo is going to die; the very first scene makes that clear.

AGE 0–2		No way.
AGE 3–4		They're still too young.
AGE 5–6	★	They're still a bit young, but some kids will start to appreciate it.
AGE 7–10	★★	Aspiring jocks will love it; others will enjoy it as well.
AGE 11–12	★★★	A perfect tearjerker for this age group.
AGE 13+	★★★	Ditto.

ADULT   ★★★   A lovely film.

SUGGESTED AGES—6–99

Bridge on the River Kwai, The (No Rating)

1957 Action/Adventure
Directed by David Lean
Starring Alec Guinness, William Holden

This David Lean film won seven Academy Awards, and though it may be a bit too raw for younger children, it is well worth watching with kids ages seven and older. Alec Guinness plays a stiff-upper-lip British colonel who is the prisoners' senior officer in a Japanese prisoner-of-war camp. The prisoners are ordered to build a bridge, which Guinness insists will be done right. William Holden plays a former P.O.W. who is ordered to destroy it. Yes, there is some violence, but you and your kids will come out whistling the "Colonel Bogey March."

SEX OR NUDITY—None.

VIOLENCE—Some. This is a prisoner of war camp. There is no real torture, but there are scenes of mistreatment. A fair amount of shooting at the end.

LANGUAGE—None.

FEAR FACTOR (SUSPENSE)—A lot. Part of what makes it so good. But it is not gratuitous nerve-rattling, just keenly crafted dramatic tension.

AGE 0–2		No way.
AGE 3–4		Ditto.
AGE 5–6	★	Only if you have to.
AGE 7–10	★★	OK at the older end.
AGE 11–12	★★★	They will appreciate this movie.
AGE 13+	★★★	A classic they'll be fascinated by.
ADULT	★★★	You will too.

SUGGESTED AGES—9–99

Brigadoon (G)

1954 Musical; Fantasy/Sci-Fi
Directed by Vincente Minnelli
Starring Gene Kelly, Van Johnson, Cyd Charisse, Elaine Stewart

Remember how this film made you feel as a kid? You'll be glad to know that it is still enchanting. *Brigadoon* is the story of an American who finds love when he stumbles upon an enchanted Scottish village that only comes to life for one day every one hundred years. The American, Tommy Albright, is engaged to marry a woman he doesn't really love, and finds himself falling in love with Fiona, a Brigadoon lass, after they dance in the heather. Tommy's cynical friend convinces him to go back to New York, but Tommy can't get Brigadoon out of his head. He returns only to find that the village has vanished. Heartsick, Tommy clings to the notion that if you love someone anything is possible. And, indeed, in the last few frames, Brigadoon reappears in the mist and we see Tommy leaving this world to join Fiona for eternity. The 1954 MGM setting may look stagey and the pace may feel slow to kids who grew up on *Star Wars*–vintage special effects, but the worst thing they'll say about it is that it's quaint. *Brigadoon* is still haunting, and seeing Gene Kelly and Cyd Charisse still casts a spell.

SEX OR NUDITY—None.

VIOLENCE—None.

LANGUAGE—None.

FEAR FACTOR (SUSPENSE)—None.

AGE 0–2		No, although if they wake up after you've put this one in the VCR, they'll probably be spellbound.
AGE 3–4		Ditto.
AGE 5–6	★	Give it a try. They'll have no trouble with the magical aspects of the plot even if the romantic aspects aren't exactly their cup of tea.

AGE 7–10   ★★★   A great way to introduce your children to the magic of musicals, especially if they are interested in dancing.

AGE 11–12   ★★   They should be surprisingly enchanted.

AGE 13+   ★★   They'll only watch it to humor you, but it's worth a try.

ADULT   ★★★★   Even if your children don't love it, you will.

SUGGESTED AGES—7–11

Bringing Up Baby (No Rating)

1938 Comedy
Directed by Howard Hawks
Starring Cary Grant, Katharine Hepburn

This movie probably defined "screwball comedy." Directed by Howard Hawks, it has Katharine Hepburn playing a nutty heiress with a pet leopard, Baby. Hepburn sets her sights on Cary Grant, who plays an absent-minded scientist. The dialogue is fast and furious—too fast for younger children—but there is lots of slipping and falling. While there is an undercurrent of sexiness (this is Cary Grant after all) there is no sex. And the scene with Grant in a woman's bathrobe is quite hysterical.

SEX OR NUDITY—None.

VIOLENCE—None.

LANGUAGE—None.

FEAR FACTOR (SUSPENSE)—None.

AGE 0–2		No way.
AGE 3–4		Sorry, still no.
AGE 5–6	★	They'll barely understand it.
AGE 7–10	★★	Getting there, but still probably a bit too sophisticated.
AGE 11–12	★★★	Right on target.
AGE 13+	★★★	Ditto.
ADULT	★★★	A hoot.

SUGGESTED AGES—7–99

Bugs Bunny Classics (No Rating)
1941–48 Animated
Directed by Chuck Jones
Starring the voice of Mel Blanc

So we're pushovers. We love Bugs and aren't a bit hesitant to admit it. All our kids have to do, especially if we're a bit down or grumpy, is suggest "Kill the Wabbit." There are at least twenty-five different collections of Bugs Bunny cartoons, and you can't go wrong with any of them!

SEX OR NUDITY—None.

VIOLENCE—Tons—but most kids have no problem understanding it is cartoon violence of a benign sort.

LANGUAGE—None.

FEAR FACTOR (SUSPENSE)—Minimal. Children ages two or younger may be a bit afraid the very first time they experience Bugs and friends.

AGE 0–2	★★	Think of it as an acquired taste worth acquiring.
AGE 3–4	★★★★	Perfect.
AGE 5–6	★★★★	Still perfect.
AGE 7–10	★★★★	Ditto.
AGE 11–12	★★★★	They'll protest for about a minute that they're too old.
AGE 13+	★★★	They may be a bit too jaded for classic cartoons, but will still enjoy them.
ADULT	★★★★	Try not to laugh louder than your kids.

SUGGESTED AGES—2–99

Butch Cassidy and the Sundance Kid (PG)

1969 Western
Directed by George Roy Hill
Starring Paul Newman, Robert Redford, Katharine Ross

Paul Newman and Robert Redford reinvigorated the "buddy" movie with this amusing, stylish film about bank and railroad robbers in the American West at the turn of the century. After their various robberies make them wanted men, they flee to Bolivia with schoolteacher Katharine Ross accompanying them and adding an undercurrent of sexual tension. The film is both dramatic and funny, with a plot most kids can follow. A modern classic that's easy to watch, with a line we often quote, "Who are those guys?"

SEX OR NUDITY—Minimal.

VIOLENCE—Some. Plenty of gunplay, a few fistfights; and of course that slow-motion ending.

LANGUAGE—None.

FEAR FACTOR (SUSPENSE)—Minimal. More funny than scary.

AGE 0–2		Sorry, no way.
AGE 3–4	★	Lots of horses, explosions, but too violent.
AGE 5–6	★★	A stretch for this group too.
AGE 7–10	★★★	They'll love it.
AGE 11–12	★★★	Ditto.
AGE 13+	★★★★	They'll probably understand why this film *made* Newman and Redford.
ADULT	★★★★	Relive the pleasure.

SUGGESTED AGES—8–99

Captains Courageous (No Rating)

1937 Action/Adventure Drama
Directed by Victor Fleming
Starring Spencer Tracy, Freddie Bartholomew, Lionel Barrymore, Mickey Rooney, Melvyn Douglas

Spencer Tracy won a Best Actor Oscar for his portrayal of a Portuguese fisherman who befriends an obnoxious boy whom he saves after the boy falls overboard an ocean liner. Freddie Bartholomew, who plays the boy, was a major child star of the era, and is perfect as the spoiled lad who is kicked out of school and taken on a luxury liner by his wealthy father in an attempt at getting closer to his son. After being rescued by Tracy, Bartholomew must spend three months on board as the crusty skipper has no intention of returning to port and losing either his catch or income. Slowly, Bartholomew is befriended by the skipper's son (Rooney), and an extraordinary transformation takes place. A wonderful film, but be forewarned: a key character dies, and there won't be a dry eye in the house.

SEX OR NUDITY—None.

VIOLENCE—Some. The sea is rough, the captain tough.

LANGUAGE—Minimal.

FEAR FACTOR (SUSPENSE)—Some. Between the boy being swept overboard and a main character dying, some children may find this film quite disturbing.

AGE 0–2		No way.
AGE 3–4		Still too tough for this group.
AGE 5–6		Still pushing it.
AGE 7–10	★★★	Perfect, but stay close.
AGE 11–12	★★★★	Ditto.
AGE 13+	★★★★	Not too sappy for older kids.
ADULT	★★★	A terrific film.

SUGGESTED AGES—8–99

Casablanca (No Rating)

1942 Drama
Directed by Michael Curtiz
Starring Humphrey Bogart, Ingrid Bergman, Claude Rains, Dooley Wilson, Paul Henreid, Conrad Veidt

A kiss is but a kiss. . . . Happily, children seem to appreciate this great film almost as much as adults do. Maybe kids just sense that parents think it's great, and actually respect that. Younger children don't quite understand the plot, the setting, or the interplay, but older kids will at least try to stay with it. Let them try, and enjoy the film together.

Oh yes, there is a plot, and it does provide a great starting point for family discussions: Humphrey Bogart plays Rick, the owner of the café/nightclub in Casablanca, a major transit point for people trying to escape from Europe in the early days of World Way II. The Nazis, led by the dastardly Conrad Veidt, control the city, and are determined to recapture resistance leader Paul Henreid, who has escaped from a Nazi concentration camp. Where does Ingrid Bergman fit in? By now everyone, even people who haven't seen the film (and we hear there are one or two) knows that she links them all together and helps Bogart understand who he really is and what he stands for.

SEX OR NUDITY—None. Here's looking at you, kid.
VIOLENCE—Minimal. Peter Lorre is shot near the beginning, and there is that second key shooting at the end.
LANGUAGE—None. Brilliant.
FEAR FACTOR (SUSPENSE)—A lot, but it's the best kind of tension: Will the good guys win? Which man will Ingrid Bergman go off with?

AGE 0–2		Sorry, no.
AGE 3–4		Still no way.
AGE 5–6		This is even pushing it.
AGE 7–10	★★	They'll start to get it
AGE 11–12	★★★★	They'll actually appreciate it.
AGE 13+	★★★★	Insist on it, and then be prepared to hear them singing "As Time Goes By" for about a week.

ADULT   ★★★★   One of the great ones.

SUGGESTED AGES—10–99

Casper (PG)

1995 Fantasy/Science Fiction
Directed by Brad Silberling
Starring Christina Ricci, Bill Pullman, Kathy Moriarity, Eric Idle

Casper is the same friendly ghost you remember from the cartoon series, but he has been enhanced with special effects and given a trio of ghastly, ghostly uncles. The uncles do their best to scare twelve-year-old Kat and her father out of their haunted mansion, but the lonely, lovable Casper sees Kat as a kindred spirit and befriends her. A couple of evil gold diggers who want the mansion for its buried treasure, and a bizarre invention that brings ghosts back to life complicate the plot a bit, but even young kids will be able to follow it with your help. This film resembles a fun-house ride. Sensitive kids will find parts of it quite scary; thrill seekers will love it. Casper also raises thorny questions about the afterlife. Still, it will cast its spell on believers and skeptics alike with its tender treatment of ghosts and angels.

SEX OR NUDITY—None.

VIOLENCE—Minimal. Mostly the cartoonish, slapstick variety. You can safely forewarn kids that the rowdy uncles mean no harm and that they turn out to be OK in the end.

LANGUAGE—Some gratuitous profanity.

FEAR FACTOR (SUSPENSE)—None.

AGE 0–2		No.
AGE 3–4		Too scary, too complicated.
AGE 5–6	★★	Only for the stout-hearted.
AGE 7–10	★★★★	Dead on; will find it frightfully fun.
AGE 11–12	★★★	They'll like it, especially the special effects.
AGE 13+	★★	There's a ghost of a chance.
ADULT	★★★★	Parents will appreciate guest appearances by exorcist Father Guido Sarducci and ghostbuster Dan Aykroyd.

SUGGESTED AGES—7–99

Charade (No Rating)

1963 Comedy; Drama
Directed by Stanley Donen
Starring Cary Grant, Audrey Hepburn, Walter Matthau, James Coburn,
George Kennedy

Just as we were going to press, we realized that the review for *Charade* was missing; somehow it had gotten deleted from our computer disk. We thought it important enough to jump through the hoops to include it. *Charade* is a wonderfully entertaining film. Many people think it is a Hitchcock film (but it's not) because it has that unique combination of suspense and comedy. The film opens with a man being murdered on a train—the only real violence in the movie The man turns out to be Audrey Hepburn's husband. Some very nasty fellows (who may be responsible for the murder) believe that the deceased has bequeathed to the very confused widow something of value that they believe they are entitled to. Confused? Don't be. The twists and turns are surprising but very easy to follow. But you will keep wondering who is a good guy and who isn't.

SEX OR NUDITY—Minimal. A kiss and some silly pass-the-orange dancing.
VIOLENCE—Some. In addition to the opening murder on a train, there are several fights and a wonderful test of a corpse to make sure he is dead.
LANGUAGE—Minimal. Nothing to worry about.
FEAR FACTOR (SUSPENSE)—Lots of fun tension.

AGE 0–2		No way.
AGE 3–4		Ditto.
AGE 5–6		They still won't get it.
AGE 7–10	★★	They may be a bit confused.
AGE 11–12	★★★	They'll enjoy it.
AGE 13+	★★★	Perfect entertainment.
ADULT	★★★★	If you haven't seen this, you'll enjoy yourself; if you have you'll enjoy it all over again.

SUGGESTED AGES—9–99

Chariots of Fire (PG)

1981 Sports; Drama
Directed by Hugh Hudson
Starring Ben Cross, Ian Charleson, Nigel Havers, Ian Holm, Sir John Gielgud

A stirring tale of young athletes in pursuit of glory for God, country, and self, *Chariots of Fire* is based on the true stories of several members of the 1924 British Olympic team. The two key characters, Harold Abraham, a Jewish scholar-athlete, and Eric Liddell, a son of Scottish missionaries, serve as counterpoint for each other. Abraham is driven, prickly, sometimes egotistical; Liddell is calm, easygoing, almost radiant. But both are out to earn honor and to defend their religion by winning. This story is about much more than running (although the running scenes are both beautiful and inspiring). It's about class, competition, religious devotion, and patriotism. Memorable music by the Greek composer Vangelis.

SEX OR NUDITY—Minimal.

VIOLENCE—None.

LANGUAGE—Minimal.

FEAR FACTOR (SUSPENSE)—None. Only the heart-stopping suspense of wondering who will win.

AGE 0–2		No way.
AGE 3–4		No.
AGE 5–6		Still no.
AGE 7–10	★	Sophisticated, thoughtful kids will enjoy it. They will need your help with some of the historical context and Britishisms.
AGE 11–12	★★★	A bit intellectual, but still moving
AGE 13+	★★★★	A gold medal.
ADULT	★★★★	Ditto.

SUGGESTED AGES—11–99

Charlotte's Web (G)

1973 Animated
Directed by Charles Nichols
Starring the voices of Debbie Reynolds, Henry Gibson, Paul Lynde, Agnes Moorehead

Have at least two boxes of Kleenex handy when you watch this charming animated adaptation of E. B. White's classic novel (one for your child and the other for you). On the surface it is the story of a resourceful spider's efforts to keep her pig friend from being turned into bacon. Of course it is about much more than that: friendship, fear, life, and death.

SEX OR NUDITY—None.

VIOLENCE—None.

LANGUAGE—None.

FEAR FACTOR (SUSPENSE)—Some; after all, it is about death.

AGE 0–2	★	The music isn't bad, and it is a fairly simple animated cartoon.
AGE 3–4	★★★	They'll love it.
AGE 5–6	★★★	Ditto.
AGE 7–10	★★	The youngest of this group will still enjoy it, but older kids may think of themselves as too old.
AGE 11–12	★	Only as nostalgia.
AGE 13+	★	Ditto.
ADULT	★★	Lovely; just be prepared to discuss death.

SUGGESTED AGES—2–10

Citizen Kane (No Rating)

1941 Drama
Directed by Orson Welles
Starring Orson Welles, Joseph Cotten

Virtually every "best" list includes *Citizen Kane* at or near the very top. We agree; the only question is at what age will kids start to appreciate it. Our answer is, for most children, about ten to twelve. That doesn't mean all kids, or that even the few who profess to get it—seeing you enthralled, some children will *want* to love it—won't understand most of it. But the story of Charles Foster Kane's rise to power, fame, and loneliness will touch most older kids in some way. And for all, there is "Rosebud."

SEX OR NUDITY—None.

VIOLENCE—None.

LANGUAGE—None.

FEAR FACTOR (SUSPENSE)—None.

AGE 0–2		Sorry, no way.
AGE 3–4		Ditto.
AGE 5–6		Still no way.
AGE 7–10	★	We're starting to get there.
AGE 11–12	★★	We're on our way!
AGE 13+	★★★	Easy sledding, especially for aspiring film buffs.
ADULT	★★★★	Go enjoy yourself. In the long run, they'll appreciate your nagging them to stick with it.

SUGGESTED AGES—10–99

Close Encounters of the Third Kind (PG)
1980 Fantasy/Science Fiction
Directed by Steven Spielberg
Starring Richard Dreyfuss, Francois Truffaut, Teri Garr, Melinda Dillon

Be sure to rent the special edition of this outstanding science fiction video: it contains spectacular new footage, including a breathtaking new ending that shows what Richard Dreyfuss's character sees when he enters the inside of the alien spaceship. (Don't worry: it's a brilliant, unthreatening churchlike cavern of lights and machinery.) In this new version, several distracting, slow-moving scenes have been trimmed and new ones added: the overall effect is a better-paced, more well-rounded film. *Close Encounters* tells the story of a regular Joe (Dreyfuss) who answers the mysterious summons of an alien spaceship. He isn't alone, he finds, as he encounters others who have also received the same "psychic implanting." Naturally, the government gets in on the act, but not, as in other Spielberg films, enough to totally screw it up. Ultimately, it is a solitary human figure, a totally average guy, who gets to be the first human to meet aliens. Cool.

SEX OR NUDITY—None.
VIOLENCE—None.
LANGUAGE—Minimal.
FEAR FACTOR (SUSPENSE)—Minimal. Most kids find alien matters less alien, and therefore less threatening than adults do; they probably won't worry too much about the humans who are compelled to come face-to-face with the aliens. They are more likely to fear the intrusive guys from the government. The sight of the ship is more awe-inspiring than frightening.

AGE 0–2		No.
AGE 3–4		No.
AGE 5–6		No. (Try *E.T.* instead.)
AGE 7–10	★★★	Depends on your child's interest in the extraterrestrial.

AGE 11–12 ★★★ A great film that should connect with most kids in this group.

AGE 13+ ★★★★ Right on. Invite them to watch the best of all the imitators that followed.

ADULT ★★★★ The special edition far exceeds the original. You're in for a treat.

SUGGESTED AGES—8–99

Clueless (PG-13)

1995 Comedy
Directed by Amy Heckerling
Starring Alicia Silverstone, Stacey Dash, Brittany Murphy, Paul Rudd

A witty, modern-day interpretation of Jane Austen's *Emma*, complete with cell phones, infomercials, and nose rings. The main character, Cher, is spoiled, self-absorbed, ditzy, and thoroughly likable. She goes about meddling in everyone else's love life, even convincing two of her teachers that each one of them is the other's secret admirer. (Happy teachers give better grades). And she gives one poor girl, the allegedly clueless one, a complete makeover so the boys will like her. When they do, and everyone seems to be in love, Cher realizes that despite all her machinations, she's the only one on the sidelines. Don't despair. There's a highly dateable guy right under her nose.

SEX OR NUDITY—Minimal.
VIOLENCE—Minimal. A brief, silly fistfight at a party.
LANGUAGE—Some. Enough to earn a PG-13 rating.
FEAR FACTOR (SUSPENSE)—None.

AGE 0–2		No way.
AGE 3–4		Still no way.
AGE 5–6		Still no way.
AGE 7–10	★	Maybe. But we'd wait until they're at least in double digits.
AGE 11–12	★★★	This is a smart, funny movie; they ought to love it.
AGE 13+	★★★	Ditto.
ADULT	★★★	You will, too.

SUGGESTED AGES—11–99

Cocoon (PG-13)

1985 Fantasy/Science Fiction
Directed by Ron Howard
Starring Wilford Brimley, Brian Dennehy, Don Ameche, Steve Guttenberg, Tahnee Welch, Hume Cronyn, Jessica Tandy

Don Ameche won a Best Supporting Actor Oscar for his portrayal as a senior citizen, who, with a group of his equally elderly friends, stumbles upon the Fountain of Youth. It happens to be located in the swimming pool of a nearby estate, just a heartbeat away from their old-age home. This is a very good-natured science fiction fantasy with a superb cast. There is transformation, life-and-death choices to be made by both humans and aliens, and plenty of humor. Some reviewers—though few kids or people we've watched with—complain that the ending is too schmaltzy or similar to *Close Encounters of the Third Kind*, which came out in 1977. We don't think it's a problem; go enjoy!

SEX OR NUDITY—None. A wonderfully creative love scene—with no human-like sex—between an alien and an earthling. Lots of groans and glowing, but no touching.

VIOLENCE—None.

LANGUAGE—Some. Encounters with aliens tend to bring out some cussing.

FEAR FACTOR (SUSPENSE)—Minimal.

AGE 0–2		No way.
AGE 3–4		Ditto.
AGE 5–6	★	Maybe, but they're probably too young.
AGE 7–10	★★	Good, but younger kids may not get pieces.
AGE 11–12	★★★	Charming.
AGE 13+	★★★	Ditto.
ADULT	★★★	You'll enjoy it even more.

SUGGESTED AGES—7–99

Cool Runnings (PG)
1993 Sports; Comedy
Directed by Jon Turtletaub
Starring John Candy, Doug E. Doug

Start with a wonderfully improbable premise based on a true story: a team of four unlikely athletes from Jamaica compete in the 1988 Winter Olympics in Calgary. They are entering the competition in a sport they've never even seen (bobsledding) on something they've never experienced (snow). Add the very physical comedy of John Candy as their coach and former bobsledder who is trying to deal with his own past as a failed Olympian. The result is a fairly amusing comedy and an upbeat "message" film.

SEX OR NUDITY—None.
VIOLENCE—None.
LANGUAGE—Minimal. A bit of excessive expression—not unexpected—from John Candy.
FEAR FACTOR (SUSPENSE)—None.

AGE 0–2		No way.
AGE 3–4	★	Eh, nothing harmful, but they probably won't understand the premise.
AGE 5–6	★★	Right on.
AGE 7–10	★★	Ditto.
AGE 11–12	★★★	Surprisingly entertaining.
AGE 13+	★★★	Perfect, especially for John Candy fans.
ADULT	★★	You could do worse.

SUGGESTED AGES—5–99

Court Jester, The (No Rating)

1956 Musical; Comedy
Directed by Norman Panama, Melvin Frank
Starring Danny Kaye, Glynis Johns, Basil Rathbone, Angela Lansbury

Set in England at the time of Robin Hood, Danny Kaye is hysterically funny as a former circus performer posing as a court jester in the service of a tyrant king. There he tries to discover the evil king's plans, but also falls in love with the princess. The film is quite funny, a bit politically incorrect, and a touch hyper. But overall it has great songs, funny routines, and is terrific entertainment.

SEX OR NUDITY—None.
VIOLENCE—Some. Lots of arrows, duels, and general mayhem; but not violent in any really objectionable way.
LANGUAGE—None.
FEAR FACTOR (SUSPENSE)—Minimal.

AGE 0–2		A bit too young.
AGE 3–4	★	They'll actually start to enjoy this.
AGE 5–6	★★	Pretty much on target for this group.
AGE 7–10	★★★	Right on!
AGE 11–12	★★	May find it a bit silly for their "mature" tastes.
AGE 13+	★★	Ditto.
ADULT	★★	A pleasant enough hour and a half.

SUGGESTED AGES—4–99

Crimson Tide (R)

1995 Drama
Directed by Tony Scott
Starring Denzel Washington, Gene Hackman, Matt Craven, George Dzundza

This has been described as a high testosterone, macho flick. (It is from the same producer-director team that created *Top Gun*.) Unfair! This film is an intelligently written, terrifically acted drama about an American nuclear submarine captain (Gene Hackman) who is challenged by his executive officer (Denzel Washington) during a confrontation with a rogue Russian warship. Don't worry about the plotting, which actually holds together quite well, or the R rating. Candidly, we can't quite figure out why it has an R rating: there is little actual violence, no sex, and very little offensive language. There is just terrific tension and important issues raised by compelling characters.

For those interested in issues such as lawful versus unjust orders, mutiny, or ships and the sea, consider *Mutiny on the Bounty* and *Mister Roberts*.

SEX OR NUDITY—None.

VIOLENCE—Some fighting, including the butt of a rifle.

LANGUAGE—Some. These are Navy salts.

FEAR FACTOR (SUSPENSE)—Terrific suspense in a well-crafted drama.

AGE 0–2		No way.
AGE 3–4		Ditto.
AGE 5–6		Still no way.
AGE 7–10	★★	For older kids only.
AGE 11–12	★★★	Not an action movie but a compelling drama.
AGE 13+	★★★	Ditto.
ADULT	★★★	Well worth it.

SUGGESTED AGES—9–99

Cure, The (PG-13)
1995 Drama
Directed by Peter Horton
Starring Brad Renfro, Joseph Mazzello, Bruce Davison, Annabella Sciorra

A luminous film about a journey by two friends: one, a boy who has AIDS, the other, his only friend. Dexter, the new kid in town, is shunned when people find out about his illness. But Erik, a lonely latchkey kid who lives next door, is drawn in by Dexter's imaginative games, and the two develop a rare and unlikely friendship. Then they read a tabloid story about a doctor in New Orleans who claims to have a cure for AIDS and the two set out, Tom Sawyer–style, on a raft down the Mississippi. They don't find the cure, of course. Indeed, Dexter's illness becomes far worse. But he gets a chance to really savor life, and Erik gets the chance to know what friendship and responsibility really mean. Don't be put off by the somber subject matter: this film is as funny as it is poignant. It is a certified tearjerker, though, no question about it.

SEX OR NUDITY—None.
VIOLENCE—Minimal. A brief, comical fight with a bunch of bullies.
LANGUAGE—There is lots of profanity—the eleven-year-old variety: wildly inaccurate and liberally sprinkled with the F-word. Somehow, though, it's never gratuitous.
FEAR FACTOR (SUSPENSE)—A lot. As Dexter's condition deteriorates, the tension becomes almost unbearable. Even when he's eventually hospitalized, we know it's the end, even if Erik doesn't.

AGE 0–2		No way.
AGE 3–4		No way.
AGE 5–6		No way.
AGE 7–10	★★	Maybe. But only for the most mature kids in this age group.
AGE 11–12	★★★★	A perfect movie for kids this age to watch with parents.
AGE 13+	★★★★	This has become a cult film among teenage girls.

ADULT   ★★★★   Although the on-screen death of a child is always hard to take, you'll love this film—right up through the final, heart-wrenching moments.

SUGGESTED AGES—11–99

Damn Yankees (No Rating)

1958 Sports; Musical
Directed by George Abbott, Stanley Donen
Starring Tab Hunter, Gwen Verdon, Ray Walston, Jean Stapleton

One of the great Broadway musicals barely makes the transformation to the screen. But it does make it, and the music and dancing make it worth sitting through the rather disappointing acting. But what music and dancing! Bob Fosse, who choreographed the film, also dances—with Gwen Verdon—and the result is magic. The story is about a middle-aged fan of the Washington Senators baseball team—perennial losers to the Yankees—who sells his soul to the Devil in order to become a young baseball star for his beloved team. Walston is perfect as the Devil and Verdon couldn't be better as his seductress/emissary charged with keeping young Joe Hardy in line and in the service of the Devil.

SEX OR NUDITY—Minimal. The suggestion of sex permeates many of the numbers.
VIOLENCE—None.
LANGUAGE—None.
FEAR FACTOR (SUSPENSE)—Minimal. Will he or won't he exercise his escape clause?

AGE 0–2		Nah.
AGE 3–4	★	Maybe a few of the dance numbers will hold their attention; but probably it's pushing it.
AGE 5–6	★★	OK, but not great for this group.
AGE 7–10	★★★	They'll love the music and dancing.
AGE 11–12	★★★	Ditto.
AGE 13+	★★★	The music and dancing will still hold them, but the rest is getting a bit creaky.
ADULT	★★	So will you, but unfortunately, you'll be disappointed in a great stage musical's transition to the screen.

SUGGESTED AGES—5–99

Dirty Dozen, The (No Rating)

1967 Action/Adventure
Directed by Robert Aldrich
Starring Lee Marvin, Ernest Borgnine, Jim Brown, John Cassavetes,
Richard Jaeckel

A truly entertaining and original war flick about a group of condemned
misfits given one last chance to commute their prison (or death) sen-
tences and redeem themselves. The mission is to work as a team and
storm an impregnable Nazi castle during World War II. The former is
more difficult than the latter, but under the cool leadership of Marvin
and Jaeckel, they manage to do so.

SEX OR NUDITY—None, but one of the convicts, Telly Savalas, is a
convicted rapist.

VIOLENCE—Tons, but by current standards, it is not particularly disturbing.

LANGUAGE—Minimal. A few cusses of the mild variety.

FEAR FACTOR (SUSPENSE)—Some. Will they work as a team? Will
they accomplish the mission? We're rooting them on all the way!

AGE 0–2		Nope, sorry.
AGE 3–4		Ditto.
AGE 5–6	★★	They will actually enjoy it.
AGE 7–10	★★★★	This group will love it.
AGE 11–12	★★★★	Ditto.
AGE 13+	★★★★	Not a classic, but this film has certainly sur-vived the test of time.
ADULT	★★★★	If you like war flicks, this is a winner.

SUGGESTED AGES—6–99

Dirty Rotten Scoundrels (PG)

1988 Comedy
Directed by Frank Oz
Starring Steve Martin, Michael Caine, Glenne Headly

OK, now we're really going to be in trouble: this film is hysterically funny, utterly politically incorrect, and of dubious appropriateness despite its PG rating. Michael Caine plays an aristocratic con-man fleecing wealthy women out of their money. Steve Martin is a con man as well, but a wanna-be not yet in Caine's league. But when Martin arrives on Caine's turf—the South of France—and tries to encroach, the town simply ain't big enough for both of them. A competition ensues: whoever separates the innocent Headly from her money wins and gets to stay. What makes this so non-PC is Martin's portrayals, first as Caine's retarded younger brother, and later as a crippled sailor. If you are not offended by such portrayals, this film is a treat.

SEX OR NUDITY—Minimal. Implied but never shown.
VIOLENCE—Minimal. A whack or two.
LANGUAGE—Minimal. Nothing to worry about.
FEAR FACTOR (SUSPENSE)—None.

AGE 0–2		No way.
AGE 3–4		Still no way.
AGE 5–6		They still won't get it.
AGE 7–10	★★	If they are sophisticated, they will love it.
AGE 11–12	★★★	Perfect.
AGE 13+	★★★★	Absolutely hysterical.
ADULT	★★★	Go on, laugh.

SUGGESTED AGES—8–99

Dr. Dolittle (PG)

1998 Comedy
Directed by Betty Thomas
Starring Eddie Murphy, Oliver Platt

This updated version of the classic story about a doctor who can talk to animals is funny, sweet, and quite enjoyable. Eddie Murphy is the doc, and he hasn't been this funny in years. Oliver Platt plays his partner who is determined to sell the practice to a managed care outfit for big bucks. Platt is ready to have Murphy committed lest his partner's insistence that he can talk to animals derail the deal. This subplot is incidental; the real joy is watching Eddie Murphy give mouth-to-mouth resuscitation to a rat. The voice-overs by the animals are a scream.

SEX OR NUDITY—None.
VIOLENCE—None.
LANGUAGE—Minimal. A few butt jokes.
FEAR FACTOR (SUSPENSE)—None.

AGE 0–2	★	OK for two-year-olds—barely.
AGE 3–4	★★	Now we're getting there.
AGE 5–6	★★★	They'll love it.
AGE 7–10	★★★	Ditto.
AGE 11–12	★★	Pushing it a bit, but they'll still laugh.
AGE 13+	★★	Ditto.
ADULT	★★	Not bad.

SUGGESTED AGES—2–15

Driving Miss Daisy (PG)

1989 Drama
Directed by Bruce Beresford
Starring Morgan Freeman, Jessica Tandy, Dan Aykroyd, Patti Lupone, Esther Rolle

A rare and luminous film about a friendship that grows, gradually and subtly, between a pair of proud elderly people: Miss Daisy, a stubborn widow who is no longer able to drive herself to the beauty parlor and the synagogue, and Hoke Colburn, the patient, dignified black chauffeur her son hires to drive her. Their relationship, depicted with great skill by two of the most outstanding actors of our time, unfolds over twenty five years, years when complacency gave way to social ferment. It begins badly enough in 1948, when Miss Daisy refuses to be driven. Hoke, with a determination equal to hers, but without a smidgen of obsequiousness, finally convinces Miss Daisy to get in the car by driving slowly alongside the curb while she walks to the Piggly Wiggly, enduring the neighbors' nosy looks. Thus begins a journey that bridges time, distance, prejudice, and the loneliness that all humans are prey to. Both performances are radiant: Jessica Tandy won a Oscar at age eighty for her protrayal of Miss Daisy, a role that many say was the best of her long career; Morgan Freeman was nominated, but missed the Oscar he richly deserved.

SEX OR NUDITY—None.
VIOLENCE—None.
LANGUAGE—None.
FEAR FACTOR (SUSPENSE)—None.

AGE 0–2	No.	
AGE 3–4	No.	
AGE 5–6	No.	
AGE 7–10	No.	
AGE 11–12 ★★★★	A loud, enthusiastic yes. They'll need a little help with the subtleties of the historical context, but you and they will be richly rewarded for it.	

AGE 13+   ★★★★   Ditto.

ADULT   ★★★★   Luminous.

SUGGESTED AGES—10–99

Dumb and Dumber (PG-13)
1994 Comedy
Directed by Peter Farrelly
Starring Jim Carrey, Jeff Daniels, Lauren Holly

If you want to know why your kids think Jim Carrey is the funniest man alive, rent this no-brainer of a film. You'll find yourself laughing out loud in spite of yourself. The plot, if you can call it that, is about a couple of dimwits who travel across the country to return a briefcase full of ransom money. A series of slapstick pratfalls, goofy malapropisms, and juvenile jokes about bodily functions ensues. You may blanch at the bathroom humor, especially one sequence involving a potent laxative, but you'll have a hard time keeping a straight face as the two title characters pose as a pair of bon vivants on the town in Aspen.

SEX OR NUDITY—Minimal. Much innuendo, no real action.
VIOLENCE—Minimal. Two comic but graphic scenes: a death by rat poison and a fantasy fight scene where Carrey rips out the heart of his rival.
LANGUAGE—Some. No duh.
FEAR FACTOR (SUSPENSE)—None.

AGE 0–2		No.
AGE 3–4		Not a good idea.
AGE 5–6	★	If you must.
AGE 7–10	★★★	Yes, you must.
AGE 11–12	★★★	A howl!
AGE 13+	★★★	Still a howl!
AGE ADULT	★★★	Depending on your tolerance for dumb humor, you ought to enjoy it immensely.

SUGGESTED AGES—7–99

Dunston Checks In (PG)

1996 Animal; Comedy
Directed by Ken Kwapis
Starring Jason Alexander, Faye Dunaway, Rupert Everett, Paul Reubens

The title character in this light, entertaining farce is an orangutan. But don't let that put you off. He's also a trained jewel thief who is forced to work the five-star Majestic Hotel. What makes this film so appealing to kids (beside the sight of an orangutan helping himself to the minibar) is that none of the adults in the joint have any idea what's going on. It takes an adorable, unsupervised little boy to figure it out and rescue Dunston from his abusive owner. Kids also love this film because it shows the behind-the-scenes life of a little boy who actually lives at the hotel. There's only one poignant note: the boy's father is too preoccupied with running the hotel to pay attention to his sons. But that aspect isn't overworked, and eventually, the father gets in on the act. The final scene, a banquet calamity, involves falling chandeliers, people crashing into cakes, etc.—the kind of monkeyshines kids love because their own vacation antics look tame in comparison.

SEX OR NUDITY—None.
VIOLENCE—None.
LANGUAGE—Minimal. One mild expletive.
FEAR FACTOR (SUSPENSE)—None. Dunston's owner is so cartoonish he's never really threatening; even little children will know it's the orangutan who's got the upper hand.

AGE 0–2	★	No problem.
AGE 3–4	★★★	Will find Dunston's antics (putting a pair of underpants on his head, stealing foil-wrapped bedtime mints) unspeakably funny.
AGE 5–6	★★★★	Ditto.
AGE 7–10	★★★★	Right up their alley, especially if their brand of humor involves things like seeing a grown-up getting a tranquilizer dart in the rump.

AGE 11–12	★★	Not too old to enjoy it, but definitely too old to admit it.
AGE 13+	★	Nah, too old.
ADULT	★★★	More fun than you'd expect. Dunaway, Reubens, and Alexander turn in solidly amusing performances.

SUGGESTED AGES—4–10

Empire Strikes Back, The (PG)

1980 Fantasy/Science Fiction
Directed by Irvin Kershner
Starring Mark Hamill, Carrie Fisher, Harrison Ford

The second (of three) *Star Wars* films in the original trilogy. (As we write this, a new film is being previewed.) Luke and the Rebel Alliance are still battling Darth Vader and the forces of the Dark Side. But now we have wonderfully interesting subplots: Luke's training as a Jedi knight by Yoda and the romance blooming between Princess Leia and Han Solo. Great special effects, a compelling story, and wonderful music. Always a treat.

SEX OR NUDITY—Minimal. Just wordplay between the princess and Han.
VIOLENCE—A lot. Cosmic battles large and small. Luke's arm is severed by a light saber.
LANGUAGE—Minimal.
FEAR FACTOR (SUSPENSE)—Some. Do we ever doubt the outcome? Just remember that this episode ends with a cliff-hanger: the sight of Han Solo's frozen form might be upsetting.

AGE 0–2		Still too young.
AGE 3–4	★★	Watch them play with light sabers.
AGE 5–6	★★★★	They'll be humming, "Dum, dum, dum-da-dum, dum-da-dum" for about a week.
AGE 7–10	★★★★	Ditto.
AGE 11–12	★★★★	Maybe the perfect age.
AGE 13+	★★★★	They won't even pretend to be too old.
ADULT	★★★★	Nor should you.

SUGGESTED AGES—4–99

E.T. The Extra-Terrestrial (PG)

1982 Fantasy/Science Fiction
Directed by Steven Spielberg
Starring Henry Thomas, Dee Wallace, Peter Coyote, Robert McNaughton, Drew Barrymore

This film has it all: it's exciting, funny, scary, thrilling, and poignant. It may also be too much of all of those things for some kids. But kids who are able to be scared without becoming upset will probably rank it as one of the best movie-watching experiences of their lifetime. It features a little alien who is left behind on earth when his spaceship has to make a hasty departure and the little boy who, through sheer faith and humanity, forges a deep friendship with him. It's a powerful mix, one that taps into kids' most powerful feelings: fear of abandonment, longing for friendship, and coping with loss. These topics are treated with great sensitivity and respect for children; they are also leavened with some side-splitting humor. Be prepared: there are moments when it looks for sure like E.T. is a goner. Go ahead and cry. He'll be back, but only to leave for good at the end. (You can, at least, reassure worried kids that E.T. only *looks* dead.)

SEX OR NUDITY—None.

VIOLENCE—None.

LANGUAGE—Minimal. One tame utterance, though your kids are sure to repeat it later with glee.

FEAR FACTOR (SUSPENSE)—A lot. Your child will be on your lap (and you'll be biting your nails) for the last thirty minutes of the film. It's scary—really scary—when the government guys seize E.T. and poke him with all kinds of wires. And it's even scarier when he appears to be dead. And it's heart-wrenching when it looks like E.T.'s rescue appears to have failed. In other words, this film will put you and your child through an emotional wringer.

AGE 0–2		No.
AGE 3–4	★	You may be tempted to let them watch along with older siblings, but it's not really for them.

AGE 5–6	★★	They'll howl with laughter as they watch E.T. try to figure out things they mastered long ago. Sensitive kids, though, may find the fear factor too high to bear. You decide.
AGE 7–10	★★★★	Even if they saw it when they were little, they'll get a kick out of it, and out of seeing Drew Barrymore in her adorable, lisping, little girl screen debut.
AGE 11–12	★★★★	Go for it.
AGE 13+	★★★★	Ditto.
ADULT	★★★★	Lay in a hearty supply of Reese's Pieces and tissues and enjoy!

SUGGESTED AGES—6–99

Fantasia (No Rating)

1940 Animated
Directed by Ben Sharpsteen

A fascinating experiment that combined classical music with Walt Disney's best animation. It has eight segments, each based on a different classical piece played by the Philadelphia Orchestra and conducted by Leopold Stokowski. Some of the segments, such as Mickey Mouse as the Sorcerer's Apprentice, are more traditional cartoons. Others are quite abstract. None have any dialogue, although there is a narration that provides a bit of musical perspective. Several of the sequences may be a bit spooky for younger children. But in an era of show-tune-inspired animated mega-hits and MTV videos, this film is a wonderful antidote. A surprising number of kids will get it, and you can share their joy of discovery.

SEX OR NUDITY—None.

VIOLENCE—None.

LANGUAGE—None.

FEAR FACTOR (SUSPENSE)—Minimal. From dancing brooms?

AGE 0–2	★	Wait on this one.
AGE 3–4	★★	OK, but some find the Sorcerer's Apprentice segment too scary.
AGE 5–6	★★★	Will probably be captivated by the music and images.
AGE 7–10	★★	Ditto at the younger age range; the older kids may think themselves too old for a "cartoon."
AGE 11–12	★★	Most won't want to admit they find it interesting.
AGE 13+	★	Probably won't sit still.
ADULT	★★	You'll appreciate that this was made almost sixty years ago.

SUGGESTED AGES—4–9

Ferris Bueller's Day Off (PG-13)

1986 Comedy
Directed by John Hughes
Starring Matthew Broderick, Jennifer Grey, Alan Ruck, Mia Sara, Charlie Sheen

Matthew Broderick plays a popular, successful high schooler who goes to elaborate lengths to cut class and spend the day cavorting around Chicago. Jennifer Grey is his little sister who does her best to make sure he gets caught. The kids are sharp, the adults dim-witted, and the humor positively charming. Relive high school and then try to explain it to your kids; and enjoy!

SEX OR NUDITY—None.

VIOLENCE—None.

LANGUAGE—Some. Lots of "basic" curses in uncomfortable combinations.

FEAR FACTOR (SUSPENSE)—Minimal.

AGE 0–2		No way.
AGE 3–4		Ditto.
AGE 5–6		Still no way.
AGE 7–10	★★	If they don't have an older sibling, they won't appreciate it.
AGE 11–12	★★★★	This is what they aspire to.
AGE 13+	★★★★	They will *love* this movie.
ADULT	★★★	Will bring back memories of high school.

SUGGESTED AGES—7–99

Fiddler on the Roof (No Rating)

1971 Musical
Directed by Norman Jewison
Starring Topol, Molly Picon, Leonard Frey, Paul Michael Glaser, Norma Crane

This faithful, full-bodied interpretation of the Broadway hit may be even better on film, if only because the filmmakers are able to show the vast, beautiful, and punishing Russian landscape. If your children don't know the story of a Jewish peasant family trying to cling to its traditions and customs under the brutal assault of the czar, they should. This film is as much about being Jewish as it is about tradition and the irresistible force of change. And it's as timeless and timely as it ever was.

SEX OR NUDITY—None.
VIOLENCE—None.
LANGUAGE—None. Oy vey!
FEAR FACTOR (SUSPENSE)—There is political oppression and great sadness in this film, especially as the daughters leave their home, but no real fear.

AGE 0–2		No.
AGE 3–4		No.
AGE 5–6		No.
AGE 7–10	★★	Yes. They'll at least like the music.
AGE 11–12	★★★	They'll be pleased at how much they understand.
AGE 13+	★★★	Insist on it; they'll love it.
ADULT	★★★★	You'll probably be surprised by what you notice this time around.

SUGGESTED AGES—8–99

Field of Dreams (PG)

1989 Sports; Drama
Directed by Phil Alden Robinson
Starring Kevin Costner, Amy Madigan, James Earl Jones, Ray Liotta,
Burt Lancaster

A beautiful film with a gentle tone about a man (Kevin Costner) who
"hears a voice" and obsessively builds a baseball field on his Iowa farm.
He hopes to bring back long-dead baseball stars, including Shoeless Joe
Jackson, and deal with the death of his own father. Even if you care
nothing about baseball, you and your older children will truly enjoy this
film together. "Build it and they will come" has become part of our popular lexicon, a phrase that underscores the theme of faith that runs
through this film.

SEX OR NUDITY—None.

VIOLENCE—None.

LANGUAGE—Minimal. Nothing to worry about.

FEAR FACTOR (SUSPENSE)—Minimal. Not really, but long-dead people do go in and out of the mist.

AGE 0–2		Sorry, no.
AGE 3–4		Ditto.
AGE 5–6		Still pushing it for this age group.
AGE 7–10	★★	May be too slow for some kids this age.
AGE 11–12	★★★	They'll love it.
AGE 13+	★★★	If you rent it, they will come . . . and stay with it!
ADULT	★★★	A terrific film.

SUGGESTED AGES—7–99

Flamingo Kid, The (PG-13)

1984 Drama
Directed by Garry Marshall
Starring Matt Dillon, Richard Crenna, Hector Elizondo, Janet Jones, Bronson Pinchot

A smart, entertaining coming-of-age film set in 1963. Matt Dillon plays a plumber's son from Brooklyn who gets a summer job at a fancy Long Island beach club. There he comes under the influence of a wealthy car salesman-cum-card player (Richard Crenna). Dillon is torn between the flashy lifestyle of his new patron and the "boring" but solid values of his father. The performances from the entire cast are terrific, and the music and settings will transport you back to the era.

SEX OR NUDITY—Some. One brief but fairly explicit scene.
VIOLENCE—None.
LANGUAGE—Some. Not much, but a few words that may be of concern.
FEAR FACTOR (SUSPENSE)—None.

AGE 0–2		No way.
AGE 3–4		Ditto.
AGE 5–6		Still no way.
AGE 7–10	★★	Barely, but only for the older kids.
AGE 11–12	★★★	They'll love it.
AGE 13+	★★★★	A royal flush!
ADULT	★★★	You'll be pleasantly surprised

SUGGESTED AGES—10–99

Flight of the Navigator (PG)

1986 Action/Adventure
Directed by Randal Kleiser
Starring Joey Cramer, Veronica Cartwright, Cliff De Young, Sarah Jessica Parker

A lovely fantasy about a twelve-year-old boy who goes playing in the forest and returns home to find that eight years have passed but he hasn't aged. To complicate matters, a UFO has landed, NASA is unable to open the spacecraft, and David has the key to the mysteries within. In some ways this film will be compared to *E.T.* and *Close Encounters of the Third Kind*; it shouldn't be. Rather, it is a simple story with a youthful hero and some sweet twists.

SEX OR NUDITY—None.

VIOLENCE—None.

LANGUAGE—None.

FEAR FACTOR (SUSPENSE)—A lot. It starts with a missing child and proceeds to a child being separated from his family in order to to explain the mysteries of the UFO.

AGE 0–2		They're still a bit too young.
AGE 3–4	★	They'll appreciate the talking robot.
AGE 5–6	★★	They'll appreciate this film.
AGE 7–10	★★	Perfect for this group.
AGE 11–12	★★	Ditto.
AGE 13+	★	Not that they're getting a bit too old, but they'll compare it to other, better films.
ADULT	★★	Not bad.

SUGGESTED AGES—4–11

Fly Away Home (PG)

1996 Animal; Drama
Directed by Carroll Ballard
Starring Anna Pacquin, Jeff Daniels, Dana Delany

A lovely fantasy about a girl who flies an ultra-light aircraft to lead a flock of pet geese home from Canada to North Carolina. (To enjoy this film as fantasy, you'll have to put aside recollections of the tragic real-life cross-country flight of Jessica Dubroff and her father.) When Amy rescues a nest of goose eggs from a bulldozer and takes them home, they hatch and mistake her for their mother. Her father, trying hard to forge a relationship with his daughter, puts up with having a flock of baby geese in the house, but he soon realizes they need to learn how to live like real geese. And this means going south when winter comes. He rigs up a plane for Amy and the two of them fly south with the birds in tow. They encounter hunters and suspicious military personnel en route, but no real dangers. Great, soaring film.

SEX OR NUDITY—None.

VIOLENCE—None.

LANGUAGE—None. One mild expletive.

FEAR FACTOR (SUSPENSE)—Minimal. Amy crashes in a test flight, but is unhurt. The dangers she encounters in her flight are brief, and not especially threatening. The film opens with the death (not actually shown) of her mother.

AGE 0–2		They're too young.
AGE 3–4	★	Maybe. It moves a little slowly for most kids this age.
AGE 5–6	★★★	Just right; they'll love antics of the baby birds and the flying sequences.
AGE 7–10	★★★★	Ditto. They'll also start to pick up on the emotional nuances.
AGE 11–12	★★★	Touching and perfect.
AGE 13+	★★★	It could be a hard sell, but well worth it.

ADULT   ★★★★   Once you put aside parental anxieties, you'll be charmed and moved.

SUGGESTED AGES—5–12

Forrest Gump (PG-13)

1994 Drama
Directed by Robert Zemeckis
Starring Tom Hanks, Robin Wright, Sally Field, Gary Sinise

Tom Hanks won an Oscar as Best Actor for his portrayal of a slow-witted innocent who becomes an all-American football star, war hero, Ping Pong champion, and business tycoon. Each accomplishment is both unexpected and believable—*if* you suspend disbelief and just enjoy Hanks in this terrific role. Each achievement puts him in the center of the major social, cultural, and political events of the last four decades. Using some nifty documentary footage and special effects, Forrest Gump manages to stand next to, and interact with, many of the major figures of our time. Beyond the ongoing series of entertaining—and, via Forrest's participation, personalized—historical vignettes, it is also a terrific story about love and friendship. Enjoy!

SEX OR NUDITY—Some. A bare butt, Gump's girlfriend in her bra, a hooker scene, and some inferences of sex.

VIOLENCE—Some. The shooting of George Wallace and some pretty graphic scenes of fighting in Vietnam can be tough on younger kids.

LANGUAGE—None.

FEAR FACTOR (SUSPENSE)—Some. A little boy being tormented by bullies and Gump's efforts to save a war buddy are pretty disturbing.

AGE 0–2		No way.
AGE 3–4		Ditto.
AGE 5–6	★	They'll barely get any of it.
AGE 7–10	★★★	They'll start to appreciate it, but be prepared for lots of questions.
AGE 11–12	★★★	They should begin to appreciate this film.
AGE 13+	★★★★	Perfect.
ADULT	★★★★	Enjoy!

SUGGESTED AGES—7–99

Four Musketeers, The (PG)

1974 Action/Adventure
Directed by Richard Lester
Starring Oliver Reed, Raquel Welch, Richard Chamberlain, Michael York, Charlton Heston, Faye Dunaway

This sequel to the 1974 version of *The Three Musketeers* has the same sensibility (it was filmed simultaneously), as well as the same cast. More treachery, more swashbuckling. Several of the principal characters die at the end, which might prove disturbing to younger children.

SEX OR NUDITY—None.

VIOLENCE—Some, but nothing to worry about. Sword fights and gunfights.

LANGUAGE—Minimal.

FEAR FACTOR (SUSPENSE)—Minimal.

AGE 0–2		Nope.
AGE 3–4	★	Barely.
AGE 5–6	★★	On target.
AGE 7–10	★★★	Even better for this group.
AGE 11–12	★★★	Ditto.
AGE 13+	★★	They may think it a bit dated.
ADULT	★★	Not bad.

SUGGESTED AGES—5–15

Freaky Friday (G)

1977 Fantasy/Science Fiction
Directed by Gary Nelson
Starring Jodie Foster, Barbara Harris, John Astin

Winning and whimsical, this film takes a look at what just might happen if parents and kids switched places for a day. What makes this so much fun is how well the mother and daughter mimic each other's quirks and mannerisms. It's silly, corny, maybe a little dated (the mother is a somewhat ditzy housewife whose main responsibilities are making a pot roast and showing up at her husband's business affairs.) But it's still a hoot.

SEX OR NUDITY—None.

VIOLENCE—None.

LANGUAGE—None.

FEAR FACTOR (SUSPENSE)—None.

AGE 0–2		Not really for them, but no harm if they happen to toddle in while older siblings are watching.
AGE 3–4	★★	Maybe a little over their heads.
AGE 5–6	★★★	Perfect.
AGE 7–10	★★★	Ditto.
AGE 11–12	★	Pushing it a bit.
AGE 13+	★	No, they're too sophisticated for this one.
ADULT	★★★	This is the kind of movie you saw as a kid.

SUGGESTED AGES—4–10

Free Willy (PG)

1993 Animal
Directed by Simon Wincer
Starring Jason James Richter, Jayne Atkinson, Michael Madsen, Lori
Petty

Forget everything you've heard about this film and its dead-in-the water
sequels. It's a charming flick about a tough, unhappy kid who finds he
has a lot in common with a whale held captive in a seedy sea creatures
show. Sounds implausible, doesn't it? Somehow it works, and the ending is a bona fide tearjerker.

SEX OR NUDITY—None.
VIOLENCE—Minimal. There are some rough characters, but the action
never gets rough.
LANGUAGE—Minimal. Pretty tame.
FEAR FACTOR (SUSPENSE)—None.

AGE 0–2		Over their heads.
AGE 3–4		Ditto.
AGE 5–6	★★	Just right—especially for animal lovers.
AGE 7–10	★★★	Ditto.
AGE 11–12	★	You'd be pushing it.
AGE 13+		They are too sophisticated for this film.
ADULT	★★	You'll get sucked in.

SUGGESTED AGES—6–10

Freshman, The (PG)

1990 Comedy
Directed by Andrew Bergman
Starring Marlon Brando, Matthew Broderick, Bruno Kirby, Penelope
Ann Miller, Maximilian Schell

Broderick plays a college student at NYU, new to New York City, and
in need of money. He winds up working for a mob family headed by
Brando (who does a wonderful parody of his Don Corleone role). The
plot takes several hysterical turns and climaxes in a banquet of endan-
gered animals. Don't worry too much. This is not a classic, but it is quite
loony and very satisfying. In fact, it is one of our dark-horse favorites!

SEX OR NUDITY—Some. There's a talk about sex, and some mild activity, but nothing to worry about.

VIOLENCE—None.

LANGUAGE—Minimal.

FEAR FACTOR (SUSPENSE)—Minimal.

AGE 0–2		No way.
AGE 3–4		Ditto.
AGE 5–6		Still no way.
AGE 7–10	★★★	Absolutely.
AGE 11–12	★★★	Perfect.
AGE 13+	★★★★	Ditto.
ADULT	★★★	Enjoy.

SUGGESTED AGES—7–99

Friendly Persuasion (No Rating)

1956 Drama
Directed by William Wyler
Starring Gary Cooper, Dorothy McGuire, Marjorie Main, Anthony Perkins

A charming story about a Quaker family living in southern Indiana at the outbreak of the Civil War. Each member of the family has to balance his or her own sense of identity with the changes being forced upon their lives and values. Most significantly, it is about the family's struggle to maintain their Quaker pacifism. It is a beautiful story, well acted, but sometimes slow.

SEX OR NUDITY—None.
VIOLENCE—Minimal. Some fighting and shooting. A young boy gets bitten on the rump by pet goose.
LANGUAGE—None.
FEAR FACTOR (SUSPENSE)—Minimal.

AGE 0–2		No way.
AGE 3–4		Ditto.
AGE 5–6		Still too slow for this crowd.
AGE 7–10	★	Older kids will start to appreciate this film.
AGE 11–12	★★	A tender story with important issues—*if* they hang in there.
AGE 13+	★★	Ditto.
ADULT	★★	Lovely.

SUGGESTED AGES—9–99

From Russia with Love (No Rating)

1963 Action/Adventure
Directed by Terence Young
Starring Sean Connery, Robert Shaw, Daniela Bianchi, Lotte Lenya

The second of the James Bond films (*Dr. No* was made a year earlier), and probably our favorite. Few gadgets but plenty of fighting, smart dialogue, and decent acting. The real question is whether *any* James Bond flick should be included in this list of best family films. Our answer is yes. (We've included two; the other being *Goldfinger*.) The reason is that they were fun—indeed, still are—and a wonderful window onto an era. Yes, there's violence, sexual innuendo, dated plots and mores. So? We like these two films; so will most kids. By today's standards, they are quite innocent. But use your discretion.

SEX OR NUDITY—Minimal. No real sex or nudity beyond some kissing, lots of flirting, and innuendo.
VIOLENCE—A lot. Lots of killing, but nothing gruesome.
LANGUAGE—None.
FEAR FACTOR (SUSPENSE)—Some. Surprisingly, there is a bit more dramatic tension than in the other Bond films.

AGE 0–2		No way.
AGE 3–4		Ditto.
AGE 5–6	★★	They'll enjoy it.
AGE 7–10	★★★	They'll love it.
AGE 11–12	★★★	"Bond, James Bond," will be the refrain in the house for days.
AGE 13+	★★★	They'll be fascinated and will compare this to the current crop of Bond films.
ADULT	★★	Think of it as a trip down memory lane.

SUGGESTED AGES—6–99

Funny Girl (G)

1968 Musical
Directed by William Wyler
Starring Barbra Streisand, Omar Sharif, Kay Medford, Anne Francis, Walter Pidgeon

Even if you're not a Barbra Streisand fan, there's a lot to love about this film: great songs, a lavish production, and Omar Sharif's eyes. Besides, it's a poignant story about ambition, success, and the tragedy of an ill-fated love. The plot, in case you forget: ugly duckling Fanny Brice becomes a leading lady through dint of sheer talent, chutzpah, and comic panache. Success is hers, but she is hopelessly in love with a hopeless gambler. But that doesn't keep our girl down in the end.

SEX OR NUDITY—None. Intimacy is implied, but not shown.

VIOLENCE—None.

LANGUAGE—None.

FEAR FACTOR (SUSPENSE)—None.

AGE 0–2		No.
AGE 3–4		Still no.
AGE 5–6		Still no.
AGE 7–10	★★	Just barely able to appreciate it.
AGE 11–12	★★★	Bingo.
AGE 13+	★★	Just for aspiring actors.
ADULT	★★	Only if you liked it the first time around.

SUGGESTED AGES—8–99

General, The (No Rating)

1927 Comedy
Drama
Directed by Buster Keaton
Starring Buster Keaton, Marion Mack, Glen Cavender

We have a bit of a problem: we're not big Buster Keaton fans. Yet so many of our friends told us we were wrong not to include at least one Buster Keaton film that we asked them to recommend one. This was their recommendation, and we still have mixed feelings about including it. It is is a silent comedy based on a true story about a stolen train during the Civil War. It didn't quite hold our attention. But we'll admit the possibility that we're wrong, and ask readers to let us know their Buster Keaton favorite and whether this particular film deserves more than the two stars we've given it.

SEX OR NUDITY—Minimal.
VIOLENCE—A lot.
LANGUAGE—None.
FEAR FACTOR (SUSPENSE)—Minimal.

AGE 0–2		No way.
AGE 3–4		Ditto.
AGE 5–6	★★	Kids seem to appreciate this more than we do.
AGE 7–10	★★	Ditto.
AGE 11–12	★★	The jury is out.
AGE 13+	★★	Ditto.
ADULT	★★	Let us know.

SUGGESTED AGES—5–99

George of the Jungle (PG)

1997 Comedy
Directed by Sam Weisman
Starring Brendan Fraser, Leslie Mann, Thomas Haden Church, the voice of John Cleese

Good, dumb fun, with a few slapstick bits that will leave you laughing harder than you might expect (and a few slightly crude bits, too). Brendan Fraser's George is the same dimwitted, lovable native you remember from television, but this George also has an elephant who thinks he's a dog (he bounds through the jungle, slides to a stop at George's feet, and sits there panting and wagging his tail) and a pet ape who has the voice and mannerisms of an English butler. These two sidekicks offer invaluable advice and assistance on how to woo a beautiful heiress who falls into George's life (standard stuff like barring your teeth and beating on your chest).

SEX OR NUDITY—Minimal. Implied, not shown.
VIOLENCE—Minimal. Only the cartoonish kind.
LANGUAGE—Minimal. Very mild.
FEAR FACTOR (SUSPENSE)—None.

AGE 0–2		No real harm done.
AGE 3–4	★★★	They ought to love it.
AGE 5–6	★★★	Ditto.
AGE 7–10	★★★	Don't let them tell you they're too old.
AGE 11–12	★★	*Titanic*, it's not. But it's fun.
AGE 13+	★★	A chance to see Brendan Fraser in loincloth.
ADULT	★★★	You may like it better than your kids—especially if you liked the cartoon series.

SUGGESTED AGES—4–11

Ghostbusters (PG)

1984 Fantasy/Science Fiction; Comedy
Directed by Ivan Reitman
Starring Bill Murray, Dan Aykroyd, Sigourney Weaver, Harold Ramis, Rick Moranis

A very funny—but rather scary for younger children—story about three friends who set up a business as "paranormal investigators" to rid New York City of ghosts, ghouls, poltergeists, and other supernatural creatures. And there are plenty to get rid of! The special effects are terrific, the humor zany, and the attitude very hip. Kids may be more familiar with the cartoons they know from television; this film has more of an edge to it, and is much funnier and scarier.

SEX OR NUDITY—Some. Talk and sexual flirting with ghosts, but nothing too worrisome.
VIOLENCE—Some. The ghouls get busted! Yuck!
LANGUAGE—Some. A fair amount of profanity.
FEAR FACTOR (SUSPENSE)—Some. It can get a bit scary for younger kids.

AGE 0–2		No way.
AGE 3–4	★	Still pushing it; they'll want to watch, particularly if they have older siblings. Be careful if they get scared easily.
AGE 5–6	★★	They'll like it, but stay close.
AGE 7–10	★★★	Perfect.
AGE 11–12	★★★	Even more perfect.
AGE 13+	★★★	So who ya going to call?
ADULT	★★	Not bad.

SUGGESTED AGES—6–99

Glory (R)
1989 Drama
Directed by Edward Zwick
Starring Matthew Broderick, Denzel Washington, Morgan Freeman

When Robert Gould Shaw, an aristocratic Union officer, is put in charge of a regiment of black soldiers, his disappointment is palpable. Even though he's an avowed abolitionist, like many others in 1863, he has serious doubts about whether black men have the courage and discipline to make good soldiers. He also has hidden doubts about himself, having been deeply shaken by the violence he has seen on the battlefield. But as his men—an assortment of freeman and escaped slaves—prove themselves to him, they develop a mutual, if guarded, trust. On a July afternoon, in what turns out to be a nearly suicidal battle, that trust is put to the test. The performance of the 54th Massachusetts Regiment was a pivotal moment in the war, a show of bravery that turned the tide both on the battlefield and in the public mind. It was decisive in the military's decision to recruit more black soldiers, who eventually numbered more than one hundred thousand. Shaw's growth as a man and as a leader is as much at the heart of this film as is the true story of a hitherto unheralded group of freedom fighters.

It's worth remembering and telling your children that this event took place a century before the civil rights movement.

SEX OR NUDITY—None.
VIOLENCE—A lot. The final battle is wrenching in its intensity, not because it is gory (although it is) but because viewers will have come to care so deeply for the members of the 54th Regiment.
LANGUAGE—Minimal. A realistic but temperate amount for a war film.
FEAR FACTOR (SUSPENSE)—A lot.

AGE 0–2	No.
AGE 3–4	No.
AGE 5–6	No.
AGE 7–10	No.

AGE 11–12 ★★★★ Yes. They'll find it absorbing, satisfying, and eye-opening.

AGE 13+ ★★★★ Ditto.

ADULT ★★★★ A great way to open a discussion about the roots of racism, especially applicable if your child is studying American history.

SUGGESTED AGES—12–99

Gold Rush, The (No Rating)
1925 Comedy; Drama
Directed by Charlie Chaplin
Starring Charlie Chaplin, Georgia Hale, Mack Swain, Tom Murray

This is the film that Chaplin most wanted to be remembered for. It is a semi-talky, with narration and some lip-synched dialogue, about the Little Tramp in the Yukon. It has some of his classic routines, including the leather shoe feast. Most children take a moment or two to get into Chaplin films, but once they do they become mesmerized. You'll be able to enjoy this with your child over and over again, each time discovering something new.

SEX OR NUDITY—Minimal.
VIOLENCE—Some. The usual array of both slapstick and dramatic moments.
LANGUAGE—None.
FEAR FACTOR (SUSPENSE)—Some. Cliff-hangers—literally.

AGE 0–2		Not quite.
AGE 3–4	★	Sure, why not.
AGE 5–6	★★	Getting there.
AGE 7–10	★★★★	Perfect.
AGE 11–12	★★★	They'll like it but may be a bit hesitant about a silent film.
AGE 13+	★★★	Ditto.
ADULT	★★★★	A classic to be shared.

SUGGESTED AGES—5–99

Goldfinger (No Rating)

1964 Action/Adventure
Directed by Guy Hamilton
Starring Sean Connery, Honor Blackman, Gert Frobe

As mentioned in the write-up for *From Russia with Love*—the only other James Bond film we've included in this book—we debated whether to include *any* Bond flick. The earlier ones are entertaining, and only later did the films go over the edge in gadgetry and explosions.

Goldfinger was last of the "tame" Bond movies. You need to suspend disbelief to buy into Q's wonderful gadgets. The level of sexiness increases with this movie as well: Honor Blackman plays Pussy Galore, the head of a band of beautiful blond pilots part of Goldfinger's scheme to rob Fort Knox. And of course there is Odd Job with his deadly bowler. Just remember, the name is Bond, James Bond.

SEX OR NUDITY—Some kissing followed by a few postcoital bathrobe scenes. And, of course, the famous naked body painted in gold.
VIOLENCE—Some. Bodies fall, but surprisingly tame.
LANGUAGE—Minimal. No problems.
FEAR FACTOR (SUSPENSE)—Minimal. Entertaining, but not scary.

AGE 0–2		Nope.
AGE 3–4		Still nope.
AGE 5–6	★★	They'll like it.
AGE 7–10	★★★	They'll love it.
AGE 11–12	★★★	Perfect.
AGE 13+	★★★	May offend the feminists in this group, but others will enjoy it.
ADULT	★★	Surprisingly good fun.

SUGGESTED AGES—5–99

Gone with the Wind (G)

1939 Drama
Directed by Victor Fleming
Starring Vivien Leigh, Clark Gable, Leslie Howard, Olivia de Havilland

You don't need us to tell you this is epic entertainment of the highest caliber. But you may not think of renting it to watch with the kids. Consider it. We watched in two installments, sort of like our own miniseries. What followed, after the lights came up, were some of the best family discussions we've ever had. Kids may need your help with historical context, especially as the story moves into Reconstruction. Well worth the time invested.

SEX OR NUDITY—None. Implied, but not shown.

VIOLENCE—Some. Unforgettable scenes of wartime Atlanta and of Scarlett killing a Yankee varmint. But tame by today's standards.

LANGUAGE—None. Oh, fiddle dee dee!

FEAR FACTOR (SUSPENSE)—Some. The burning of Atlanta, one the most riveting in film history, is indeed terrifying. So is the attack on Scarlett's buggy.

AGE 0–2		As Scarlett would say, don't be a goose.
AGE 3–4		Ditto.
AGE 5–6		Afraid not.
AGE 7–10		Getting closer.
AGE 11–12	★★★★	Will need your help with some historical details, but otherwise perfect.
AGE 13+	★★★★	Just plain perfect.
ADULT	★★★★	What can we say?

SUGGESTED AGES—10–99

Good Morning, Vietnam (R)

1988 Comedy; Drama
Directed by Barry Levinson
Starring Robin Williams, Forest Whitaker, Tung Thanh Tran, Bruno Kirby

This film almost didn't make it onto our list because of the R rating and the violence. (Not to mention the profanity.) But we decided that it was too good, too moving, and too funny not to include. It's based on the true story of Adrian Cronauer, a fast-talking Radio Armed Forces disc jockey who rides to fame and official opprobrium with his irreverent send-ups of top brass, grunts, and Charlie Cong. It's also about the insanity of war (this confusing war in particular) and the need for laughter in the grimmest of situations.

SEX OR NUDITY—Minimal.
VIOLENCE—A lot. There's a gruesome terrorist attack on a café and a searing montage of shots showing villages being blown up, set to hauntingly beautiful music.
LANGUAGE—A lot. Hey, it's a war film.
FEAR FACTOR (SUSPENSE)—A lot. Cronauer is lost in the jungle once, but comes out unscathed. The real tension is between him and the censors.

AGE 0–2		No way.
AGE 3–4		No way.
AGE 5–6		No way.
AGE 7–10		No way.
AGE 11–12	★★★	Yes, an enthusiastic yes. But beware of the violence.
AGE 13+	★★★★	Perfect. Robin Williams's comforting presence makes this tour of duty through the war zone bearable, funny, and eventually moving.
ADULT	★★★★	Brilliant.

SUGGESTED AGES—12–99

Grease (PG)

1978 Musical; Comedy
Directed by Randal Kleiser
Starring John Travolta, Olivia Newton-John, Stockard Channing, Didi Conn, Eve Arden, Sid Caesar

A terrific musical comedy that made an energetic, entertaining transition from the stage to the screen. There is only one problem: it is basically about sex among high school kids. It is also about being accepted versus being yourself. But it's still about sex—talking about it, trying to do, sometimes actually doing it. Set in the 1950s, there is a certain innocence. But the language is still, well, what high school kids actually sounded like and pretty much still sound like. Plus there is constant smoking, a bit of drinking, and plenty of insulting. Yep, pretty realistic. But it is a wonderfully enjoyable movie: John Travolta dances and Oliva Newton-John really sings! The only questions you have to answer are: Is your child ready for this and do you want to be the one to explain it all to him or her? We've come down on the affirmative—for our kids. But you have to make the call for your family.

SEX OR NUDITY—A lot. No nudity, but lots of talk and suggestive behavior.
VIOLENCE—None.
LANGUAGE—A lot. The usual array of high school cursing circa 1955—which makes it fairly tame by today's standards (or lack of standards).
FEAR FACTOR (SUSPENSE)—Minimal. Will the hot rod race end safely? Is she pregnant or isn't she?

AGE 0–2		No way.
AGE 3–4	★	Music and dancing are super, but they won't get it.
AGE 5–6	★★	They will appreciate the energy, and hopefully not understand too much.
AGE 7–10	★★★	They'll get most of it; be prepared to explain the rest.

AGE 11–12 ★★★★ They'll love it.
AGE 13+ ★★★★ Ditto.
ADULT ★★★ So will you.

SUGGESTED AGES—6–99

Great Dictator, The (No Rating)
1940 Comedy; Drama
Directed by Charlie Chaplin
Starring Charlie Chaplin, Paulette Goddard, Jack Oakie

This film may be Chaplin's greatest legacy. It is not his funniest, but in many ways it is his most important. Made at the outbreak of World War II, it is a fascinating blend of slapstick and social commentary. Chaplin stars in two roles: a Jewish barber living in the ghetto, and dictator Adenoid Hynkel of Tomania. Parents will have to do a fair amount of explaining to children of virtually all ages, but it is worth it. This film is a classic as both satire and entertainment.

SEX OR NUDITY—Minimal. Some kissing.
VIOLENCE—A lot. The film opens with war scenes set in the trenches of World War I, but the real violence is that perpetrated against Jews in the ghetto. It is not graphic, but it is insidious.
LANGUAGE—Minimal.
FEAR FACTOR (SUSPENSE)—Minimal.

AGE 0–2		No way.
AGE 3–4		Still pushing it.
AGE 5–6	★	They'll appreciate the slapstick, but the dual roles and context will go way over their heads.
AGE 7–10	★★	They'll appreciate and enjoy more.
AGE 11–12	★★★	Perfect.
AGE 13+	★★★	Ditto.
ADULT	★★★	You will marvel at the insights and audacity that Chaplin brought to these critical issues as early as 1940.

SUGGESTED AGES—6–99

Great Escape, The (No Rating)

1963 Action/Adventure
Directed by John Sturges
Starring Steve McQueen, James Garner, Richard Attenborough, Charles Bronson, James Coburn, David McCallum

We listed all these stars—and they represent just *some* of the terrific actors in this all-star cast—because this film is that unique combination of ensemble acting and great adventure. This film worked when we first saw it as kids in the mid-1960s and it still works today. Based on a true story, it is the nail-biting drama of an extraordinary escape from a German prisoner of war camp during World War II. Be prepared to explain some history to kids as they are sure to have questions after seeing this super film.

SEX OR NUDITY—None.
VIOLENCE—Some. Yes, the good guys do get killed.
LANGUAGE—Minimal.
FEAR FACTOR (SUSPENSE)—Some. We *really* root for the Allies to escape.

AGE 0–2		No way.
AGE 3–4		Still no way.
AGE 5–6	★	If they have an older sibling in the room, they'll watch because they will see the others mesmerized.
AGE 7–10	★★★	They'll love it!
AGE 11–12	★★★★	They'll still love it, and will probably shed a tear.
AGE 13+	★★★★	Ditto, plus they'll understand the context.
ADULT	★★★★	Enjoy it yet again!

SUGGESTED AGES—7–99

Great Gatsby, The (PG)

1974 Drama
Directed by Jack Clayton
Starring Robert Redford, Mia Farrow, Bruce Dern, Karen Black, Sam Waterston

Sumptuous adaptation of F. Scott Fitzgerald's novel about Jay Gatsby, an enigmatic millionaire who loves the self-absorbed and unattainable Daisy Buchanan. Some kids will need background information on the Roaring Twenties, Prohibition, and such, and most will need your help sorting out the subtle plot. Still, it's worth a go, especially if it's on your child's summer reading list. (Or is that cheating?)

SEX OR NUDITY—None. Discreetly implied, but never shown.
VIOLENCE—Some. A devastating hit-and-run accident and a shooting at the end. Not graphic, though.
LANGUAGE—None. Rather limited.
FEAR FACTOR (SUSPENSE)—Minimal.

AGE 0–2		No way.
AGE 3–4		Still no way.
AGE 5–6		Ditto.
AGE 7–10		Too slow moving, even for mature kids in this age group.
AGE 11–12	★★★	A good choice, especially if they're assigned the book.
AGE 13+	★★★	Yes. Insist on it.
ADULT	★★★	An all-star cast; a classic story always worth seeing again.

SUGGESTED AGES—12–99

Gunga Din (No Rating)

1940 Action/Adventure
Directed by George Stevens
Starring Cary Grant, Victor McLaglen, Douglas Fairbanks, Jr., Sam Jaffe

Loosely based on Rudyard Kipling's famous poem, this is a classic Hollywood action/adventure film set in nineteenth-century India. On one level, this is the story of three carousing friends serving in the British army and battling a savage cult. On another level, it is about class warfare: the British versus the "savages" and British officers versus enlisted men. But perhaps most interestingly, it is probably the original buddy movie.

SEX OR NUDITY—None.

VIOLENCE—A lot. Lots of sword and gun battles.

LANGUAGE—None.

FEAR FACTOR (SUSPENSE)—Some. We care about Cary Grant and friends; and this *is* a war flick.

AGE 0–2		No way.
AGE 3–4	★	Barely suitable if you don't mind lots of fighting.
AGE 5–6	★★	They'll start to appreciate it.
AGE 7–10	★★	This group will appreciate it.
AGE 11–12	★★★	Ditto.
AGE 13+	★★★	They'll love it.
ADULT	★★★	So will you.

SUGGESTED AGES—5–99

Guys and Dolls (No Rating)

1955 Musical
Directed by Joseph Mankiewicz
Starring Marlon Brando, Jean Simmons, Frank Sinatra, Stubby Kaye, Sheldon Leonard, Vivian Blaine

One of the great Broadway shows, *Guys and Dolls* made a pretty good transition to film. Brando, in his musical debut, plays Sky Masterson, a professional gambler. He makes a bet with his buddies that he can win over the Salvation Army woman who is determined to turn him away from his gambling ways. Ultimately, Masterson is torn between his lifestyle and the woman who grows to be the object of his heart. Brando isn't half bad, but the rest of the cast is super! And the songs—from "Luck Be a Lady Tonight" to "Sit Down You're Rocking the Boat"— are great!

SEX OR NUDITY—Minimal. Talk, but nothing more explicit than a kiss.
VIOLENCE—None.
LANGUAGE—None.
FEAR FACTOR (SUSPENSE)—None.

AGE 0–2		Nope.
AGE 3–4		Not quite.
AGE 5–6	★	They won't get much, but the tunes may hold them a bit.
AGE 7–10	★★★	Perfect.
AGE 11–12	★★★	Ditto.
AGE 13+	★★★	High schools and summer camps all across the country put this on, so expect some interesting comparisons.
ADULT	★★★	A classic musical!

SUGGESTED AGES—7–99

Heidi (G)

1937 Drama
Directed by Allan Dwan
Starring Shirley Temple, Jean Hershot, Arthur Treacher

Insist on the original. There are no less than four versions of Johanna Spyri's heartwarming tale of a young Swiss girl from a bucolic Alpine farm who is sent, against her will, to be a companion to a young city girl in a wheelchair. This one, available in both black and white and in a new colorized version, is the best. (The others are serviceable, but they don't have Shirley Temple.)

SEX OR NUDITY—None.

VIOLENCE—None.

LANGUAGE—None.

FEAR FACTOR (SUSPENSE)—Minimal. When Heidi is separated from her beloved grandfather, it's more heart-wrenching than fearful.

AGE 0–2		Not quite ready for this.
AGE 3–4	★★	Give it a try.
AGE 5–6	★★★	Wonderful.
AGE 7–10	★★	Girls through age ten will love it. Boys are another matter.
AGE 11–12	★★	Pushing it.
AGE 13+	★	Probably too old for it.
ADULT	★★★	But you're not. Never will be.

SUGGESTED AGES—4–11

High Noon (No Rating)

1952 Western
Directed by Fred Zinnemann
Starring Gary Cooper, Thomas Mitchell, Lloyd Bridges, Grace Kelly

The winner of four Academy Awards, this is one of a handful of truly classic Westerns. Gary Cooper (who won Best Actor) plays the sheriff of a small town, who on his wedding—and retirement—day, learns that four killers are coming to town to seek revenge against him. Although the town professes to admire and even love their sheriff, no one is willing to help him. The showdown is, of course, to be at high noon, and the many shots of clocks add to the tension. A terrific film with themes worth discussing with kids of almost any age.

SEX OR NUDITY—None.

VIOLENCE—Some. Yep, a big shoot-out.

LANGUAGE—None.

FEAR FACTOR (SUSPENSE)—A lot. The tension truly builds.

AGE 0–2		No way.
AGE 3–4		Ditto.
AGE 5–6	★★	They'll start to appreciate it.
AGE 7–10	★★★	They'll love it.
AGE 11–12	★★★	Ditto.
AGE 13+	★★★	This group will recognize that it is more than a simple Western or action flick.
ADULT	★★★	So will you.

SUGGESTED AGES—6–99

Homeward Bound: The Incredible Journey (G)

1993 Animal; Drama
Directed by Duwayne Dunham
Starring Robert Hayes, Kim Griest, Jean Smart, and the voices of Michael J. Fox, Sally Field, Don Ameche

A talking animal movie that will surprise you with its believability, drama, and poignancy. Three pets—Chance, a brash young puppy, Shadow, a wise older dog, and Sassy, a snobby cat—are left at a friend's ranch when their owners go on a trip to San Francisco. The animals decide that they've been marooned and set out on a cross-country journey to find their owners. Improbable as this may sound, the filmmakers bring it to life with incredible live-action stunts and the amusing voices of the squabbling pets. Be prepared for strong emotions to be stirred up at the end when the pets are finally reunited with their owners. One of the most delightful children's movies in recent years.

SEX OR NUDITY—None.

VIOLENCE—None.

LANGUAGE—None.

FEAR FACTOR (SUSPENSE)—Some. Many near-catastophes, including one where Sassy is swept over a waterfall and given up for lost, and one especially painful-looking scene where Chance gets a snoutful of porcupine quills removed.

AGE 0–2		Probably too scary for them.
AGE 3–4	★	Sensitive children will find the suspense too much to take; other kids will love the action sequences. Your call.
AGE 5–6	★★★★	Right up their alley.
AGE 7–10	★★★★	All but the oldest children in this age group will love it.
AGE 11–12	★★	Maybe.
AGE 13+	★	Nah. Only real animal lovers or very patient older siblings will be willing to watch.

ADULT   ★★★★   You may resist it at first, but you'll find it sur-
                        prisingly charming.

SUGGESTED AGES—4–9

Honey, I Shrunk the Kids (PG)

1989 Fantasy/Science Fiction; Comedy
Directed by Joe Johnston
Starring Rick Moranis, Matt Frewer, Marica Srassman, Kristine Sutherland

Great special effects are what's good and bad about this film. The kids, accidentally reduced to insect size by their absent-minded professor father, battle giant honeybees, a torrent of water from a garden hose, and other hazards so convincingly big and fearsome that younger kids will be frightened. Don't let this deter you, though, from renting this movie for older ones. It's a great adventure flick where everyday objects—bits of cereal, blades of grass—are re-created in loving and extreme exaggeration. (You can forget the sequel, however; it's all special effects and no character development.)

SEX OR NUDITY—None.
VIOLENCE—Minimal. No violence per se, but plenty of suspenseful, anxiety-provoking near-disasters.
LANGUAGE—Mild. The kind of stuff your kids say to each other all the time.
FEAR FACTOR (SUSPENSE)—Some. Can be intense for younger kids.

AGE 0–2		Nah, it'll give them nightmares.
AGE 3–4		Ditto.
AGE 5–6	★★	OK, but not for kids prone to fearful reactions.
AGE 7–10	★★★	Bingo.
AGE 11–12	★★	The outer limit.
AGE 13+	★★	Too bad, they're probably too old for this one.
ADULT	★★	Good thing you're not.

SUGGESTED AGES—6–10

Hoosiers (PG)

1986 Sports; Drama
Directed by David Anspaugh
Starring Gene Hackman, Barbara Hershey, Dennis Hopper

Rated by *USA Today* readers as their favorite sports video, *Hoosiers* is the Cinderella story of how a real-life Indiana high school basketball team made it to the state finals. It's also the comeback story of coach Norman Dale (Gene Hackman), a man with a shady past, and Shooter (Dennis Hopper), the town drunk and father of one of the players. This is less a sports story than a tale of growth and redemption, with basketball as the vehicle. The climax will surprise jaded sports-video watchers, but that's another one of the charms of this unusual video.

SEX OR NUDITY—A little romance, no sex or nudity.

VIOLENCE—A punch or two is thrown; no one gets hurt.

LANGUAGE—Surprisingly tame.

FEAR FACTOR (SUSPENSE)—Not to worry.

AGE 0–2		No way.
AGE 3–4		Ditto.
AGE 5–6	★	Even basketball diehards will get restless and wander out to shoot some real hoops.
AGE 7–10	★★	With help from you, they ought to appreciate it.
AGE 11–12	★★★	Complicated but worth the effort.
AGE 13+	★★★★	Bingo.
ADULT	★★★★	Yup.

SUGGESTED AGES—7–99

Hopscotch (R)

1980 Comedy
Directed by Ronald Neame
Starring Walter Matthau, Glenda Jackson, Sam Waterston, Ned Beatty

Don't let the R rating scare you off; except for one character who curses incessantly (and he's the bad guy who gets his comeuppance), this film deserves a PG. This is a caper movie about a nice-guy CIA agent (Walter Matthau) who is sent to an unwanted desk job by his idiot hard-nosed boss (Beatty). Rather than take retirement gracefully, Matthau comes up with a way of getting even: publishing his tell-all memoirs. The plot is contrived, but the film is good-natured and funny.

SEX OR NUDITY—None.

VIOLENCE—None.

LANGUAGE—Lots of profanity from Ned Beatty, but it is so clear that the cursing contributes to his being a jerk that the inappropriate use of language is one of the lessons learned.

FEAR FACTOR (SUSPENSE)—Minimal.

AGE 0–2		No way.
AGE 3–4		Still no way.
AGE 5–6	★	A bit of slapstick, but not enough to hold their interest.
AGE 7–10	★★★	They'll enjoy it, even if they don't appreciate the Nixon-era references.
AGE 11–12	★★★	Ditto.
AGE 13+	★★★	A real hoot for this group as they start to understand the historical references.
ADULT	★★★	A joy to share.

SUGGESTED AGES—7–99

Indian in the Cupboard, The (PG)

1995 Fantasy/Science Fiction
Directed by Frank Oz
Starring Hal Scardino, Litefoot, Rishi Bhat, David Keith, Lindsay Crouse

This charming fantasy is based on Lynne Reid Banks's wonderful book about Omri, a nine-year-old boy who discovers that he can bring his toys to life by placing them inside an old cupboard. First he transforms a plastic toy Indian into a living, breathing three-inch-tall man. Then he brings a toy cowboy to life, setting off a miniature cowboy-and-Indian war. Eventually, Omri realizes he is responsible for the two living toys and the consequences of bringing them to life. The message is moving, funny, and poignant but not heavy.

Footnote: Seeing the film is one way to get reluctant readers interested in Banks's book and its sequels.

SEX OR NUDITY—None.
VIOLENCE—None.
LANGUAGE—Very mild and in context.
FEAR FACTOR (SUSPENSE)—Kids may be frightened when the Indian is trapped under a floorboard with Omri's brother's pet rat.

AGE 0–2		No.
AGE 3–4	★	Probably not.
AGE 5–6	★★★	Although it's a little slow-moving, for this age group, they ought to be charmed.
AGE 7–10	★★★★	Bingo. For boys and girls alike.
AGE 11–12	★★★★	Not too old to enjoy it.
AGE 13+	★★★	Probably too old for this one; may be willing to watch if they've read the book.
ADULT	★★★★	Enchanting.

SUGGESTED AGES—5–12

In-Laws, The (PG)
1979 Comedy
Directed by Arthur Hiller
Starring Peter Falk, Alan Arkin, Richard Libertini

This may be one of the five funniest comedies for kids and parents to share. In fact, it may be one of the five funniest films, period. Peter Falk claims to be a CIA agent, and enlists his soon-to-be-in-law Alan Arkin, a mild-mannered dentist, in a truly wacky scheme of international espionage. Not to be missed is South American dictator Libertini's art collection and talking hand. Don't ask, don't tell, but be prepared to double over in laughter.

SEX OR NUDITY—A painting with nude breasts.
VIOLENCE—Very slapstick chases and shoot-outs.
LANGUAGE—Nothing to be concerned about.
FEAR FACTOR (SUSPENSE)—Will Libertini execute the captured spies?

AGE 0–2		Sorry, no, and too bad.
AGE 3–4	★	Why not? They won't get much, but they will appreciate your laughing so hard.
AGE 5–6	★★★	Even this age will understand how hysterical this is.
AGE 7–10	★★★★	They will love it!
AGE 11–12	★★★★	Ditto.
AGE 13+	★★★★	They will agree that this is one of the funniest videos around, and they'll be amazed by your sense of humor.
ADULT	★★★★	Double ditto!

SUGGESTED AGES—4–99

It's a Mad, Mad, Mad, Mad World (No Rating)

1963 Comedy
Directed by Stanley Kramer
Starring Spencer Tracy, Milton Berle, Sid Caesar, Buddy Hackett, Ethel Merman, Phil Silvers, Peter Falk

An all-star cast in a very silly, usually very funny movie about several groups of people in pursuit of hidden bank loot. Spencer Tracy plays the detective on their tail. It has gags, pratfalls, and the classic schtick of some of the best comedic actors of the 1960s.

SEX OR NUDITY—Nothing to worry about.
VIOLENCE—Lots of crashes, a few fights, all of it slapstick.
LANGUAGE—A few exclamations, but nothing rauchy.
FEAR FACTOR (SUSPENSE)—Minimal.

AGE 0–2		No, sorry.
AGE 3–4	★	They won't understand much, but they may enjoy the slapstick.
AGE 5–6	★★	Better. They won't miss much of the humor.
AGE 7–10	★★★	Perfect.
AGE 11–12	★★★	Ditto.
AGE 13+	★★★	Just fine.
ADULT	★★★	More of a nostalgia trip than a first-rate comedy.

SUGGESTED AGES—6–99

James and the Giant Peach (PG)

1995 Animated
Directed by Henry Selick
Starring the voices of Susan Sarandon, Richard Dreyfuss, Simon Callow, Miriam Margolyes, David Thewlis

We didn't like this as much as our kids did, but we're not fans of the dark, edgy work of producer Tim Burton. Or maybe it's because the parents in this film are wiped out in the opening moments with such obvious delight. That's probably the only really scary scene in the movie. The rest of this film—a trans-Atlantic fantasy that involves the wily James and a host of larger-than-life insects aboard, you guessed it, a giant peach—is just charming. Exciting. Not as good as Roald Dahl's book, but pretty darn good.

SEX OR NUDITY—None.

VIOLENCE—The parents are gored by a rampaging rhino right before James's eyes.

LANGUAGE—None.

FEAR FACTOR (SUSPENSE)—Just right.

AGE 0–2		The opening scene is too intense.
AGE 3–4	★★	Maybe. James's mean old aunts are awfully mean to behold.
AGE 5–6	★★★	Perfect.
AGE 7–10	★★★	Ditto. Maybe they'll even read the book.
AGE 11–12	★	Nope.
AGE 13+		No, sorry.
ADULT	★★★	Relax and enjoy. It's just a movie, right?

SUGGESTED AGES—4–10

Jungle Book, The (G)

1967 Animated
Directed by Wolfgang Reitherman
Starring the voices of Phil Harris, George Sanders, Sterling Holloway, Louis Prima, Sebastian Cabot

Solidly entertaining from beginning to end, this film tells the story of Mowgli, the orphan boy who is adopted by a host of jungle creatures. But when Shere Khan, a vicious, human-hating tiger, threatens them, the animals decide that Mowgli must go back to the village. Bagheera, a real softy of a panther, agrees to act as Mowgli's escort, only to have his efforts undermined by Baloo, an easygoing bear. Jazzy songs with inspired lyrics will have little kids dancing (and possibly you, too) in front of the television. Great drama and pathos at the end.

A note for film buffs: This was the last cartoon feature supervised by Walt Disney himself. (This film is not to be confused with the 1942 original or the 1994 live-action version.)

SEX OR NUDITY—None.

VIOLENCE—None.

LANGUAGE—None.

FEAR FACTOR (SUSPENSE)—A wily snake almost ensnares Mowgli; a final showdown with Shere Khan and his henchmen may send little ones to your lap.

AGE 0–2	★★★★	A guaranteed hit. (Your child will want to watch this so often, you'll probably want to buy it.)
AGE 3–4	★★★★	Sure to become a favorite, this film explores two popular fantasies of kids this age: living in the wild and befriending animals.
AGE 5–6	★★★	If they didn't see it when they were little, convince them to give it a try. They'll be glad you did.
AGE 7–10	★★	They'll probably think they're too sophisticated for it, even if they're not.
AGE 11–12		Ditto.

AGE 13+   Sorry, no.

ADULT   ★★★★   A complete delight. Even if you stop watching
                           alongside your child after the umpteenth time
                           he watches it, you'll find yourself coming in
                           just so you can sing along with songs like "The
                           Bear Necessities."

SUGGESTED AGES—2–10

Junior (PG-13)
1994 Comedy
Directed by Ivan Reitman
Starring Arnold Schwarzenegger, Danny DeVito, Emma Thompson

Think of this as *From Here to Maternity*. Schwarzenegger plays a fertility researcher who tests a new drug on himself and becomes pregnant. The comic possibilities of Schwarzenegger with mood swings, morning sickness, and newfound feelings of tenderness are heightened when he discovers that the frozen ovum used for this improbable experiment belongs to his fellow researcher and love interest. This is good, silly fun, but you may be in for a discussion about the birds and the bees afterward.

SEX OR NUDITY—Either discreetly off-screen or in a petri dish.
VIOLENCE—Virtually none.
LANGUAGE—Very mild.
FEAR FACTOR (SUSPENSE)—None.

AGE 0–2		Would be premature.
AGE 3–4		Ditto.
AGE 5–6	★	Probably not.
AGE 7–10	★★	May develop some wildly inaccurate ideas about sex, but will love seeing the Terminator in maternity drag.
AGE 11–12	★★★	Assuming they've had Sex Ed 101, they'll get all the jokes.
AGE 13+	★★★	They'll understand more than you'd like them to.
ADULT	★★★	Go ahead, laugh.

SUGGESTED AGES—8–99

Jurassic Park (PG-13)

1993 Fantasy/Science Fiction; Action/Adventure
Directed by Steven Spielberg
Starring Sam Neill, Laura Dern, Jeff Goldblum, Richard Attenborough,
Wayne Knight, B. D. Wong

When this film was first released in cinemas, Spielberg was reputed to
have cautioned parents that the film was too intense for children under
ten (including, supposedly, his own kids). It's still pretty powerful—the
PG-13 rating is for "intense science fiction terror"—even on a small
screen. But it will be hard to keep young dinosaur aficionados away from
this riveting film about what just might happen if we were to clone these
ancient beasts. The plot: A millionaire dreamer builds a theme park
where prehistoric creatures dwell safely behind electrified fences in a
computer-controlled environment. When an unscrupulous employee
shuts down the computer system in order to smuggle out a few dinosaur
embryos, intense science fiction terror results. The beasts rampage
through the park, terrorizing everyone, including a pair of cute kids who
happen to be the park owner's grandchildren. This is one heck of an
exciting film—but it is not for the faint of heart.

SEX OR NUDITY—None.
VIOLENCE—A lot. This is a real monster movie. People die grisly
deaths, but this film is more terrifying than violent.
LANGUAGE—Minimal. Language is the least of your worries with this
film.
FEAR FACTOR (SUSPENSE)—A lot. Several unforgettable, nightmare-
inducing scenes, including one where the two children are trapped in a
car being attacked by a hungry carnivore, and one where they are chased
through a kitchen by two vicious raptors.

AGE 0–2	No way. Stick to Barney.
AGE 3–4	Ditto.
AGE 5–6	Don't. The thrill won't be worth the night-mares.

AGE 7–10	★	Your call. Older kids in this age group can handle it without problems.
AGE 11–12	★★★★	A great, old-fashioned adrenaline rush.
AGE 13+	★★★★	They'll recognize this for the modern classic that it is.
ADULT	★★★★	You'll just have to keep reminding yourself that they never kill off the kids in movies.

SUGGESTED AGES—10–99

Karate Kid, The (PG)

1984 Sports; Drama
Directed by John G. Avildsen
Starring Ralph Macchio, Noriyuki "Pat" Morita, Elizabeth Shue

Don't turn up your nose at this one. This is as sweet, refreshing, and exciting as a kid's movie gets. Daniel is a lonely, restless teenager who moves to Los Angeles. He is almost certain to get into trouble until the odd Japanese janitor in his apartment building takes Daniel under his wing. Mr. Miagi, a master karate teacher whose methods are somewhat unorthodox, puts Daniel on a regimen of work, shining cars, painting fences, and ultimately, karate. The movie culminates with a big fight scene where Daniel faces the bullies who've been tormenting him since he arrived. But the movie's message is oddly pacifist: Mr. Miagi, a deadly fighter, fights only after all attempts to make peace have failed, and he teaches his young protégé to do likewise. The best part of the movie, however, isn't the fighting or the preaching; it's the friendship that blossoms between the boy and the old man.

The sequels, with the exception of *The Last Karate Kid*, in which Mr. Miagi trains a girl warrior, aren't up to this one.

SEX OR NUDITY—None.
VIOLENCE—Some. It is about martial arts, after all.
LANGUAGE—Minimal.
FEAR FACTOR (SUSPENSE)—Minimal. There's a certain amount of tension in the obligatory fight scene, even though we know our boy will win.

AGE 0–2		No.
AGE 3–4		No. Stick with the Power Rangers for the time being.
AGE 5–6	★	Only for karate enthusiasts.
AGE 7–10	★★★★	Right on.
AGE 11–12	★★	Still OK.

| AGE 13+ | ★ | Nah. They're probably too cool to be caught watching this. |
| ADULT | ★★★ | You'll be pleasantly surprised. |

SUGGESTED AGES—7–10

Kid, The (No Rating)

1921 Comedy; Drama
Directed by Charlie Chaplin
Starring Charlie Chaplin, Jackie Coogan, Edna Purviance

We almost didn't include this film in the book, but in the end decided it was too much of a classic to omit. The reason we were hesitant is simple: A child is abandoned by his unwed mother, unwittingly kidnapped by car thieves, learns to be a scam artist in cahoots with his "adoptive" father (Chaplin), and is later taken away from Chaplin by the orphan asylum baddies. Phew! That combination can be difficult for kids as well as for adults. But there is enough humor and love to make this—Chaplin's first feature—a treat for both parent and child.

SEX OR NUDITY—Minimal. Kissing.

VIOLENCE—Some. Several very funny fights between the kid and bully, and between the bully's thug brother and the Little Tramp.

LANGUAGE—None.

FEAR FACTOR (SUSPENSE)—Some. Sit close to your child as the recurring theme of abandonment can be disturbing.

AGE 0–2		No.
AGE 3–4	★	The slapstick will be appreciated by this group.
AGE 5–6	★★	These kids will enjoy this enormously.
AGE 7–10	★★	Ditto.
AGE 11–12	★★	This group may think themselves too mature.
AGE 13+	★★	They'll probably appreciate it more as a classic.
ADULT	★★	So will you.

SUGGESTED AGES—4–99

King Kong (No Rating)

1933 Fantasy/Science Fiction
Directed by Ernest Shoedsack
Starring Fay Wray, Robert Armstrong

Of course we're talking about the original 1933 version, not the lame 1976 remake. The story is a twist on the classic tale of Beauty and the Beast. This film works even in light of today's advanced special effects. It is dramatic and poignant, and you shouldn't let the fact that it is in black and white discourage your kids from watching it.

SEX OR NUDITY—Minimal. Kong loves Fay Wray!

VIOLENCE—Some. Plenty of shooting.

LANGUAGE—None.

FEAR FACTOR (SUSPENSE)—Some. Only of the dramatic kind, writ large.

AGE 0–2		Nope.
AGE 3–4	★	They may get a kick out of Kong.
AGE 5–6	★★	We're getting there.
AGE 7–10	★★★	This is a perfect antidote to the new *Godzilla*.
AGE 11–12	★★★	You bet!
AGE 13+	★★★	Ditto.
ADULT	★★★	Great nostalgia!

SUGGESTED AGES—5–99

Lady and the Tramp (G)
1955 Animated
Directed by Hamilton Luske
Starring the voices of Peggy Lee, Barbara Luddy

The charming story of the romance between a pedigreed pup and a mutt from the wrong side of the tracks. It's also a cleverly disguised story about sibling rivalry since it's a new baby in the house that sends Lady on the lam. She's ill-equipped for the mean streets and comes to learn a lot from her streetwise pal. This is a classic that is as good today as it was the day it came out.

SEX OR NUDITY—None.
VIOLENCE—None.
LANGUAGE—None.
FEAR FACTOR (SUSPENSE)—None. One mildly upsetting scene of a rat in the baby's bedroom.

AGE 0–2	★★★	Could easily become a favorite.
AGE 3–4	★★★★	Perfect.
AGE 5–6	★★★★	Ditto.
AGE 7–10	★★★	Getting a little old for such fare.
AGE 11–12		Don't even think about it.
AGE 13+		No way.
ADULT	★★★	Could easily become a favorite of yours, too.

SUGGESTED AGES—1–8

Land Before Time, The (G)
1988 Animated
Directed by Don Bluth
Starring the voices of Helen Shaver, Fred Gwynne, Pat Hingle

After an earthquake and an attack by Tyrannosaurus Rex, Little Foot, an adorable baby brontosaurus, is separated from his mother. He sets off, a little frightened but undaunted, for the lush plains of the Great Valley, where he hopes to find his mother. Along the way he meets other young dinosaurs and gets into scrapes and adventures that teach (subtly) the value of cooperation and caring for each other. At the journey's end, Little Foot realizes that his mother has died; it's a truly sad moment, but not overdone. Even the littlest viewers will understand that Little Foot has found a new family and new strength of his own.

SEX OR NUDITY—None.

VIOLENCE—None.

LANGUAGE—None.

FEAR FACTOR (SUSPENSE)—Minimal. The T-Rex attack may be scary for some children, but it's over in a wink.

AGE 0–2	★★★	The nice slow pace and sweet songs will keep them involved. The story deals with issues right up their alley: separation and independence.
AGE 3–4	★★★★	Perfect for them, too.
AGE 5–6	★★	Probably too slow for a lot of kids this age.
AGE 7–10		Wouldn't want to be caught dead watching this, even though it's delightful.
AGE 11–12		Sorry, no.
AGE 13+		Ditto.
ADULT	★★★★	Surprisingly good.

SUGGESTED AGES—2–6

Lassie (PG)

1994 Animal
Directed by Daniel Petrie
Starring Thomas Guiry, Helen Slater, Jon Tenney

An updated film-length version of the television series, but without the Campbell's Soup advertisements. When the Turner family leaves Baltimore to explore the rural life in Franklin Falls, Virginia, they acquire Lassie, a dog whose daring is exceeded only by her powers of extrasensory perception. The film grafts 1990s-style step-family dynamics onto the classic rural struggle between good and evil. But it's still the Lassie you remember, alerting humans to danger and nudging windows open with her nose, who saves the day. And just like in the television series, there's no actual violence, but there is melodrama that can be upsetting to big and little dog-lovers.

Note: Many tears will be shed before the film's (happy) conclusion. An especially heartbreaking scene includes a shot of Lassie's waterlogged body disappearing under the rapids. The agony is prolonged and Lassie's death seems certain as the family carves her name in a special tree. Have plenty of tissues handy and keep Rover on your lap the whole time.

SEX OR NUDITY—None.

VIOLENCE—Minimal. After a brief, blurry battle of bared teeth and flying fur, Lassie prevails.

LANGUAGE—None. Very mild.

FEAR FACTOR (SUSPENSE)—Minimal. Can be intense.

AGE 0–2		No.
AGE 3–4		Too intense for them.
AGE 5–6	★★★	Yes, but not for the tenderhearted.
AGE 7–10	★★★★	Exciting and entertaining. Be prepared for them to ask to get a dog and move to the country.
AGE 11–12	★★★	For those willing to admit they liked *Homeward Bound*.

AGE 13+   ★   Probably not.
ADULT   ★★   You'll miss June Lockhart and little Timmy.
                      But the scenery is better in this version.

SUGGESTED AGES—6–99

Lawrence of Arabia (PG)

1962 Drama
Directed by David Lean
Starring Peter O'Toole, Omar Sharif, Anthony Quinn, Alec Guiness

This film won seven Academy Awards, including Best Picture, and yet we find many people lukewarm about it. Our bottom line is: this is a terrific film with a few scenes that may be a bit rough for kids. But as a history lesson complete with extraordinary acting and stunning cinematography, there aren't many better films.

The plot centers on the true-life exploits of T. E. Lawrence, a British Army officer who was at first an advisor to the Bedouin tribes in the Middle East during World War I. Lawrence took on Arab dress and mannerisms, and evolved into a true, albeit strange, leader. Watching the film, one could conclude that Peter O'Toole did the same. Considered a classic for good reason, parents should be prepared to explain the historical context. The only really touchy part involves a scene where O'Toole has been raped by a prison commander. We don't see it happen, but there is enough context for kids to deduce that something terrible has happened. Despite that, this film is a must-see.

SEX OR NUDITY—None.

VIOLENCE—A lot. The film's many killings, while not gruesome in the horror-film sense, are powerful.

LANGUAGE—None.

FEAR FACTOR (SUSPENSE)—Some. Just great drama.

AGE 0–2		No way.
AGE 3–4		Still no way.
AGE 5–6	★	They are a bit young, but the desert and battle scenes are stunning.
AGE 7–10	★★★	They will appreciate it.
AGE 11–12	★★★	Ditto.
AGE 13+	★★★★	These kids will understand why it is considered a classic.

ADULT ★★★★ See it again!

SUGGESTED AGES—6–9

League of Their Own, A (PG)

1992 Sports; Drama
Directed by Penny Marshall
Starring Geena Davis, Tom Hanks, Madonna, Lori Petty, Rosie
O'Donnell

The All Girls Professional Baseball League was a little-known bit of feminist trivia until this engaging film came along. Founded as a World War
II novelty, the league once gave women the chance to play the Great
American pastime for money. This film not only chronicles one glorious
season of the short-lived league, it captures all the rivalry and personal
ambitions of the players. There are two sisters—one a gifted home-run
hitter, the other a terrific fielder—who are both teammates and rivals,
there's the floozy (All The Way Maye, portrayed by Madonna) with a
heart of gold and a line drive to match, and the reluctant coach (a former
home-run king turned alcoholic) who is redeemed by the end of the season. An all-star cast, they got game.

Note: This film makes a great girls' slumber party rental.

SEX OR NUDITY—Minimal. In the classic 1940s style, it happens off-
screen.
VIOLENCE—Minimal. A mild fistfight.
LANGUAGE—Minimal. It is a sports film, after all.
FEAR FACTOR (SUSPENSE)—None. Only the kind generated by not
knowing who's going to win the World Series.

AGE 0–2		No.
AGE 3–4		No.
AGE 5–6		Still no.
AGE 7–10	★★★	Little Leaguers in pigtails ought to love it.
AGE 11–12	★★★★	A home run.
AGE 13+	★★★★	Ditto.
ADULT	★★★★	Ditto.

SUGGESTED AGES—8–99

Lion King, The (G)

1994 Animated
Directed by Rob Minkoff, Roger Allers
Starring the voices of Jonathan Taylor Thomas, Matthew Broderick, James Earl Jones, Jeremy Irons, Whoopi Goldberg

"Hakuna matata," the Swahili phrase for "no worries," is often invoked in this masterful film, but it may, in fact, be too worrisome for some children. *The Lion King,* one of the best and most memorable Disney films in the past decade, deals with a somber theme: the death of a parent. In this case, the parent is Mufasa, the lordly king of the African beasts. Mufasa's adorable young son, Simba, believes he's responsible for his beloved father's death. Simba is convinced of his guilt by his Uncle Scar, the real culprit, who caused Mufasa's death in order to take over the kingdom. Simba is so guilt- and grief-stricken, he flees. Eventually, after a lot of soul-searching, Simba regains his regal bearings and returns to oust his villainous uncle and take his rightful place in the circle of life.

This film has all the weight of Greek tragedy, but is animated by a cuddly lion and a couple of hilarious sidekicks. It's also lightened by brilliantly funny, highly hummable, and often deeply meaningful songs. It is a memorable, moving dramatization of some of life's cruelest realities. Still, it is entertaining and, in the end, uplifting.

SEX OR NUDITY—None.
VIOLENCE—Minimal. The stampede death of Mufasa is violent, but not graphic.
LANGUAGE—None.
FEAR FACTOR (SUSPENSE)—The on-screen death of Simba's father may trouble some children and parents. But it is integral to the story and is poignant rather than gory. Two other scenes—where Simba is chased by hyenas and battles with Scar—may be more frightening.

AGE 0–2　　　　　　Even though it features a cuddly lion cub, it's too intense for children this young.

AGE 3–4   ★★   Preschoolers may find the theme—the death of a parent—and the accompanying grief too much to bear. Your call.

AGE 5–6   ★★★★   Educational, entertaining, and deep, which is really saying a lot for a film for first- and second-graders. Most kids this age are mature enough for it, but they'll need your help to understand and process some of the feelings it stirs up.

AGE 7–10   ★★   They'll get all the jokes and even the film's message about taking your parents' advice, but may fancy themselves too old for this G-rated movie. They're not.

AGE 11–12   ★★★   Ironically, this film may be best suited to adolescents and teenagers as it deals with breaking away from family, forging a new identity, and returning to find your place in the world. It was a surprise hit with teens, who may enjoy seeing it again on video.

AGE 13+   ★★   Ditto.

ADULT   ★★★★   As with most Disney films, the script and lyrics are seeded with jokes just for the parents. You too may find it stirs up some feelings about your role in the circle of life; keep some tissues handy.

SUGGESTED AGES—5–99

Little Big League (PG)

1994 Sports; Drama
Directed by Andrew Scheinman
Starring Luke Edwards, Timothy Busfield, Ashley Crow, Jason Robards

Unlike many baseball films, which use the game as a backdrop for a lot of shenanigans, *Little Big League* is practically a love song to America's pastime. This solidly entertaining comedy/fantasy is about Billy Heywood, a twelve-year-old baseball buff who inherits a major league team. The fans boo him and the players ignore him until he walks out to the mound and gets rid of a sulking, stubborn pitcher. He starts to win respect by showing off his encyclopedic knowledge of the game, and eventually gives one of the best locker-room pep talks in recent memory (about how the players ought to be grateful that they get to play baseball). Once the turnaround is underway however, Billy lets the success go to his head, forgetting that he's still a kid. Eventually everyone gets straightened out—just in time for the Big Game.

SEX OR NUDITY—None, although Billy rents a raunchy video on a road trip with the team.
VIOLENCE—None.
LANGUAGE—Minimal. Very tame.
FEAR FACTOR (SUSPENSE)—None.

AGE 0–2		No.
AGE 3–4		A little high and outside for this age group.
AGE 5–6	★★★	Ought to be a solid hit with Little Leaguers.
AGE 7–10	★★★★	A home run.
AGE 11–12	★★★	It may be a little softball for this age group.
AGE 13+	★★	Probably not a big hit.
ADULT	★★★★	One of those rare family films that doesn't condescend to anyone—parents *or* kids.

SUGGESTED AGES—5–10

Little Big Man (PG)

1970 Western
Directed by Arthur Penn
Starring Dustin Hoffman, Faye Dunaway, Chief Dan George, Martin Balsam, Richard Mulligan

Dustin Hoffman plays Jack Crabb, a 121-year-old man who reminisces about his life as survivor of Custer's Last Stand, adopted Indian, gunslinger, Western pioneer, and medicine show hustler. It is very funny, sometimes poignant, and wonderful to watch. It is told principally in the form of flashbacks, which some children may need explained, and richly mixes historical fact and fiction, which will also require some explaining. There is a lot of frontier action/violence, but it is rarely too rough by today's standards. A marvelous movie—enjoy!

SEX OR NUDITY—Minimal. A breast touched; several inferences of sexual activity.
VIOLENCE—Lots of guns, arrows, and killings, but nothing gruesome.
LANGUAGE—Minimal.
FEAR FACTOR (SUSPENSE)—Minimal. Some major characters do get killed off, but there is more sorrow than tension.

AGE 0–2		Nope.
AGE 3–4		Ditto.
AGE 5–6	★	Barely appropriate.
AGE 7–10	★★★	They'll love it.
AGE 11–12	★★★	Ditto.
AGE 13+	★★★★	A real treat and an interesting take on history.
ADULT	★★★★	Wonderfully entertaining.

SUGGESTED AGES—7–99

Little Mermaid, The (G)

1989 Animated
Directed by John Musker, Ron Clements
Starring the voices of Jodi Benson, Pat Carroll, Buddy Hackett

One of the best of Disney's more recent productions, this film features unforgettable scenes of romance, magic, tempest, and crustacean choreography. It tells the story of Ariel, an independent young mermaid who falls in love with a human. Ariel makes a pact with Ursula, the sea witch, in which she trades her voice for the chance to be human. Enjoy the terrific songs, lush drama, good family dynamics, and a winning cast of aquatic sidekicks, but be forewarned: some small children find Ursula too much to take.

SEX OR NUDITY—None.

VIOLENCE—None. No violence per se. But there is an especially scary moment in which Ursula rises up with all the fury of tsunami.

LANGUAGE—None. Clean as a whistle.

FEAR FACTOR (SUSPENSE)—Some. Ursula can be truly menacing.

AGE 0–2		No. Rent *The Jungle Book* instead.
AGE 3–4	★	It'll be hard to keep kids away from this one. Still, we recommend waiting a year.
AGE 5–6	★★★	Smooth sailing.
AGE 7–10	★★★	Ditto.
AGE 11–12		Nope.
AGE 13+		Ditto.
ADULT	★★★	Outstanding.

SUGGESTED AGES—5–10

Little Princess, A (PG)

1995 Drama
Directed by Alfonso Cuaron
Starring Liesel Matthews, Liam Cunningham

In a word: magical. Based on the book by Francis Hodgson Burnett, *A Little Princess* is the story of Sara Crewe, the pampered daughter of a dashing British captain stationed in India, who is sent to Miss Minchin's School for Girls in New York when her widowed father is called to war. Sara succeeds in upending Miss Minchin's strict prohibition against gaiety by enchanting her fellow boarders with her exotic imaginary tales. But when Sara's father is lost in battle and she becomes a penniless orphan, Sara is forced to become Miss Minchin's overworked, underfed servant girl. Her belief in magic, sorely tested by the grim realities of her new life, is never extinguished and, in the end, triumphs gloriously.

Note: Boys, who normally steer clear of any movie with the word "princess" in the title, can rest assured; this film has mystery, adventure, and nary a tiara is in sight.

SEX OR NUDITY—None.

VIOLENCE—None.

LANGUAGE—None. "Snotty two-faced bully" is as coarse as it gets.

FEAR FACTOR (SUSPENSE)—Minimal. One disturbing scene (a corpse-strewn battlefield), one white-knuckle moment (when Sara falls off a plank shakily suspended over a chasm between two buildings), and two brief appearances by an imaginary ten-headed monster.

AGE 0–2		Save it until they're older.
AGE 3–4		Despite the title, it's not really for them, either.
AGE 5–6	★★★	Ought to be captivated.
AGE 7–10	★★★★	Ditto.
AGE 11–12	★★	They may see it if you insist and be pleasantly surprised by how good a G-rated movie can be.
AGE 13+	★★	Ditto.

ADULT   ★★★★   Fine acting, incredibly beautiful, fanciful sets, a good story, and a happy ending. What more can you want?

SUGGESTED AGES—5–11

Little Women (PG)

1994 Drama
Directed by Gillian Armstrong
Starring Winona Ryder, Susan Sarandon, Kirsten Dunst, Trini Alvarado, Claire Danes

Luminous and enchanting, this is the latest and probably the most loving adaptation of Louisa May Alcott's classic story. With their father away at war, the four March girls and their indefatigable mother maintain their dignity, values, and devotion to one another despite straitened financial circumstances. The story is told largely from the vantage point of Jo, an aspiring writer whose lively theatrical productions keep the girls in high spirits and later form the basis for her writing career (just as author Louisa May Alcott's did). This interpretation of Alcott's classic is updated to underscore the family's commitment to feminism, integration, and other currently fashionable issues, yet still features quaint touches, solid historical content, and homespun warmth.

Note: As readers will no doubt recall, Beth, the sensitive, beloved sister, dies after being exposed to typhoid. It is a tear-drenched and wrenching scene, but she dies a radiant, peaceful death.

SEX OR NUDITY—None.

VIOLENCE—None.

LANGUAGE—None. "Oh, blast!" is as salty as it gets.

FEAR FACTOR (SUSPENSE)—Minimal. One scary scene where the youngest daughter, Amy, falls through the ice while skating.

AGE 0–2		Save it for about ten years.
AGE 3–4		Ditto.
AGE 5–6	★	Too slow-going for most kids this age.
AGE 7–10	★★★★	Absolutely charming, but probably only for girls.
AGE 11–12	★★★★	Ditto.
AGE 13+	★★★★	Ditto, especially if they loved the book.
ADULT	★★★★	Be prepared for a good long cry.

SUGGESTED AGES—8–99

Longest Day, The (No Rating)

1962 Action/Adventure
Directed by Ken Annakin, Andrew Marton, Bernhard Wicki
Starring John Wayne, Rod Steiger, Henry Fonda, Robert Ryan, Sean Connery, Peter Lawford, Robert Mitchum

A three-hour, Oscar-winning, grand-scale retelling of the D-Day invasion. This historically accurate story of the Allied landing at Normandy boasts an all-star international cast, great cinematography, and, for its day, spectacular special effects. Many kids are aware of Steven Spielberg's brilliant but too-gruesome epic, *Saving Private Ryan*. This classic, made thirty-five years earlier, also has human drama but relatively less gore, and should trigger dozens of questions from your kids. Be prepared and enjoy.

SEX OR NUDITY—None.

VIOLENCE—A lot. Even the good guys get killed.

LANGUAGE—Some. A bit salty.

FEAR FACTOR (SUSPENSE)—Some. You care about these characters and want them to make it through alive; some don't.

AGE 0–2		No way.
AGE 3–4		Ditto.
AGE 5–6	★	Still pushing it.
AGE 7–10	★★★	Right on target.
AGE 11–12	★★★	Ditto.
AGE 13+	★★★★	This group will really appreciate it.
ADULT	★★★★	A classic.

SUGGESTED AGES—7–99

Look Who's Talking (PG-13)

1989 Comedy
Directed by Amy Heckerling
Starring John Travolta, Kirstie Alley, Olympia Dukakis, George Segal, and the voice of Bruce Willis

A silly, feel-good movie that succeeds admirably. A suddenly single mother-to-be goes into labor in a cab and the cabby falls for her and her baby. He spends the rest of the movie enthralled with them both. She spends the rest of the movie resisting the notion that the perfect father for her baby is right under her nose. That's the plot. But your kids will love the baby's wry, sardonic voice-overs (even if you don't exactly find them hysterical), and you'll all be rolling in the aisles as the baby is accidentally driven off in the back of a cab as it is towed to the pound. The film's ending, featuring voice-overs from a swarm of sperm making their way toward an egg, may raise some interesting questions.

Note: Resist pleas to see the sequels; they're mighty tepid by comparison.

SEX OR NUDITY—Minimal. It's sex, after all, that got the whole ball rolling.
VIOLENCE—None. Only the cartoonish kind.
LANGUAGE—Minimal. A little more than we'd like.
FEAR FACTOR (SUSPENSE)—None. Harmless, screwball fun.

AGE 0–2		Just because it has a baby in it doesn't make it right for this age group.
AGE 3–4		Wait a year.
AGE 5–6	★★	OK.
AGE 7–10	★★★	They'll find the baby's comments unspeakably funny.
AGE 11–12	★★	They're just on the edge of finding this sort of thing too immature for their tastes.
AGE 13+	★	Nah.
ADULT	★★	Relax. *Gone With the Wind* it's not. But it's fun.

SUGGESTED AGES—5–11

Lucas (PG-13)

1986 Drama
Directed by David Seltzer
Starring Corey Haim, Kerri Green, Charlie Sheen, Winona Ryder

Unsappy, unsentimental, unpredictable take on a group of high school kids coming of age in the 1980s. Corey Haim plays Lucas, a small, precocious fourteen-year-old who has skipped several grades and has a crush on a very pretty, older, new girl at school. In an attempt to win her affection—as opposed to her friendship, which he has—he tries out for the football team. The characters are not one-dimensional, nor are the relationships. Very good performances by virtually everyone in the cast, plus some very early roles by actors who went on to become big stars. A surprisingly enjoyable film for parents and (principally older) kids.

SEX OR NUDITY—Some. A locker-room scene with bare bottoms. Lots of talk about sex.
VIOLENCE—Lucas is tormented by some bullies, and football is considered by some to be inherently violent.
LANGUAGE—Yup, the usual array of high school cussing.
FEAR FACTOR (SUSPENSE)—Lucas gets knocked unconscious in the football game.

AGE 0–2		Nope.
AGE 3–4		Ditto.
AGE 5–6	★	Seeing the younger Lucas deal with big kids may strike a chord, but generally this group is too young.
AGE 7–10	★★★	They'll appreciate it.
AGE 11–12	★★★★	They'll love it!
AGE 13+	★★★★	Ditto.
ADULT	★★★	A pleasant surprise.

SUGGESTED AGES—7–99

Madeline (No Rating)

1989–1994 Animated
Narrated by Christopher Plummer

Originally made for HBO, this series of thirty-minute cartoons is surprisingly entertaining and fairly true to the original Ludwig Bemelmans books. Written in rhyme, the simple animation and music make these shows quite charming. For the uninitiated, Madeline and her French schoolgirl friends embark on many adventures, from going to London (and rescuing a horse) to attending a famous cooking school.

Note: Don't confuse this video with the bland 1998 feature film.

SEX OR NUDITY—None.

VIOLENCE—None.

LANGUAGE—None.

FEAR FACTOR (SUSPENSE)—None.

AGE 0–2	★	Nice music and simple animation may hold them.
AGE 3–4	★★	Perfect.
AGE 5–6	★★	Pushing it a bit.
AGE 7–10		They'll not only see themselves as too old, but probably are.
AGE 11–12		No way.
AGE 13+		Ditto.
ADULT	★	Think of this as a pleasant siesta.

SUGGESTED AGES—1–6

Maltese Falcon, The (No Rating)

1941 Drama
Directed by John Huston
Starring Humphrey Bogart, Mary Astor, Peter Lorre, Sydney Greenstreet, Elisha Cook, Jr.

Humphrey Bogart in his quintessential role as private eye Sam Spade. After his partner is murdered, Spade finds himself in the middle of a group of conniving, double-crossing characters in search of the statue known as the black bird, or the "stuff that dreams are made of." This film noir is energetically sinister but not scary. The performances are spectacular. Be prepared to keep explaining what is going on. The plot is not terribly confusing, but it is quick-moving. Encourage your children to hang in there.

SEX OR NUDITY—None.
VIOLENCE—Some. Several murders, but nothing graphic or disturbing.
LANGUAGE—None.
FEAR FACTOR (SUSPENSE)—Some. Film noir tension, but nothing to be really afraid of.

AGE 0–2		No way.
AGE 3–4		Ditto.
AGE 5–6		Ditto.
AGE 7–10	★★	Older kids will start to get and appreciate it.
AGE 11–12	★★★	Should really start to connect.
AGE 13+	★★★★	Perfect.
ADULT	★★★★	A classic.

SUGGESTED AGES—9–99

Man in the Moon, The (PG-13)

1991 Drama

Directed by Robert Mulligan

Starring Reese Witherspoon, Sam Waterston, Tess Harper, Emily Warfield, Jason London

A bittersweet gem of a story about a young girl's first love and the heartache that goes with it. Dani is the fourteen-year-old kid sister who, though she longs to be like Maureen, her perfect older sister, runs off to the swimming hole as soon as it's chore time. It's there that she meets Court, the cute seventeen-year-old boy who has just moved to the farm next door. Dani's puppy love crush on Court grows into something far deeper—a kind of altruistic love—then, after a "perfect" first kiss, he tells her he's too old for her. Later he comes to Dani's house for dinner, meets Maureen, and the two of them fall hopelessly in love. Maureen's guilt is as palpable as Dani's hurt. Tragedy strikes, and the two sisters, once so close, find out how hard—and how wonderful—it is to forgive.

SEX OR NUDITY—Some. It's talked about and attempted, then finally consummated, but with discretion and no nudity.

VIOLENCE—Some. There's only one violent scene. It's both bloody and wrenching, but not gratuitous.

LANGUAGE—Minimal. Very, very tame.

FEAR FACTOR (SUSPENSE)—Minimal. Dani's father, in a fit of anger, takes a belt to her, but the blows are not shown.

AGE 0–2		No way.
AGE 3–4		No way.
AGE 5–6		Still no way.
AGE 7–10		The subject matter makes it inappropriate for even the oldest and most sophisticated kids in this age group. Wait a year or two instead.
AGE 11–12	★★★	Fine for sophisticated kids.
AGE 13+	★★★★	They'll love it. (They will especially like seeing teen heartthrobs Witherspoon and London in early roles.)

ADULT ★★★★ It's perfect. Absolutely perfect. A great vehicle for discussing love, lust, and loyalty.

SUGGESTED AGES—12–99

Marx Brothers, The (No Rating)

1929–1937 Comedy
Starring Groucho, Harpo, Chico, Zeppo, Margaret Dumont

Sadly, most of the Marx Brothers films simply don't work for most kids. The wonderful dialogue goes by too quickly or is over the heads of most kids. Happily, there is enough physical humor to entertain most children. The plots (if one can call them plots) make almost no sense to kids (or adults), and the musical interludes barely sustain anyone's interest. Nevertheless, there is enough silliness for parents and children to share on a rainy afternoon.

Duck Soup (1933) Groucho is named ruler of Freedonia, hires Harpo and Chico as spies, and then declares war on neighboring Sylvania. Harpo's antics with the lemonade vendor and his mirror dance with Groucho are classics.

A Night at the Opera (1935) There is a bit more music in this hilarious film–after all, it is ostensibly about the opera. But don't let that keep you from two classic Marx Brothers scenes: the contract-ripping duel between Groucho and Chico, and the stateroom-stuffing scene.

A Day at the Races (1937) Groucho is a horse doctor who becomes the head of a sanitorium. The principal patient is, of course, Margaret Dumont. Chico's selling race tips is a classic, but this film is a bit weaker than many of the others.

Horse Feathers (1932) What's the password? Swordfish, of course. Groucho is the president of Huxley College, and he is determined to have a winning football team.

Monkey Business (1931) The brothers stow away on an ocean liner. Trying to talk their way through immigration, they each in turn imitate Maurice Chevalier. Hysterical.

Animal Crackers (1930) Hooray indeed for Captain Spaulding. The brothers are guests at an estate owned by, you guessed it, Margaret Dumont. The best scene is the wacky bridge game between Chico and Harpo.

The Cocoanuts (1929) This was the brothers' first film. Set in a Florida resort hotel, it set the tone for many of their later antics. It includes their classic viaduct routine, which is lost on most children, but the kids will love watching you double over with laughter.

SEX OR NUDITY—None.
VIOLENCE—Minimal.
LANGUAGE—None.
FEAR FACTOR (SUSPENSE)—None.

AGE 0–2		No way.
AGE 3–4		Ditto.
AGE 5–6	★	Some of the slapstick will connect with them.
AGE 7–10	★★	This is probably the perfect age. They won't understand much of the repartee, but the sight gags are wonderful.
AGE 11–12	★	The visual elements still work, but there aren't enough of them to sustain interest, and too much of the dialogue goes over their heads.
AGE 13+	★★	Now they should start appreciating the dialogue.
ADULT	★★★	Let the kids watch you laugh!

SUGGESTED AGES—6–99

Mary Poppins (G)

1964 Musical
Directed by Robert Stevenson
Starring Julie Andrews, Dick Van Dyke, Glynis Johns, Ed Wynn

Quite possibly the best Disney film ever. Children's films nowadays are judged by what they don't have: violence, sex, profanity. This film has none of that. More important is what it has: charm, sincerity, fantasy, humor, and no small amount of poignancy as a British nanny works her magic, then leaves on the next updraft. Julie Andrews is luminous, Dick Van Dyke is charming. The special effects, revolutionary in their time, may seem a tad stiff, but this film will cast its spell over your children nonetheless.

SEX OR NUDITY—None.

VIOLENCE—None.

LANGUAGE—None.

FEAR FACTOR (SUSPENSE)—None.

AGE 0–2	★	No problem.
AGE 3–4	★★★★	Perfect.
AGE 5–6	★★★★	Ditto.
AGE 7–10	★★★	No problem.
AGE 11–12		It's a shame, but they're too old for this one.
AGE 13+		Ditto.
ADULT	★★★★	But you're not.

SUGGESTED AGES—2–99

Mask, The (PG-13)

1994 Comedy
Directed by Charles Russell
Starring Jim Carrey, Peter Riegert, Cameron Diaz, Peter Greene, Amy
Yasbeck

One of Jim Carrey's better rubber-face performances enhanced by the
special effects of a magical mask that transforms the meek Stanley Ipkiss
into Superdude. There is a plot that involves bad guys, but it adds little
to the overall experience. In fact, the bad guys are quite yucky, and the
movie has a tawdry side to it. It is quite violent and at times disturbing;
the PG-13 rating is justified and serves as a legitimate warning. Be forewarned: This is not the animated television series. Despite those warn-
ings, it is quite entertaining.

SEX OR NUDITY—Some. Talk about sex, overtones of sex, lots of leer-
ing at Cameron Diaz.
VIOLENCE—A lot. Bad guys with bad weapons, plus revenge by Carrey
in his Mask role.
LANGUAGE—Some. Cursing, particularly by the bad guys.
FEAR FACTOR (SUSPENSE)—A lot. Carrey with the mask on is not
wholly benign. Also, the bad guys are rather disturbing

AGE 0–2		No way.
AGE 3–4		Ditto.
AGE 5–6	★★	They'll like the goofy parts but may be dis-turbed by the rougher moments.
AGE 7–10	★★★	They'll love it, but the younger kids, though scared, will try to be stoic and may need your support.
AGE 11–12	★★★	They'll love it.
AGE 13+	★★	Pushing it a bit.
ADULT	★★	Carrey is terrific in or out of costume, but the rest is nasty.

SUGGESTED AGES—7–99

Mask of Zorro, The (PG-13)
1998 Action/Adventure
Directed by Martin Campbell
Starring Antonio Banderas, Anthony Hopkins

Forget about plot, don't worry about historical context, and certainly don't compare this to the television series of the 1950s and 1960s. *The Mask of Zorro* is a gas, with terrific swordplay, plenty of humor, and style. With the exception of one gruesome scene, involving a severed head and a bottled hand (yes, bottled) by the main villain, this is a perfectly entertaining film for parents and kids of all ages.

Anthony Hopkins plays the original Zorro, who is forced into retirement. Years later, he takes on a protégé, a new Zorro, played with a unique, campy style by Antonio Banderas. There is a plot of sorts, which most kids will be able to follow, but it is really quite secondary. The action, banter, and scenery are just first-rate.

Our only hesitation is that bottled-head-and-hand scene, which is more yucky than gruesome, and can be avoided with a judicial sneeze or covering of the eyes.

SEX OR NUDITY—Minimal. A few kisses and some deft swordwork cutting away of a woman's dress, but nothing is revealed.
VIOLENCE—Lots, but no blood.
LANGUAGE—None.
FEAR FACTOR (SUSPENSE)—Not really, but beware of the bottled head and hand.

AGE 0–2		No way.
AGE 3–4	★★	They'll enjoy it.
AGE 5–6	★★★	They'll enjoy it even more.
AGE 7–10	★★★★	Older kids will love it.
AGE 11–12	★★★	It works just fine fine for this group.
AGE 13+	★★	This group will appreciate just how attractive the stars are.
ADULT	★★	Not bad.

SUGGESTED AGES—4–99

Meet Me in St. Louis (No Rating)
1944 Musical
Directed by Vincente Minnelli
Starring Judy Garland, Margaret O'Brien, Lucille Bremer, Mary Astor, Tom Drake

OK, here's where we get into trouble: This is a chick flick. We have yet to find a father or son who say they really like this movie. Sure, the music is lovely and the portrayal of four sisters living in St. Louis at the time of the 1904 World's Fair is heartwarming. Even Margaret O'Brien's continual scene-stealing performance as five-year-old Tootie is terrific. But for guys—sorry, it's slow.

SEX OR NUDITY—None.
VIOLENCE—Minimal. A slap and a bite.
LANGUAGE—None.
FEAR FACTOR (SUSPENSE)—Minimal. Tootie gets injured and blames her sister's beau.

AGE 0–2		Nope.
AGE 3–4	★	The music may hold some kids—barely.
AGE 5–6	★	Ditto.
AGE 7–10	★★	OK for girls of this age. Guys? Forget about it.
AGE 11–12	★★	Split decision.
AGE 13+	★★	Ditto.
ADULT	★★	Mom may give it more stars; Dad would rather watch water boil.

SUGGESTED AGES—7–99

Mighty, The (PG)

1998 Drama
Directed by Peter Chesholm
Starring Sharon Stone, Kieran Culkin, Gillian Anderson, Harry Dean Stanton, Gena Rowlands

A surprisingly touching story of friendship, brains and brawn, and the power of fantasy. Max is a giant of a kid who can scarcely read and who is taunted at school as the son of Killer Kane, a notorious criminal who killed Max's mother. His unlikely, and only, friend is Kevin, a brilliant boy the other kids call "Freak" because of a birth defect that has stunted his growth. The two team up—with Kevin riding on Max's shoulders—as Freak the Mighty, going on imaginary quests, performing knightly good deeds, and doing battle with a bunch of bullies. The story takes a chilling turn when Killer Kane is released from jail and kidnaps Max and Kevin tries to rescue him. And it takes a tragic if predictable turn when Kevin's disease kills him. This blend of realistic drama and fantasy, based on Rodman Philbrick's book, *Freak the Mighty,* is very, very moving.

SEX OR NUDITY—None.

VIOLENCE—Some. Max's father nearly strangles a woman, setting off a flashback of Max's mother's death.

LANGUAGE—Tame.

FEAR FACTOR (SUSPENSE)—Some. When Max's father appears abruptly in his bedroom, you'll jump. And when he kidnaps his son, the enormous Max is rendered helpless.

AGE 0–2		No way.
AGE 3–4		Ditto.
AGE 5–6		Wait a while.
AGE 7–10	★★★	Great if they can stand the suspenseful parts.
AGE 11–12	★★★	Perfect.
AGE 13+	★★	Try it; there's enough action and enough story to overcome any objections about this being a "kid's movie."
ADULT	★★★	An original. Almost as good as the book.

SUGGESTED AGES—8–99

Mighty Ducks, The (PG)

1992 Sports
Directed by Stephen Herek
Starring Emilio Estevez, Joss Akland, Lane Smith, Heidi King, Joshua Jackson

This, the first in a series of three very popular films featuring the kids' version of the Disney-owned hockey team, is a better-than-average sports drama about a ragtag team that achieves victory. In this twist on a familiar plot, the coach is a lawyer who, to make amends for a drunken driving arrest, must do community service on the ice. You know the rest. The team muddles along, pulls together, almost falls apart, and wins in time for the coach to find personal redemption and a girlfriend in the bargain. Predictable, but still pretty darn good.

Note: The first sequel, *D2*, deals with the effects of success on the Ducks; it's not bad at all. Can't say the same about the final installment: *D3*.

SEX OR NUDITY—None.

VIOLENCE—Minimal. Nothing like the NHL version.

LANGUAGE—Minimal. Pretty tame.

FEAR FACTOR (SUSPENSE)—None.

AGE 0–2		Not yet.
AGE 3–4		Ditto.
AGE 5–6	★★	Sure, why not?
AGE 7–10	★★★	This is the target audience.
AGE 11–12	★★	Harmless.
AGE 13+	★	Won't want to be caught watching.
ADULT	★★	Not outstanding, but at least entertaining.

SUGGESTED AGES—6–11

Mister Roberts (No Rating)

1955 Drama
Directed by John Ford and Mervyn LeRoy
Starring Henry Fonda, James Cagney, William Powell, Jack Lemmon, Betsy Palmer, Ward Bond

A comedy-drama set aboard a Navy cargo ship anchored in a remote Pacific harbor during World War II. Henry Fonda plays an officer yearning for action at odds with his very peculiar captain played by James Cagney. Jack Lemmon won an Oscar for his role as the irrepressible Ensign Pulver.

The plot centers on Fonda's efforts to get transferred and get a well-deserved liberty for the men, Lemmon bragging how he will get even with the captain for a million slights, and Cagney's paranoia and demand for complete control. It is worth it for kids just to hear Fonda lecturing Lemmon about finishing a job. A bit talky, but very well done.

SEX OR NUDITY—Minimal. Horny sailors trying to make it with nurses on a nearby island.
VIOLENCE—Minimal. A fistfight.
LANGUAGE—Minimal. For sailors, they're pretty low-key.
FEAR FACTOR (SUSPENSE)—Minimal.

AGE 0–2		Nope.
AGE 3–4		Ditto.
AGE 5–6		Still too slow and talky for this group.
AGE 7–10	★★	Older kids may enjoy this.
AGE 11–12	★★	Ditto.
AGE 13+	★★★	They'll be surprisingly entertained.
ADULT	★★★★	Find a kid—any kid—and enjoy.

SUGGESTED AGES—9–99

Modern Times (No Rating)

1936 Comedy; Drama
Directed by Charlie Chaplin
Starring Charlie Chaplin, Paulette Goddard, Henry Bergman

This is Charlie Chaplin's last "silent" film, although it is not entirely silent; there is some dialogue along with title cards and spectacular music (composed by Chaplin.) The Little Tramp takes on industrialism and modern life with wit, imagination, and grace. It is often hysterical and always entertaining. It is very physical humor that kids connect with immediately. The sets are classics, particularly those featuring factory assembly line and gears. See if the kids pick up the fact that many of today's most expressive actors, from Kevin Kline to Jim Carrey, have borrowed so much from Chaplin's mannerisms.

SEX OR NUDITY—None, but Chaplin does admire a nude statue.
VIOLENCE—Minimal.
LANGUAGE—None.
FEAR FACTOR (SUSPENSE)—Minimal.

AGE 0–2		Sorry, no.
AGE 3–4	★	The slapstick will start to work its magic.
AGE 5–6	★★	Yep, they'll get it.
AGE 7–10	★★★	They'll love it.
AGE 11–12	★★★	Ditto.
AGE 13+	★★★	They'll appreciate why it is a classic.
ADULT	★★★	You will too.

SUGGESTED AGES—4–99

Mouse and the Motorcycle, The (No Rating)

1990 Comedy; Drama
Directed by Ron Underwood
Starring Ray Walston and Fred Savage

Keith is new in town and bored with living in a hotel with his distracted parents—until he catches Ralph, a little mouse who rides through the hotel on a miniature motorcycle. A combination of live action and stop-action animation brings Ralph so fully to life that your children will believe in Ralph from the first minute they see him. And they'll get a big kick out of seeing life from the ground-level perspective of a mouse. Based on Beverly Cleary's equally funny book. (If your children like this one, try renting *Runaway Mouse*, a sequel that chronicles Ralph's adventures at summer camp.)

SEX OR NUDITY—None.
VIOLENCE—None.
LANGUAGE—None.
FEAR FACTOR (SUSPENSE)—Nothing to fear in this one.

AGE 0–2	★★	They may not be quite ready for this one, but they'll love Ralph even if they don't get the whole story.
AGE 3–4	★★★★	They ought to love it. Brings two classic childhood fantasies to life: living in a hotel and finding a secret pet.
AGE 5–6	★★★	Ditto.
AGE 7–10	★★	Fine and dandy.
AGE 11–12	★	They may be too long in the tooth for this one, even if it is charming.
AGE 13+		Nah.
ADULT	★★★★	You'll love it, too. You may even be able to get your children to read the book afterward.

SUGGESTED AGES—3–9

Mouse Hunt (PG)

1998 Animal; Comedy
Directed by Gore Verbinski
Starring Nathan Lane, Lee Evans, Christopher Walken

Upon the death of their father, the two hapless Smuntz brothers (*The Lion King*'s Nathan Lane and British comic Lee Evans) inherit a crumbling old mansion. They assume it's a white elephant and they also assume it's empty. But when the gouda cheese starts disappearing, they meet the mansion's tenacious tenant: a wily (and very cute) mouse. The mouse leads them on chase to the attic, where they discover documents showing that the house is actually an architectural treasure. The brothers decide they'll auction the house off to the highest bidder as soon as they evict their small, furry lodger.

This mouse is no ordinary rodent, however. Brought to life by the same special effects team who created *Babe*, and the director of the Budweiser frog commercials, this mouse outwits a sea of mousetraps, a vicious cat, a commando-style exterminator (played by Christopher Walken), and every trick the brothers try to play on him. (The mouse, by the way, is played by a team of real mice, animatronic models, and computer-generated images, but most kids will find the effect seamless.) By the time the mouse brings the auction to a crashing halt, children will be shrieking with delight.

One of the most refreshing aspects of this film is that the slapstick, *Home Alone*–style antics of the mouse never have the mean, sadistic edge that so many children's films have adopted lately. This is good clean fun, the kind that brings the adults down a peg without really injuring or degrading them.

SEX OR NUDITY—None. Just one hilarious scene where the mouse disappears inside a woman's cleavage.
VIOLENCE—None. Lots of slapstick, but not the sadistic variety.
LANGUAGE—Three mild but unnecessary profanities.
FEAR FACTOR (SUSPENSE)—Some. Sensitive kids may think the mouse is in danger, but they will soon see it's the humans who are at

risk. Animal lovers of all ages can be reassured that no real cats, mice, or humans were harmed during filming.

AGE 0–2	★	OK, but not for the tenderhearted.
AGE 3–4	★★★	You bet. Just warn them that the mouse doesn't make his appearance for the first fifteen minutes of the film. Most of the humor is visual, but children who don't yet know how to read may need a little help to fully appreciate the jokes.
AGE 5–6	★★★★	They'll love it.
AGE 7–10	★★★★	Not too long in the tooth to enjoy it.
AGE 11–12	★★★	Ditto.
AGE 13+	★	Probably not.
ADULT	★★★★	This film is easy to like.

SUGGESTED AGES—4–11

Mr. Deeds Goes to Town (No Rating)

1936 Comedy; Drama
Directed by Frank Capra
Starring Gary Cooper, Jean Arthur, George Bancroft

Gary Cooper plays a small-town, tuba-playing, regular guy who inherits $20 million from a distant relative. He goes off to the *big* town—New York City—where virtually everyone tries to get hold of a piece of the money and make him look like a rube. Jean Arthur plays a Pulitzer Prize–winning reporter who pretends to be a maiden in distress—a ploy irresistible to the ever-decent Cooper, of course—but who is writing the nastiest headlines in town, unbeknownst to Cooper. He decides to give the money away to needy farmers (the action takes place during the Depression) and the bad guys conspire to have Cooper committed, enabling them to steal the money. Contrived? Not a bit. Frank Capra won his second Academy Award for this film, and despite its being in black-and-white, and having a rat-a-tat dialogue, older kids will truly enjoy this movie.

SEX OR NUDITY—None.

VIOLENCE—Minimal. Three punches—does that make him insane, as charged by the villains?

LANGUAGE—None.

FEAR FACTOR (SUSPENSE)—Minimal. Will Mr. Deeds defend himself or remain silent and be judged insane?

AGE 0–2		No way.
AGE 3–4		Still no way.
AGE 5–6		Afraid not.
AGE 7–10	★★	They'll just start to appreciate Gary Cooper's simple truths and core integrity.
AGE 11–12	★★★	They will appreciate both the Capra humor and the wonderful performances.
AGE 13+	★★★★	Ditto.
ADULT	★★★★	Enjoy!

SUGGESTED AGES—10–99

Mr. Holland's Opus (PG)

1996 Drama
Directed by Stephen Herek
Starring Richard Dreyfuss, Glenne Headly, Jay Thomas, Olympia Dukakis

If you're lucky, you had a teacher like Glen Holland, a guy with passion for his subject, a teacher you never forgot. All too rarely, though, do we ever really know anything about those teachers. Here's Glen Holland's story. His dream to compose the great American symphony is sidetracked when his wife becomes pregnant and he has to stick with the high school music teaching job he abhors. After hitting plenty of sour notes, he stumbles on rock-and-roll as the way to convey his passion for music to his students, and Holland finds himself on an unplanned and very satisfying career as a teacher. Hits a crescendo when arts funding is abruptly cut from the school budget. Good family fare. Weepy ending.

Note: The film drops in historical news footage to show the passage of time, a device some kids will have a hard time following.

SEX OR NUDITY—None.
VIOLENCE—None.
LANGUAGE—None, although astute kids will pick up on a nifty bit of profanity in the sign language.
FEAR FACTOR (SUSPENSE)—None.

AGE 0–2		No.
AGE 3–4		No.
AGE 5–6		Over their heads.
AGE 7–10	★★	Only for the oldest kids in this category.
AGE 11–12	★★★	Perfect.
AGE 13+	★★★	Perfect. May give them a better appreciation for the sacrifices and rewards their own teachers experience. May even induce some kids to take up the clarinet.
ADULT	★★★	Solidly entertaining.

SUGGESTED AGES—9–99

Mr. Smith Goes to Washington (No Rating)
1939 Drama
Directed by Frank Capra
Starring Jimmy Stewart, Jean Arthur, Claude Rains, Harry Carey

The classic Frank Capra story about an idealistic, naive young man (Jimmy Stewart) who goes to Washington as a senator in place of the suddenly deceased incumbent and who finds rampant corruption. The scene where the governor, who has to choose a replacement, is confronted by his eight children who have very firm opinions and extraordinary political sophistication is a terrific introduction to politics.

Jean Arthur is the hard-boiled dame who has seen and heard everything, and who falls for the honest, incorruptible Stewart. This film is widely considered to be among Capra's and Stewart's best, and probably the finest political film ever. But it is a political drama, and that means it is talky—and that means *quick* talking, in Capra's inimitable style.

SEX OR NUDITY—None.

VIOLENCE—Minimal. The new senator punches out the reporters who snookered him.

LANGUAGE—None.

FEAR FACTOR (SUSPENSE)—Some. The climax, where Stewart stands up to corruption, is powerful.

AGE 0–2		Nope, sorry.
AGE 3–4		Ditto.
AGE 5–6		Still too young.
AGE 7–10	★★	If they're interested in history or politics, they'll start to appreciate it.
AGE 11–12	★★	Ditto.
AGE 13+	★★★★	They'll probably not choose this film on their own, but encourage them to sit through the first ten minutes and they'll be forever grateful.
ADULT	★★★★	This is what politics is all about, right?

SUGGESTED AGES—8–99

Mrs. Doubtfire (PG-13)

1993 Comedy
Directed by Chris Columbus
Starring Robin Williams, Sally Field, Pierce Brosnan

A comic tour de force by Robin Williams. After the court gives custody of his children to his wife, Daniel Hillard (Williams), an unemployed actor, poses as a Scottish nanny in order to spend time with them. It's a testament to the wonders of latex, mascara, and support hose that his ex-wife and family don't recognize him, giving Hillard the chance to be the loving, responsible parent he never was before. The tension and the comedy build as it becomes harder for him to sustain his double life. A bittersweet ending, but worth it just to see Williams dance with a vacuum cleaner.

Note: The family fights and divorce court scenes may be harrowing for children going through their own parents' divorce.

SEX OR NUDITY—None. The only frontal nudity is a quick peak at Williams's rubbery old-lady body suit.
VIOLENCE—None.
LANGUAGE—None. Mild profanity, most muttered rapid-fire under William's breath.
FEAR FACTOR (SUSPENSE)—None. A brief scene where Williams's body suit catches on fire. A birthday party that gets out of control is upsetting after the mother comes home. More wrenching are the scenes where father and children are separated.

AGE 0–2		No real harm in having them watch with older siblings, but they won't really get it.
AGE 3–4	★★	They will enjoy the slapstick and the quick-change segments.
AGE 5–6	★★★	Some of cross-dressing humor and some of the one-liners will fly over their heads, but they ought to get a big kick out of it.
AGE 7–10	★★★★	They will love it. Expect questions about

anatomical correctness and the difference between a five o'clock shadow and a hot flash.

AGE 11–12 ★★★★ Not too old to love it; rent *Tootsie* next and see how they compare the two.

AGE 13+ ★★★ Ditto.

ADULT ★★★★ Williams at his best.

SUGGESTED AGES—4–99

Mulan (G)

1998 Animated
Directed by Barry Cook, Tony Bancroft
Starring the voices of Eddie Murphy, Harvey Fierstein

Mulan, a clumsy young Chinese girl, disguises herself as a boy and runs off to take her ailing father's place in the war against the invading Huns. She survives the rigors of boot camp (and the male bawdiness she's unaccustomed to) with the help of two stowaways: a good-luck cricket, and Mushu, a hapless dragon sent by the family's spirit ancestors to protect her. Mulan eventually proves herself to be a brave and clever soldier, but her true identity is revealed when she is wounded. As she heads home in disgrace, Mulan stumbles on the avenging Huns and devises a way to stop them. In the end, Mulan saves China, restores her family's good name, gets her man, and does a little consciousness-raising in feudal China. Not bad for a day's work.

SEX OR NUDITY—None. No disgusting romance scenes to scare off young boys, either.

VIOLENCE—None. Only the bloodless, cartoon variety. The beauty of Mulan's warfare is that it is all based on clever uses of snow or fireworks, not weapons. No mean-spirited slapstick, either.

LANGUAGE—None. Nothing to worry about.

FEAR FACTOR (SUSPENSE)—Mulan is never in danger long, and humor is put to good use during tense moments.

AGE 0–2		They don't have the attention span or understanding for this one.
AGE 3–4	★★	Of all the recent Disney films, this one is the least scary and moves along at a pretty brisk pace. Some kids may fidget during the ballads (which are predictable and predictably spaced, but mercifully short).
AGE 5–6	★★★	Right on target.
AGE 7–10	★★★	They'll like it but may not want to admit it to their friends. (Consider leaving older kids in the car while you pick this one up).

AGE 11–12	★	Unfortunately, they're probably a little too old for this one.
AGE 13+		Sorry, no.
ADULT	★★★	While Mulan may sound a little too politically correct, it turns out to be lots of fun, largely because of Mushu's irreverent, well-timed humor. Even if you rent this one reluctantly, you'll be pleasantly surprised.

SUGGESTED AGES—3–10

Muppet Movie, The (G)

1979 Comedy
Directed by James Frawley
Starring Kermit the Frog, Miss Piggy, et.al.; Charles Durning, Austin
Pendleton

This was the first feature film starring the Muppets and it is still a treat.
The film's ostensible plot traces Kermit's rise from a swamp thing to a
Hollywood, um . . . fixture. At the same time that he is making his mark,
he is being pursued by a restaurant mogul played by Charles Durning,
whose speciality is frogs' legs. As always, the Muppet productions are
written on two levels—child and adult—and both work!

SEX OR NUDITY—None.

VIOLENCE—None.

LANGUAGE—None.

FEAR FACTOR (SUSPENSE)—None.

AGE 0–2	★	Barely.
AGE 3–4	★★★	Right on.
AGE 5–6	★★★★	Perfect.
AGE 7–10	★★★	They'll pretend to be too old, but will howl.
AGE 11–12	★★	This group may indeed be getting too old.
AGE 13+	★	Ditto.
ADULT	★★★	But you're not.

SUGGESTED AGES—2–12

Muppet Treasure Island (G)

1996 Comedy
Directed by Brian Henson
Starring Tim Curry, Kevin Bishop, Kermit the Frog (Steve Whitmire), Miss Piggy (Frank Oz)

Brian Henson's last Muppet film, this is a terrific adaptation of Robert Louis Stevenson's classic pirate story. Kermit the Frog is Captain Smollett, Tim Curry is the scheming Long John Silver, and Miss Piggy is Benjamina Gunn. As with all Muppet efforts, this film is written on at least two levels: lots of action and silliness for kids; hysterical word play for adults. Try to visualize Kermit as a "raging volcano, with demons no mortal man can understand." That's how he is introduced. And then we meet him . . . and of course, it is Kermit, as we love him. Plus, the music isn't half bad. Enjoy!

SEX OR NUDITY—None.

VIOLENCE—Some. Sure, this is a pirate film; but a Muppet version of violence is pretty acceptable.

LANGUAGE—None.

FEAR FACTOR (SUSPENSE)—Some. A few singing skulls and scary-looking characters.

AGE 0–2	★	Pushing it a bit.
AGE 3–4	★★	They'll love it, but might be a bit frightened by the scarier characters.
AGE 5–6	★★★	They'll just love it.
AGE 7–10	★★★	Ditto.
AGE 11–12	★★	They'll laugh and start to get the more sophisticated jokes, but might think of themselves as too old. They'll still watch, however.
AGE 13+	★	Ditto.
ADULT	★★	Enjoy.

SUGGESTED AGES—2–99

Muppets Take Manhattan, The (G)
1984 Comedy
Directed by Frank Oz
Starring the Muppets, Dabney Coleman, James Coco, Brooke Shields, Art Carney, Joan Rivers, Gregory Hines

When we told our kids we were going to watch this film—which they hadn't seen in years—the reaction, even from the twelve-year-old, was, "Cool, you mean the one with the fork in the road." Quite literally, of course, there is a giant fork in the middle of the road. Well, never mind; you'll get it when you see it. And you should see it!

This time, the Muppets decide to take their college theatrical production and stage it on the Great White Way. So they're New York bound. Their plan hits a snag when no one want to produce it on Broadway. Kermit suffers amnesia after being hit by a car and winds up working in an all-frog ad agency. Get it? Don't worry, you will. And you'll love it.

SEX OR NUDITY—None.
VIOLENCE—Minimal.
LANGUAGE—None.
FEAR FACTOR (SUSPENSE)—Minimal. Little kids may worry about Kermit's amnesia.

AGE 0–2	★	If anything can hold their interest, the Muppets will.
AGE 3–4	★★★	They'll love it.
AGE 5–6	★★★	Ditto.
AGE 7–10	★★★	This group will too, but the older kids may think they're too old.
AGE 11–12	★★	This group really will think they're too old. Too bad.
AGE 13+	★	Ditto.
ADULT	★★★	The cameos are wonderful, but then so are the Muppets.

SUGGESTED AGES—2–10

Murder by Death (PG)

1976 Comedy
Directed by Robert Moore
Starring Peter Sellers, Peter Falk, David Niven, Maggie Smith, James Coco, Alec Guinness, Elsa Lanchester

An all-star cast in a hilarious (but not slapstick) spoof of *most* of the great detective films. It is witty, well acted, and a treat to watch. Truman Capote has invited the world's greatest detectives—Peter Falk as Sam Spade, Peter Sellers as Charlie Chan, Elsa Lanchester as Miss Marple, etc.—to solve a baffling whodunit that unfolds around them over the course of one evening. Neil Simon wrote this perfectly enjoyable movie.

SEX OR NUDITY—Minimal. Some talk, no action.

VIOLENCE—Minimal. Several murders, none disturbing.

LANGUAGE—Minimal. A few cusses, nothing serious.

FEAR FACTOR (SUSPENSE)—Some. In a very humorous tone, lots of whodunit tension.

AGE 0–2		Nope.
AGE 3–4		Ditto, sorry.
AGE 5–6	★	They'll barely get it.
AGE 7–10	★★★	Great for this group, but a little scary for the younger ones.
AGE 11–12	★★★	Perfect.
AGE 13+	★★★★	Even better.
ADULT	★★★★	A hoot.

SUGGESTED AGES—7–99

Music Man, The (G)

1962 Musical
Directed by Morton Da Costa
Starring Robert Preston, Shirley Jones, Buddy Hackett

This charming film, clearly something from a less cynical time, is refreshingly sincere without being sappy. It features Robert Preston as a charismatic con man who comes to a small Iowa town and hoodwinks its members into forming a marching band. But before he can walk out on the hicks, he realizes two things: that he's fallen in love with the town librarian and, just as importantly, has fallen under the magical spell of the music. Great songs, including "76 Trombones" and "Till There Was You."

SEX OR NUDITY—None.

VIOLENCE—None.

LANGUAGE—None.

FEAR FACTOR (SUSPENSE)—None.

AGE 0–2		Not for them, but no harm if they wake up and toddle in while it's on.
AGE 3–4		Ditto.
AGE 5–6	★★	Give it a try.
AGE 7–10	★★★	Just right.
AGE 11–12	★	Might be too corny for them.
AGE 13+		Definitely too corny.
ADULT	★★★	Go ahead, hum along.

SUGGESTED AGES—6–10

Mutiny on the Bounty (No Rating)

1935 Action/Adventure; Drama
Directed by Frank Lloyd
Starring Charles Laughton, Clark Gable

An Academy Award winner for Best Picture, this earlier version is leagues ahead of the 1962 remake with Marlon Brando and Trevor Howard. This is brilliant storytelling and beautiful filmmaking, but . . . and it is a very *big* but: It may be too strong and disturbing for many kids. Laughton's portrayal of the tyrannical Captain Bligh is so powerful, and he is so despicable in his constant, abusive punishment of the sailors, that many kids and adults suffer nightmares after seeing it. Be forewarned: This is a tough, sometimes brutal movie. Even though the camera never lingers on the flogging or keelhauling, there is sufficient repetition of and attention to the punishment and physical abuse to form an understandable, albeit disturbing, basis for the mutiny that follows.

For those interested in this theme of rebellion against unjust treatment and unlawful orders, we recommend *Crimson Tide* and *Mister Roberts*.

SEX OR NUDITY—Minimal. Kissing between the officers and native women in Tahiti.

VIOLENCE—A lot. Flogging, beating, keelhauling. The battle during the mutiny is violent.

LANGUAGE—None. No "indecent" language, but Captain Bligh's verbal abuse against the crew is significant.

FEAR FACTOR (SUSPENSE)—Some. The tension between Captain Bligh and his first mate, Mr. Christian, builds continually.

AGE 0–2		No way.
AGE 3–4		Ditto.
AGE 5–6		Still no way.
AGE 7–10	★★★	Maybe, but only for the oldest and most mature children.
AGE 11–12	★★★	Same warning.
AGE 13+	★★★★	Perfect.
ADULT	★★★★	A terrific film.

SUGGESTED AGES—10–99

My Fair Lady (G)

1964 Musical
Directed by George Cukor
Starring Rex Harrison, Audrey Hepburn

Luminous musical version of George Bernard Shaw's *Pygmalion*. A stuffy British linguistics expert transforms a Cockney char woman into a graceful society lady and then falls in love with her. Unforgettable score, beautiful costumes, and the transformation of both student and pupil make this a classic sure to appeal to kids.

SEX OR NUDITY—None.

VIOLENCE—None.

LANGUAGE—None.

FEAR FACTOR (SUSPENSE)—None.

AGE 0–2		No.
AGE 3–4		Not yet.
AGE 5–6	★★	Just barely able to get it.
AGE 7–10	★★★	Perfect.
AGE 11–12	★★★	Insist on it. They'll be glad you did.
AGE 13+	★★★	Ditto.
ADULT	★★★	As wonderful as you remember it.

SUGGESTED AGES—6–99

My Favorite Year (PG)

1982 Comedy
Directed by Richard Benjamin
Starring Peter O'Toole, Mark Linn-Baker, Joe Bologna, Jessica Harper,
Lainie Kazan, Bill Macy

Set in 1954, during the heyday of live television, Peter O'Toole (in perfect casting) plays a swashbuckling movie star who has agreed to appear on a popular program. Mark Linn-Baker plays the young writer assigned to keep him out of trouble during the week prior to the show. O'Toole is the young man's personal screen idol, but he is also a drunk, a womanizer, and completely unpredictable. Bologna plays the show's comedy host, and bases his terrific performance on Sid Caesar, who had such a top-rated show in the 1950s. If you don't mind having to explain O'Toole's drunken binges and lecherous behavior to your kids, this is a very funny and charming film.

SEX OR NUDITY—Minimal. Lots of talk, a few kisses, but nothing to worry about.

VIOLENCE—Minimal. A fake-turned-real fight with Mafia hoods on live television.

LANGUAGE—Minimal. After all, this was 1950s television.

FEAR FACTOR (SUSPENSE)—Minimal. Will he make it sober to the show?

AGE 0–2		No, sorry.
AGE 3–4		Ditto.
AGE 5–6	★★	They'll appreciate the slapstick.
AGE 7–10	★★★	They'll like it.
AGE 11–12	★★★	They'll love it.
AGE 13+	★★★★	Not only will they love it, they'll start to identify with the characters.
ADULT	★★★	Ditto.

SUGGESTED AGES—5–99

My Girl (PG)

1991 Comedy; Drama
Directed by Howard Zieff
Starring Macaulay Culkin, Anna Chlumsky, Dan Aykroyd, Jamie Lee
Curtis

Many people had a problem with this film for two reasons: it features a girl obsessed with death and an engaging young boy who abruptly dies from a bee sting. Too close for comfort, some people said. Too morbid, said others. We still think it's a good family film. You will need to decide if the subject matter is right for your kids, but we think it's gentle, carefully done, and, in the end, life-affirming.

SEX OR NUDITY—None.

VIOLENCE—None.

LANGUAGE—Minimal. Very tame.

FEAR FACTOR (SUSPENSE)—Minimal. The death isn't shown, but it's sudden and quite shocking.

AGE 0–2		No way.
AGE 3–4		Not even for *Home Alone* fans.
AGE 5–6		Ditto.
AGE 7–10	★★	Not for everybody in this category. But it is 90 percent comedy and only 10 percent tragedy.
AGE 11–12	★★★	Dead on.
AGE 13+	★★	Just OK.
ADULT	★★★	Engaging, heartwarming fare. Not your usual kids' film.

SUGGESTED AGES—8–12

National Velvet (G)
1944 Sports; Drama
Directed by Clarence Brown
Starring Elizabeth Taylor, Mickey Rooney, Donald Crips, Anne Revere, Angela Lansbury

Young Liz sparkles as the plucky young girl who wins a troublesome horse and, with the help of a down-on-his luck hired man (young Mickey Rooney), trains the horse to win the Grand National Steeplechase. There are thrilling scenes of horse and rider blazing across the countryside. A feminist success story before the word "feminist" was even coined.

SEX OR NUDITY—None.

VIOLENCE—None.

LANGUAGE—None.

FEAR FACTOR (SUSPENSE)—A few spills; nothing serious.

AGE 0–2		Not yet.
AGE 3–4		Ditto.
AGE 5–6	★	Maybe. For little girls who dream of horses.
AGE 7–10	★★★	Right on.
AGE 11–12	★	Too old-fashioned and stagy for viewers as discriminating as today's kids are.
AGE 13+	★	No way.
ADULT	★★★	It's still as charming as ever.

SUGGESTED AGES—6–11

Necessary Roughness (PG-13)

1991 Sports; Comedy
Directed by Stan Dragoti
Starring Scott Bakula, Hector Elizondo, Robert Loggia, Harley Jane Kozak, Sinbad, Kathy Ireland

A major hit among ten-year-old boys. Scott Bakula plays a thirty-four-year-old who goes back to college at the urging of a new football coach. The old coach and the entire team has been expelled due to NCAA penalties. So Bakula, who is typically mistaken for a parent or a professor in each class he attends, goes back to live the dream he was forced to abandon when his father died. Needless to say, it is a team of neophytes and misfits, including supermodel Kathy Ireland as a place kicker. To complicate matters, Bakula's love interest is his by-the-book professor, and the college dean is anti-football.

SEX OR NUDITY—Minimal. Kissing; maybe a glimpse of a bare bottom in the locker room.
VIOLENCE—Some. A bar brawl and football mayhem.
LANGUAGE—Some. These *are* college football players!
FEAR FACTOR (SUSPENSE)—Minimal.

AGE 0–2		Nope.
AGE 3–4		Ditto.
AGE 5–6	★	If they like football.
AGE 7–10	★★	Perfect for this group.
AGE 11–12	★★	Ditto.
AGE 13+	★★	Just fine.
ADULT	★★	You could do a lot worse.

SUGGESTED AGES—7–99

Never Cry Wolf (PG)

1983 Action/Adventure
Directed by Carroll Ballard
Starring Charles Martin Smith, Brian Dennehy

Spectacularly photographed, this is the story of a neophyte biologist who takes an assignment to travel far into the Arctic wilderness to track the interaction of wolves and caribou. In addition to learning a great deal about the wolves he is supposed to study, he learns just as much about himself. The pacing is a bit uneven (it does get slow at points) but the scenery is so spectacular and the behavior of the wolves so interesting that this movie is a rare find: a quasi-documentary that works as a drama. One funny but potentially queasy quirk: The biologist takes to eating mice: fried, grilled, sautéed, and in a sandwich. And this is a Disney movie!

SEX OR NUDITY—Minimal. Some bare bottoms.

VIOLENCE—Minimal. Man eating mice; wolves eating caribou.

LANGUAGE—None.

FEAR FACTOR (SUSPENSE)—Some. Man against nature and against himself.

AGE 0–2		Not quite.
AGE 3–4	★	They'll appreciate the wolf behavior.
AGE 5–6	★★	Just about right.
AGE 7–10	★★★	Perfect.
AGE 11–12	★★	May find it a bit slow.
AGE 13+	★	Pushing it.
ADULT	★★	Lovely.

SUGGESTED AGES—4–99

NeverEnding Story, The (G)

1984 Fantasy/Science Fiction
Directed by Wolfgang Peterson
Starring Noah Hathaway, Barret Oliver, Tami Stronach, Moses Gunn

Enchanting science fiction fantasy about a boy who gets so lost in his reading that he actually enters the land of Fantasia. There he does gallant battle against the forces of evil alongside another young fighter. Good special effects and a story that, well, just keeps going and going. Pure fantasy of the kind kids themselves act out when no one is looking.

SEX OR NUDITY—None.
VIOLENCE—Minimal. Only the chivalrous kind.
LANGUAGE—None.
FEAR FACTOR (SUSPENSE)—Minimal. One scene where the boy's horse appears to be lost in a quagmire.

AGE 0–2		Not yet.
AGE 3–4		Just barely ready for this one.
AGE 5–6	★★★	Right on.
AGE 7–10	★★★	Great.
AGE 11–12	★★	Fine for all but the oldest in this group.
AGE 13+	★	Probably too old for it.
ADULT	★★	Depends on your tolerance for fantasy.

SUGGESTED AGES—5–10

North by Northwest (No Rating)
1959 Action/Adventure
Directed by Alfred Hitchcock
Starring Cary Grant, Eva Marie Saint, James Mason, Martin Landau

Our favorite Hitchcock film, and certainly on our short list for the top five movies—period. This is the classic "wrong man" story that takes advertizing man Cary Grant on a cross-country chase. He is both chasing the (nonexistent) Mr. Kaplan, whom he is being mistaken for, and being chased by the villians (who think he is a spy) and the police (who believe he is an assassin). Got all that? No need. Just think action, sophisticated comedy, and smoldering romance. Which is a more classic scene, being chased by the crop duster or fighting to the finish on Mount Rushmore?

SEX OR NUDITY—Minimal. Lots of talk, but no action.
VIOLENCE—Minimal. A diplomat is assassinated and there is a final fight scene.
LANGUAGE—None.
FEAR FACTOR (SUSPENSE)—A lot. Great tension, but always with a smile.

AGE 0–2		Sorry, no way.
AGE 3–4		Ditto.
AGE 5–6	★	Still a bit too young.
AGE 7–10	★★★	They'll get most of it.
AGE 11–12	★★★★	Near perfect.
AGE 13+	★★★★	Absolutely perfect.
ADULT	★★★★	Simply the best.

SUGGESTED AGES—7–99

Old Yeller (G)

1957 Animal; Drama
Directed by Robert Stevenson
Starring Tommy Kirk, Dorothy McGuire, Fess Parker, Chuck Connors

An unforgettable coming-of-age story about a boy who turns a wily stray mutt into a loyal family dog. When the boy, Arliss, is hurt falling out of a tree into a herd of rampaging wild boars, Old Yeller fights them off, becoming badly injured himself. It turns out that the boars carried rabies. Old Yeller turns vicious and Arliss must put the dog out of his misery. A neighbor gives Arliss one of Yeller's new pups, which had been born to her dog. At first Arliss rejects the adorable little thing, but eventually grows to love him.

SEX OR NUDITY—None.

VIOLENCE—Some. The death of the dog isn't shown, but we see poor Arliss shoot the gun. The chase and fight with the rabid boars is scary.

LANGUAGE—None.

FEAR FACTOR (SUSPENSE)—A lot. The scene of the dog's death and the preceding one where he snarls at Arliss and foams at the mouth are definitely frightening.

AGE 0–2		No.
AGE 3–4		Not a good idea.
AGE 5–6		Still not a good idea.
AGE 7–10	★★★	Yes, but only for the stout of heart.
AGE 11–12	★★★★	It may feel a little dated, but it teaches wonderful lessons about love and loss.
AGE 13+	★★	It will be a hard sell.
ADULT	★★★	You'll find it compelling.

SUGGESTED AGES—8–99

On the Town (No Rating)

1949 Musical
Directed by Gene Kelly and Stanley Donen
Starring Gene Kelly, Frank Sinatra, Vera-Ellen, Betty Garrett, Ann Miller, Jules Munshin

Filmed on location in post–World War II New York City, three sailors have twenty-four hours of liberty to go out on the town. They are mostly in search of romance. With music by Leonard Bernstein and lyrics by Comden & Green, this Academy Award–winning musical ranks among the best. True, there are constant overtones of sex, but the times and the musical comedy format keep it pretty innocent. It is exuberant, politically incorrect—just watch the scenes among the "primitive civilizations" at the Museum of Natural History—and terrific fun!

SEX OR NUDITY—Minimal. A sexually aggressive female cab driver has the hots for Frank Sinatra and keeps inviting him up to her apartment—where they kiss.

VIOLENCE—None.

LANGUAGE—None.

FEAR FACTOR (SUSPENSE)—Minimal. One of the gang hangs by his fingertips from the Empire State Building.

AGE 0–2		Not quite.
AGE 3–4	★	The music and dancing might hold them a bit.
AGE 5–6	★★	They'll start to enjoy it.
AGE 7–10	★★★	Perfect.
AGE 11–12	★★★	Ditto; they'll even appreciate post–WW II New York City locations.
AGE 13+	★★★	A joy.
ADULT	★★★	Ditto.

SUGGESTED AGES—5–99

On the Waterfront (No Rating)

1951 Drama
Directed by Elia Kazan
Starring Marlon Brando, Karl Malden, Lee J. Cobb, Rod Steiger, Eva
Marie Saint

The winner of eight Academy Awards, this powerful drama is unflinching in its grittiness and portrayal of corruption on the New York City waterfront. Marlon Brando plays Terry Malloy, a misfit ex-boxer who "coulda been a contender" if he hadn't taken a dive at the instruction of his mob-connected brother, Rod Steiger. Eva Marie Saint is the "pure" girl Brando loves, and Karl Malden is the waterfront priest who leads the fight against the corrupt union. A tour de force on many levels, and for older kids, a must-see.

SEX OR NUDITY—Minimal.

VIOLENCE—There's not a lot of violence, but it is graphic.

LANGUAGE—Minimal.

FEAR FACTOR (SUSPENSE)—Some. Not scary, but there is dramatic tension.

AGE 0–2		No way.
AGE 3–4		Ditto.
AGE 5–6		Still no way.
AGE 7–10	★	Still too rough for all but the oldest, most mature kids.
AGE 11–12	★★★	Definitely a contender.
AGE 13+	★★★★	The champ.
ADULT	★★★★	One of the best ever.

SUGGESTED AGES—10–99

Parent Trap, The (PG)
1998 Comedy
Directed by Nancy Meyers
Starring Dennis Quaid, Natasha Richardson, Lindsay Lohan

As kids we loved the original *Parent Trap* starring Hayley Mills. So it was with a fair amount of trepidation that we watched this new version. Happily, we enjoyed it, and the gaggle of kids we watched it with—ranging in age from seven to fifteen—all loved it. In fact, when we watched the original version the very next night, there was unanimous agreement that the new one is a bit better.

The plot is as corny in the 1990s as it was in the 1960s: twin sisters who never knew the other existed meet at summer camp. At first they are rivals, but soon become best friends determined to get their divorced parents back together. They switch places in the process unbeknownst to their parents.

Lindsay Lohan, who plays both of the eleven-year-old sisters—one raised in London, the other on a vineyard in California—is charming, feisty, and pretty convincing as two different kids. The pranks are innocent and entertaining, and the plot twists just contrived enough to keep everyone laughing.

SEX OR NUDITY—None.
VIOLENCE—None.
LANGUAGE—None.
FEAR FACTOR (SUSPENSE)—None.

AGE 0–2		Sorry, nope.
AGE 3–4	★	Barely, but they might sit still.
AGE 5–6	★★	They will enjoy the twins switching roles.
AGE 7–10	★★★	The perfect age.
AGE 11–12	★★★	They'll still enjoy it, though they might pretend to be too old for this movie.
AGE 13+	★★	May be pushing it, which is a shame.
ADULT	★★	Not bad. A bit better than the original, though we might not want to admit it.

SUGGESTED AGES—6–99

Patton (PG)

1970 Drama
Directed by Franklin Schaffner
Starring George C. Scott, Karl Malden, Stephen Young

The winner of seven Academy Awards, this film is first a grand biography, and only incidentally a war movie. That's what makes it a bit rough going for kids expecting an action flick, but well worth it when they accept it for what it is. It is not slow, but it is deliberately paced and a bit long at just over two and a half hours. But it is worth it. As a history lesson, it is remarkably true to the events of World War II, and it accurately captures General George Patton's outsized personality and persona. Encourage kids to hang in there!

SEX OR NUDITY—None.

VIOLENCE—Some battle scenes. The most disturbing incidents involve Patton slapping a soldier, and the aftermath of a battle, where nomads strip the dead bodies.

LANGUAGE—Some. Patton was profane.

FEAR FACTOR (SUSPENSE)—Minimal.

AGE 0–2		No way.
AGE 3–4		Ditto.
AGE 5–6	★	Will barely hold their interest; too talky.
AGE 7–10	★★	This group will start to get it.
AGE 11–12	★★★	They'll really begin to appreciate a well-written and well-made film.
AGE 13+	★★★★	An historical tour de force.
ADULT	★★★★	A classic.

SUGGESTED AGES—7–99

Phar Lap (PG)
1983 Animal; Sports
Directed by Simon Wincer
Starring Ron Leibman, Tom Burlinson, Martin Vaughn

An inspiring story about one of the greatest race horses of all time: the great Phar Lap of Australia. Phar Lap, a horse of dubious pedigree, is discovered by a luckless trainer who convinces the horse's owner to let him lease the horse for three years. In his first few races, the horse, whose name means lightning, is a dud. The trainer pushes the horse, sometimes too hard, while Phar Lap's handler uses a gentler touch, one that brings out the horse's indomitable will to win. Soon Phar Lap has won every race in Australia, including the Melbourne Cup. Resentment builds among frustrated gamblers, racing insiders, and those who have it in for the Phar Lap's Jewish-American owner. Then someone (we never know for sure) mysteriously kills Phar Lap on the eve of a big race in America.

SEX OR NUDITY—None.

VIOLENCE—Some. The climax of the story—the horse's death—is upsetting, but not shown.

LANGUAGE—Minimal. Your garden variety race-track language.

FEAR FACTOR (SUSPENSE)—Minimal.

AGE 0–2		No.
AGE 3–4		No.
AGE 5–6		Still no.
AGE 7–10	★★★	Yes, although sensitive kids, animal lovers, and virtually anyone with a heart will be upset by the animal's death.
AGE 11–12	★★★★	A sure bet.
AGE 13+	★★	A long shot.
ADULT	★★★★	Terrific!

SUGGESTED AGES—9–99

Philadelphia Story, The (No Rating)

1940 Comedy
Directed by George Cukor
Starring Cary Grant, Katharine Hepburn, Jimmy Stewart

One of the classic Hollywood comedies from one of the great directors. Katharine Hepburn plays a society gal who is about to get married when her ex-husband (Cary Grant) shows up and sparks are rekindled. Covering—or more accurately, spying on—the event for a newspaper is a goofy reporter (Jimmy Stewart.) He too falls in love with the bride-to-be. Hang on to your hat . . . yep, they all wore them then. A great adult comedy that may be too sophisticated for most kids. But if you think your child can appreciate a drawing-room comedy, this is the one. Winner of two Academy Awards: one for Stewart and another for best screenplay.

SEX OR NUDITY—Some. Lots of talk, little action.
VIOLENCE—Minimal. Hepburn and Grant get divorced after she breaks his golf clubs and he knocks her down. It is implied that he is drunk.
LANGUAGE—None.
FEAR FACTOR (SUSPENSE)—Minimal.

AGE 0–2		Nope, sorry.
AGE 3–4		Ditto.
AGE 5–6		Still no way.
AGE 7–10	★★	Only for the most mature.
AGE 11–12	★★★	Yep, they'll start to appreciate it.
AGE 13+	★★★★	Perfect.
ADULT	★★★★	Oh, go ahead, enjoy yourself.

SUGGESTED AGES—9–99

Pollyanna (No Rating)

1960 Drama
Directed by David Swift
Starring Hayley Mills, Jane Wyman, Karl Malden

We think this film has gotten a bad rap. But then, maybe we're a little Pollyannaish. It's a sweet but not sappy film about a young orphan girl who goes to live with her frosty old aunt and a houseful of crabby servants. Pollyanna proceeds to charm everyone in town, including a fire-and-brimstone preacher and an old miser. When she's paralyzed in a fall from a tree, the whole town turns out to send her off for the operation she needs to walk again. (Hayley Mills received a special Oscar for her performance.)

SEX OR NUDITY—None. Good heavens, no.
VIOLENCE—None. Pollyanna takes a nasty tumble from a tall tree.
LANGUAGE—None.
FEAR FACTOR (SUSPENSE)—Minimal. Sensitive children will be rightfully worried about Pollyanna.

AGE 0–2		Not enough action to hold them, but nothing to offend or frighten, either.
AGE 3–4	★	Just barely old enough to get it.
AGE 5–6	★★★	Right on target.
AGE 7–10	★★★	Good for this age, too.
AGE 11–12		No. They're way too cool for this one.
AGE 13+		Ditto.
ADULT	★★★	Good as a nostalgia trip, but not bad entertainment either.

SUGGESTED AGES—4–10

Preschool Power (Jacket Flips and Other Tips) (No Rating)

1990 Comedy; Action/Adventure
Directed by Carey Connell Sutton
Starring Blake Sutton, K'Idar Miller and the children from the North Carolina Montessori School of Winston

Real live preschoolers demonstrate neat tricks they've learned to boost independence and self-reliance. Handy skills such as buttoning, pouring, and hand-washing are shown in a clear, step-by-step sequence and set to music that encourages your child to get up and join the fun. Wise and wonderful, this series features other installments—"More Preschool Power" and "Preschool Power 3"—that show kids learning how to clean up, dress themselves, and how to bake. Songs stress cooperation and the joy of accomplishment. A great confidence booster for the pre-kindergarten crowd.

SEX OR NUDITY—None.

VIOLENCE—None.

LANGUAGE—None

FEAR FACTOR (SUSPENSE)—None.

AGE 0–2	★★★	Although they're a little young for some of the activities, they'll still like seeing what's ahead.
AGE 3–4	★★★★	Great stuff! They'll feel empowered to try new age-appropriate tasks, and they can use the songs and the models for help.
AGE 5–6		They'll be insulted if you bring this one home for them.
AGE 7–10		No.
AGE 11–12		No.
AGE 13+		No.
ADULT	★★★★	You needn't watch it with them every time, but you can help them feel more comfortable trying the tasks shown if you do it along with them the first time.

SUGGESTED AGES—1–4

Pride of the Yankees, The (No Rating)

1947 Sports; Drama
Directed by Sam Wood
Starring Gary Cooper, Teresa Wright, Babe Ruth, Walter Brennan

A beautiful tearjerker about a man who was far more than a great base-ball player—and Lou Gehrig was indeed that. It is about honor and decency and courage, both on the field and in the face of a debilitating and ultimately fatal disease. It is also a story about the American Dream. Gehrig grew up poor in New York City, his parents immigrants from Germany. His mother worked as a cook at Columbia University with the hope that working there would help her son gain admission and ulti-mately become an engineer. Gehrig did go to Columbia, but his talent as an athlete took him in a different direction. This superb biography won an Academy Award for Best Editing, and the old baseball footage inter-woven into the film—along with Babe Ruth playing himself—is a treat.

SEX OR NUDITY—None.

VIOLENCE—Minimal. A fraternity fight.

LANGUAGE—None.

FEAR FACTOR (SUSPENSE)—Minimal. Gehrig faces death stoically.

AGE 0–2		No way.
AGE 3–4		Still not right for this group.
AGE 5–6	★★	If they have an interest in baseball, they'll love it.
AGE 7–10	★★★	Bravo.
AGE 11–12	★★★	A home run.
AGE 13+	★★★	Ditto.
ADULT	★★★	A classic.

SUGGESTED AGES—6–99

Princess Bride, The (PG)

1987 Comedy; Fantasy/Science Fiction
Directed by Rob Reiner
Starring Cary Elwes, Mandy Patinkin, Chris Sarandon, Christopher Guest, Wallace Shawn, Andre the Giant

A wonderful, sometimes hysterical take on the classic fairy tale–adventure story. It is the story of the beautiful princess separated from her true love, promised to the evil nobleman, and finally, after many harrowing adventures, reunited with the man she truly loves. It is swashbuckling, sometimes satirical, often a spoof, but always very well done. Indeed it seems to be written on two levels—adult and child—and it works on both.

SEX OR NUDITY—Minimal. One kiss that, as the narrator says, is more passionate than the five most passionate kisses of all time.
VIOLENCE—Some. Great sword fights, some head bonking.
LANGUAGE—Minimal. One relatively mild curse.
FEAR FACTOR (SUSPENSE)—Many adventures, but nothing terribly upsetting. A giant ratlike creature wrestles with our hero and is then roasted in the fire swamp.

AGE 0–2		They're a bit too young.
AGE 3–4	★★	They'll start to appreciate this.
AGE 5–6	★★★	It is just goofy enough for this group.
AGE 7–10	★★★★	Perfect.
AGE 11–12	★★★★	Ditto.
AGE 13+	★★★	They won't want to watch it but they will be glad they did.
ADULT	★★★★	Enjoy yourself.

SUGGESTED AGES—4–99

Prisoner of Zenda, The (No Rating)

1937 Action/Adventure
Directed by John Cromwell
Starring Ronald Colman, Madeleine Carroll, Douglas Fairbanks, Jr.,
C. Aubrey Smith, Raymond Massey, Mary Astor

This is the third of five versions of this film, and the only one worth watching. Colman plays two roles: the king-to-be of a small Eastern European nation, and his lookalike English cousin who substitutes for him at the coronation. This film is a swashbuckling adventure-romance complete with dastardly plots, double-dealing, and old-fashioned heroes and villains. Enjoy!

SEX OR NUDITY—None.
VIOLENCE—Some. Gun battles, swordplay, a slap.
LANGUAGE—None.
FEAR FACTOR (SUSPENSE)—Minimal.

AGE 0–2		Nope.
AGE 3–4	★	The swordplay will entertain, but they'll be confused by the role switching.
AGE 5–6	★★	They'll enjoy it.
AGE 7–10	★★	Ditto.
AGE 11–12	★★	Same for this group, but they may think it a bit dated.
AGE 13+	★★	Ditto.
ADULT	★★	We like this film, but don't love it.

SUGGESTED AGES—5–99

Producers, The (No Rating)

1968 Comedy
Directed by Mel Brooks
Starring Zero Mostel, Gene Wilder, Kenneth Mars, Dick Shawn

This is Mel Brooks's first film as a director, and his absolutely hysterical screenplay won him an Oscar. The plot, which takes a bit of explaining to younger kids, centers on Zero Mostel, a down-on-his-luck Broadway producer, who realizes that a meek accountant, played by Gene Wilder, has stumbled on a brilliant way to make money. All they have to do is find a show that is sure to fail, sell 25,000 percent ownership in it, and pocket the cash. Since no one ever audits a show that loses money, the duo, now partners, are sure they have hit the jackpot when they discover a musical called *Springtime for Hitler*. This is one of the funniest films ever made, and even if the kids don't quite follow the convoluted logic, they will certainly appreciate the classic performances of the entire cast.

SEX OR NUDITY—Minimal. The non-English speaking Swedish sexpot who is Mostel's new secretary dances and coos, but nothing more. You may have to explain the director's cross-dressing.

VIOLENCE—Minimal. A slap. The crazy author of the play shoots up the Bialystock and Bloom office.

LANGUAGE—None.

FEAR FACTOR (SUSPENSE)—None

AGE 0–2		No way.
AGE 3–4	★	Still not right for this group.
AGE 5–6	★★	It is a musical, and while this group won't appreciate too much of the humor, they will understand some.
AGE 7–10	★★★	These kids will get it.
AGE 11–12	★★★	Most in this group should love it.
AGE 13+	★★★★	Older kids will appreciate the genius.
ADULT	★★★★	So will you. This movie gets better every time you see it!

SUGGESTED AGES—5–99

Raiders of the Lost Ark (PG)
1981 Action/Adventure
Directed by Steven Spielberg
Starring Harrison Ford, Karen Allen, Paul Freeman, Ronald Lacey

The first and the best of three swashbuckling, action-packed adventure stories featuring archaeologist extraordinaire Indiana Jones. It's got an inventive plot, great characters, the bona fide thrills of the old Saturday morning television shows, and one of the most exciting chase scenes in movie history. Indy's quest is for nothing short of the Holy Grail, a treasure in danger of falling into Nazi hands. The film is funny, exhilarating, and satisfying.

Most kids love this film so much, they start begging for parents to rent the sequel, *Indiana Jones and the Temple of Doom*, before the credits have finished rolling on this one. Be forewarned: the second film in this series is much edgier and contains what we consider a good deal of gratuitous violence (eyeballs on a plate, a bad guy beheaded by a whirling propeller blade). *Indiana Jones and the Last Crusade*, the third in the series, which pairs Harrison Ford with Sean Connery as his fictional father, returns to the exciting, but not so violent, tone of the first. Some say the final film is the best.

SEX OR NUDITY—None. References to it and what looks like a precursor to it, but no actual sex.

VIOLENCE—Some. A poisonous snake pit is the most intense scene, but it's rivaled by others that are thrilling but not as scary.

LANGUAGE—Minimal. Pretty darn tame.

FEAR FACTOR (SUSPENSE)—It's a nonstop adrenaline rush.

AGE 0–2		No. It will give them nightmares.
AGE 3–4		Ditto.
AGE 5–6		It will be hard to keep little guys away from this one, but we recommend holding off a year or two.
AGE 7–10	★★★★	Go for it! But don't be surprised if they climb up on your lap halfway through.

AGE 11–12	★★★	They would climb on your lap, too, if they could.
AGE 13+	★★★	Ditto.
ADULT	★★★★	Now, whose lap are you going to sit on?

SUGGESTED AGES—8–99

Red Pony, The (No Rating)
1949 Drama
Directed by Lewis Milestone
Starring Robert Mitchum, Myrna Loy, Peter Miles, Louis Calhern

A moving and long-forgotten coming-of-age story about a boy and his pet horse. Based on John Steinbeck's novella, this unforgettable film is about a farmboy, Tom Tiflin, who receives a beautiful red pony for his birthday. He names the pony Gavilan and, with the help of Billy Buck, a hired hand, Tom trains the pony, earning the respect of his standoffish father and grandfather. One day the pony takes sick, and Tom blames Buck. Eventually he forgives his friend as they try in vain to save the horse. Tom nearly loses faith after this crushing loss, but with the help of the older men, comes to see it as his passage to manhood.

There's also a lovely made-for-television version of this film starring Henry Fonda. Both films are terrific. We picked this one because its stark, black-and-white tableau and rich Copland score seemed more aesthetically appropriate. You can't go wrong with either one.

SEX OR NUDITY—None.

VIOLENCE—Some. There is one very frightening scene where a flock of vultures descends on the boy and his pony, clawing at them with their talons. But they are quickly rescued by the boy's father.

LANGUAGE—None.

FEAR FACTOR (SUSPENSE)—Some. The pony's imminent death is clear to us long before Tom admits it.

AGE 0–2		No.
AGE 3–4		No.
AGE 5–6		No.
AGE 7–10	★★	Yes, but not for the faint-of-heart.
AGE 11–12	★★★★	They may love it so much they'll be willing to read the book.
AGE 13+	★★★★	Ditto.
ADULT	★★★★	As good as it gets.

SUGGESTED AGES—8–99

Rescuers, The (G)

1977 Animated
Directed by Wolfgang Reitherman, John Lounsbery
Starring the voices of Bob Newhart, Eva Gabor, Geraldine Page

The Rescue Aid Society is run by mice out of the basement of the United Nations. One day a note in a bottle appears, containing a plea for help from a girl named Penny. Off go the delegates from Hungary (Eva Gabor) and the Society's janitor (Bob Newhart.) The villain is Madame Medussa (Geraldine Page), who is using the kidnapped Penny to search for a diamond treasure hidden by pirates. Lovely Disney animation, good music (but quite simple by the post–*Little Mermaid* standards), and great voices.

SEX OR NUDITY—None.
VIOLENCE—Minimal. Nothing to speak of.
LANGUAGE—Minimal. "Shut up" is as raw as this gets.
FEAR FACTOR (SUSPENSE)—Minimal. The evil alligators may be a bit much for the youngest children.

AGE 0–2	★★	Sure, for the older kids.
AGE 3–4	★★	Perfect for this group.
AGE 5–6	★★	Just fine.
AGE 7–10	★	Barely OK for the younger kids.
AGE 11–12		Nope.
AGE 13+		No.
ADULT	★★	Fine to share with little ones.

SUGGESTED AGES—2–7

Rescuers Down Under, The (G)

1990 Animated
Directed by Hendel Butoy, Mike Gabriel
Starring the voices of Bob Newhart, Eva Gabor, George C. Scott, John Candy

A perfectly adequate sequel to the 1977 hit *The Rescuers*. This time the unlikely duo (Newhart and Gabor) from the Rescue Aid Society go down to Australia to search for a young boy who has been kidnapped by the evil George C. Scott, who is using him to obtain a rare, valuable eagle. The animals portrayed are indigenous to Australia and are pretty nifty. The best scene is the view from the back of a soaring eagle.

SEX OR NUDITY—None.
VIOLENCE—None.
LANGUAGE—None.
FEAR FACTOR (SUSPENSE)—Minimal.

AGE 0–2	★	OK for the older kids in this group.
AGE 3–4	★★	Perfect.
AGE 5–6	★★	Ditto.
AGE 7–10	★	Barely OK for the youngest in this group.
AGE 11–12		No way.
AGE 13+		Ditto.
ADULT	★	You could do worse.

SUGGESTED AGES—2–7

Return of the Jedi (PG)

1983 Fantasy/Science Fiction
Directed by Richard Marquand
Starring Mark Hamill, Harrison Ford, Carrie Fisher, Billy Dee Williams

In this, the final installment of Lucas's epic tale, the loose ends from the first two films are neatly tied up. Thanks largely to the presence of the teddy-bear cute Ewoks, the film has a young, jovial tone at times, but it features perhaps the darkest moment of the trilogy: the death of Darth Vader, the revelation of his face, and the fact that he is Luke Skywalker's father. A few other scenes may be scary to small children, but if they've watched the others, there is nothing here that should upset them. There's Jabba, of course, who seems larger and more loathsome; the crew of bizarre creatures that inhabits his corner of the galaxy; the toothy monster beneath his throne, and the desert monster, an ingenious and repulsive hole in the sand that looks like an enormous digestive tract. Boffo entertainment that will leave you wanting more.

SEX OR NUDITY—None.

VIOLENCE—The usual: lots of laser swordplay, shooting, and explosives.

LANGUAGE—Minimal. Very tame.

FEAR FACTOR (SUSPENSE)—Some. All of the heroes are captive at one point, and Luke comes perilously close to death in a duel with Darth Vader.

AGE 0–2		No.
AGE 3–4		Not quite yet.
AGE 5–6	★★★	Fine and dandy.
AGE 7–10	★★★★	Even better.
AGE 11–12	★★★	A little past their prime for this one.
AGE 13+	★★★	Ditto.
ADULT	★★★★	But you're not.

SUGGESTED AGES—6–99

Road Construction Ahead (No Rating)
1991 Drama
Directed by Focus Video

This simple video about how a road is built has reached cult classic status among the preschool male population. Plenty of digging, dumping, bulldozing, and, best of all, blasting, is set to peppy music and accompanied by the chatty, informative narration of a guy in a hard hat named George. There are also big trucks, heavy equipment, and neat finishing touches including a great shot of the machine that sprays the road with a bright yellow line. You will enjoy watching it once; your son will not be able to watch it enough.

SEX OR NUDITY—None.

VIOLENCE—None.

LANGUAGE—None.

FEAR FACTOR (SUSPENSE)—None.

AGE 0–2	★★★	Little guys who love trucks will love this video.
AGE 3–4	★★★★	It'll become a favorite.
AGE 5–6	★★	Probably getting too old for this one.
AGE 7–10		Ditto.
AGE 11–12		No.
AGE 13+		No.
ADULT	★★	Road Construction 101 for mothers; a great way to bond for both parents.

SUGGESTED AGES—2–5

Robert McCloskey Library, The (No Rating)
1990 Animated
Directed by Children's Circle (800-543-7843)

This quiet, old-fashioned, fifty-five minute video includes adaptations of *Lentil, Make Way for Ducklings, Blueberries for Sal, Time of Wonder,* and *Burt Dow: Deep-Water Man,* as well as a profile of the author at the end of the tape. (You'll enjoy learning about Caldecott-winning author McCloskey; your kids may want to skip this part.) The stories are not fully animated; they are more like still shots with quick cuts, pans, and scans set to a slow, soothing narration. In other words, perfect for inviting young children into a relaxed storytelling atmosphere. (A good choice for viewing before naptime or bedtime.)

SEX OR NUDITY—None.

VIOLENCE—None.

LANGUAGE—None.

FEAR FACTOR (SUSPENSE)—None.

AGE 0–2	★★★	Gentle and quiet; may not be active enough for some children.
AGE 3–4	★★★★	They ought to be spellbound. The real plus for kids this age is that they can see the connection between the books and the video.
AGE 5–6	★★	Probably too juvenile for most kids this age.
AGE 7–10		No.
AGE 11–12		No.
AGE 13+		No.
AUDLT	★★★	You'll appreciate the quiet quality of the storytelling. And it will remind you of those early stories put to film on "Captain Kangaroo."

SUGGESTED AGES—2–6

Rocketeer, The (PG)

1991 Fantasy/Science Fiction
Directed by Joe Johnston
Starring Bill Campbell, Jennifer Connelly, Alan Arkin, Timothy Dalton,
Paul Sorvino

With the look and feel of a 1930s Saturday serial, this adventure pits an
innocent, do-good stunt flyer against evil Nazi spies. On the eve of
World War II, our protagonist has found a prototype jet backpack that
the bad guys are searching for. Timothy Dalton is the villain, and he
bases his character on Errol Flynn. Lots of energy, good special effects,
and bad guys you love to hate.

SEX OR NUDITY—Minimal. The requisite kiss.

VIOLENCE—Some. Gun battles, sword fights, and a fistfight or two.

LANGUAGE—Minimal. "Hell" is used several times.

FEAR FACTOR (SUSPENSE)—Some. One of the bad guys is killed in his
hospital bed by an even worse bad guy.

AGE 0–2		No way.
AGE 3–4	★	They'll like the swashbuckling and flying sequences.
AGE 5–6	★★	They'll enjoy this.
AGE 7– 10	★★★	Perfect for this group.
AGE 11–12	★★	May be a little too retro for kids who think of themselves as cool or mature.
AGE 13+	★★	Ditto.
ADULT	★★	Not bad.

SUGGESTED AGES—5–16

Rocky (PG)

1976 Sports
Directed by John G. Avildsen
Starring Sylvester Stallone, Talia Shire, Burt Young, Carl Weathers, Burgess Meredith.

We were surprised to see that this old warhorse was only rated PG. Sure, it's about boxing, but it's also about having a dream, a little talent, and a lot of heart. You know the story: punk fighter gets the chance of a lifetime to fight the world heavyweight champ and, against all odds, wins. Yes, the final scenes in the ring are bloody, but upon watching it again after all these years, we decided they weren't bad at all, especially by current standards. It's your call, but we think the real story—about becoming a hero—transcends all the punching.

Note: Forget about the sequels; they don't do justice to the original, which won the Academy Award for Best Picture in 1976.

SEX OR NUDITY—Minimal. Delicately done.
VIOLENCE—A lot. The meat locker scene, while memorable, is only bloody. The final scene is, well, a knock-down, drag-out fight.
LANGUAGE—Some. Not as bad as you think.
FEAR FACTOR (SUSPENSE)—Some. You worry about the guy, but you know how it's going to end.

AGE 0–2		No way.
AGE 3–4		Ditto.
AGE 5–6		Sorry, we still don't think so.
AGE 7–10	★★★	Only for the older ones in this group.
AGE 11–12	★★★★	The champ.
AGE 13+	★★★★	They'll be surprised at how involved they get.
ADULT	★★★	You will be, too.

SUGGESTED AGES—8–99

Rookie of the Year (PG)

1994 Sports
Directed by Daniel Stern
Starring Thomas Ian Nicholas, Daniel Stern, Gary Busey, Dan Hedaya

Twelve-year-old Henry breaks his arm, ending his Little League season. When it heals, he somehow has a fastball so swift and accurate that it lands him in the Major Leagues, pitching for the Chicago Cubs. This is a sweet, rather predictable film that is a fine diversion for a rainy afternoon. It isn't the best sports film for kids or parents, but you could do a lot worse.

SEX OR NUDITY—None.

VIOLENCE—None.

LANGUAGE—None.

FEAR FACTOR (SUSPENSE)—None.

AGE 0–2		Nope, sorry.
AGE 3–4	★	OK if they understand baseball.
AGE 5–6	★★	Perfect for this group.
AGE 7–10	★★	Ditto.
AGE 11–12	★★	Still two stars, but pushing it.
AGE 13+	★	Pushing it.
ADULT	★★	Not bad.

SUGGESTED AGES—4–14

Roxanne (PG)

1987 Comedy
Directed by Fred Schepisi
Starring Steve Martin, Daryl Hannah, Rick Rossovich, Shelley Duvall, Michael J. Pollard

A modern take on the classic tale of *Cyrano de Bergerac*. Steve Martin, who also wrote the screenplay, plays a sweet, smart fire chief in a small ski town. He also has an enormously long nose. One of the firemen who works for him is quite handsome, rather dim-witted, and in love with the beautiful Roxanne (Daryl Hannah). Martin is chivalrous in helping the dim bulb win Roxanne, all the while pining for her himself. It is a lovely story, at times quite funny.

SEX OR NUDITY—Some. Much is implied, little is seen, although we do glimpse Hannah's bare bottom running through the bushes.
VIOLENCE—Some. Martin dispenses with bullies and thugs with his tennis racquet.
LANGUAGE—Some. This film is full of mild cursing.
FEAR FACTOR (SUSPENSE)—None.

AGE 0–2		No way.
AGE 3–4		Still no way.
AGE 5–6		Nah, still pushing it for this group.
AGE 7–10	★★	They'll find Martin funny.
AGE 11–12	★★★	Ditto.
AGE 13+	★★★	This group will really appreciate this film.
ADULT	★★	Pleasant enough.

SUGGESTED AGES—8–99

Rudy (PG)

1993 Sports
Directed by David Anspaugh
Starring Sean Astin, Jon Favreau, Ned Beatty, Charles S. Dutton, Robert Prosky

Finally, a sports film that's not all about winning and losing. One of the best family sports films ever made, *Rudy* is the true story about a "five foot nuthin' " who dreams of wearing the Notre Dame football uniform. That's it. Rudy, a fireplug of a kid with virtually no athletic ability, doesn't even expect to play; all he wants to do is be a part of the practice team so that he can contribute in some way to the Fighting Irish. But he can't even get into Notre Dame. So he saves his money, applies to a nearby school, and takes a job helping the equipment manager. Finally, he tries out as a walk-on. He takes such a pounding, the coach doesn't know what to make of him. But Rudy hangs in there, showing more heart than the starters, and finally the coach agrees to let him practice with the team. This means Rudy takes a pounding five days a week but still can't get into the games. He's ridiculed by his family and friends but never quits. Finally, it's the last game of Rudy's senior year. In an unabashedly emotional climax, the team stages a protest and convinces the coach to let Rudy dress for the game. Never has sitting on the bench been such an inspiring accomplishment.

SEX OR NUDITY—None.

VIOLENCE—Minimal. Rudy's best friend is killed in a fiery accident at the steel mill. A brief, not especially scary scene.

LANGUAGE—Some. Nothing your kids haven't already heard in the locker room at school.

FEAR FACTOR (SUSPENSE)—None.

AGE 0–2		No.
AGE 3–4		No.
AGE 5–6	★	Probably too slow for kids this age.
AGE 7–10	★★★	They'll just start to get it, but they will appreciate this film.

AGE 11–12	★★★★	An inspiring story for all the underdogs of the world.
AGE 13+	★★★★	Ditto.
ADULT	★★★★	You'll resist at first, thinking this is another rags-to-riches cliché, but this determined kid will win you over. You will be reaching for the tissues by the end.

SUGGESTED AGES—8–99

Sandlot, The (PG)

1993 Sports
Directed by David Mickey Evans
Starring Tom Guiry, Mike Vitar, Patrick Renna, Chauncey Leopardi, Denis Leary, Karen Allen, James Earl Jones

It's a dry, dusty summer day in 1962 and all Scotty Smalls wants to do is join the other boys in a game of sandlot baseball. But he's new in town, can't play the game, and his stepfather is too busy to teach him. Enter Benjamin Franklin Rodriguez, the best kid on the team. Ben offers to teach Scotty what he needs to know to join the sandlot team and thereby make friends with a bunch of neighborhood guys who turn out to be just as gawky as he is. The setting for this quirky coming-of-age story is a Los Angeles sandlot next to a mysterious vacant lot, home of The Beast, a ferocious dog who eats any ball that goes over the fence. Eager to impress his new friends, Scotty borrows his stepfather's prized possession: a baseball signed by Babe Ruth. Naturally, the ball goes over the fence and Scotty has to retrieve it. His new friends rig up a contraption that uses an Erector set and a catcher's chest protector to lower Scotty into the Beast's lair. The darn thing breaks, and Scotty falls just inches from The Beast's reach. Finally, Scotty braves the horror of confronting the dog's owner to try to reclaim the ball. The owner, it turns out, is a former member of the Negro League who invites the boys in to hear stories about his old friend, Babe Ruth. This simple, nostalgic film makes a great diversion on a hot, nothing-to-do summer day.

SEX OR NUDITY—None.

VIOLENCE—None.

LANGUAGE—None.

FEAR FACTOR (SUSPENSE)—Minimal. You only get glimpses of The Beast—a toothy, slobbering jaw, a giant furry paw—but it may be enough to scare little children. Older kids will recognize The Beast as a kind of legendary brute whose bark is worse than his bite.

AGE 0–2		No way.
AGE 3–4		Too scary for them, too.
AGE 5–6	★★★	A good choice for older kids in this age group.

AGE 7–10	★★★★	A home run.
AGE 11–12	★★★	Former Little Leaguers may be willing to watch it with younger siblings, but may not want to let in on how much they like it.
AGE 13+	★★	Probably pushing it.
ADULT	★★★	May take you back to the summer of 1962.

SUGGESTED AGES—6–12

Searching for Bobby Fischer (PG)

1993 Drama
Directed by Steven Zaillian
Starring Joe Mantegna, Laurence Fishburne, Joan Allen, Max Pomeranc

This film, based on the real-life story of a seven-year-old chess prodigy Josh Waitzkin, starts when the little boy confounds the streetwise chess players in New York's Washington Square Park. Then he stumps the polished players at the city's stuffy chess clubs. Before long, he's the number one player in the country. But suddenly he develops a crippling fear of losing. In this gentle, heartening film, Josh and his parents find a way to balance his gift for chess with his seven-year-old joie de vivre.

Note: *Searching for Bobbie Fischer* is a heartwarming video that makes an ideal Saturday night family rental. It offers fertile grounds for discussion about the ethics of competition and the importance of letting children be children. But it's not one kids will watch on their own; the style is so quiet and subtle that children will need an adult nearby for questions and interpretations.

SEX OR NUDITY—None.

VIOLENCE—None.

LANGUAGE—None.

FEAR FACTOR (SUSPENSE)—None.

AGE 0–2		No.
AGE 3–4		No.
AGE 5–6		Too subtle and slow-moving for kids this age.
AGE 7–10	★★★	Chess enthusiasts in this age range will love it, others may need your help.
AGE 11–12	★★★★	Right on.
AGE 13+	★★★	Ditto.
ADULT	★★★★	An all-star cast, a touching story. Enjoy.

SUGGESTED AGES—7–99

Secret Garden, The (G)

1993 Drama
Directed by Agnieszka Holland
Starring Kate Maberly, Heydon Prowse, Andrew Knott, Laura Crossley, Maggie Smith

This is one of those deeply satisfying children's films that is as much for parents as it is for their children. It's also hauntingly beautiful and more than a little sad. The story, based on Frances Hodgson Burnett's classic book, is about Mary Lennox, a young orphan girl sent to live in a lonely mansion in England. The lord of the manor is aloof and often gone, traveling the world in an effort to forget the death of his young bride. Left on her own, Mary has little to do but explore the manor, where she discovers the dead woman's bedroom and a key to a secret garden. She also uncovers the manor's great secret: the woman's nine-year-old son who lives in a remote corner of the mansion, confined to his bed. Mary, determined that the boy should see the garden his mother left for him, embarks on a quest that changes and heals the boy, his father, and her own motherless heart.

SEX OR NUDITY—None.
VIOLENCE—None.
LANGUAGE—None.
FEAR FACTOR (SUSPENSE)—None.

AGE 0–2		Too young.
AGE 3–4		Still too young.
AGE 5–6		Still probably too young.
AGE 7–10	★★★★	Perfect.
AGE 11–12	★★★★	Ditto.
AGE 13+	★★★	They may think they're too sophisticated for this one. They're not. No one is.
ADULT	★★★★	Enchanting.

SUGGESTED AGES—7–99

Seven Brides for Seven Brothers (No Rating)

1954 Musical; Western
Directed by Stanley Donen
Starring Howard Keel, Jane Powell, Russ Tamblyn

A tremendously energetic—some say macho—musical set in Oregon in the 1850s. Howard Keel sets out to get himself a bride in one day. Jane Powell goes off with Keel to live on the timber ranch he shares with his six brothers. There she manages both to civilize the group and give them a new appreciation of women. The dance numbers are spectacular, particularly "The Barn Raising." This film was nominated for a number of Oscars and won for Best Score. Enjoy.

SEX OR NUDITY—Minimal. The requisite kiss.

VIOLENCE—Minimal. Just some macho posturing.

LANGUAGE—None.

FEAR FACTOR (SUSPENSE)—None.

AGE 0–2		No, sorry.
AGE 3–4	★	They may sit still for a few numbers.
AGE 5–6	★★	Fine for this group.
AGE 7–10	★★	Ditto.
AGE 11–12	★★	A bit dated for this group.
AGE 13+	★★	Ditto.
ADULT	★★	A nice musical, but it's not our favorite.

SUGGESTED AGES—4–99

Shane (No Rating)

1953 Western
Directed by George Stevens
Starring Alan Ladd, Jean Arthur, Van Heflin, Jack Palance, Brandon de Wilde

A classic Western with Alan Ladd starring as the ex-gunslinger who has hung up his guns, and then comes to the defense of beleaguered home-steaders. De Wilde plays the homesteaders' young son who idolizes Shane, and Palance is nearly perfect as the creepy thug hired by the avaricious land baron. The story is compelling, and the Oscar-winning cinematography is gorgeous.

SEX OR NUDITY—None.
VIOLENCE—Lots of shooting in the classic Western sense
LANGUAGE—None.
FEAR FACTOR (SUSPENSE)—Some. The tension builds beautifully.

AGE 0–2		No way.
AGE 3–4		Ditto.
AGE 5–6		Still no way.
AGE 7–10	★★★	They'll appreciate both Shane and the young boy's infatuation with him.
AGE 11–12	★★★	Ditto.
AGE 13+	★★★★	Perfect for this group.
ADULT	★★★★	One of the best Westerns ever made.

SUGGESTED AGES—7–99

Shiloh (PG-13)

1997 Animal; Drama
Directed by Dale Rosenbloom
Starring Blake Heron, Scott Wilson, Rod Steiger

What should you do if a dog follows you home? What if you know the dog is being mistreated by his owner? What if, despite your parents' insistence that you return the dog, he comes back? Such are the ethical dilemmas eleven-year-old Marty Preston must face when he comes across a winsome beagle pup owned by Judd Travers, a brutish, hard-drinking hunter. In this updated version of Phyllis Reynolds Naylor's Newbury Award–winning book, Marty struggles to do the right thing, only to find that his decision to secretly keep the dog creates even bigger problems. A tearjerker about love, lies and responsibility.

SEX OR NUDITY—None.

VIOLENCE—Some. Many children will wince at Judd Travers's abusive treatment of the adorable Shiloh, and all but the toughest will be upset by a dogfight scene. But most of the kicks, blows, and bites are heard rather than seen.

LANGUAGE—Some. Travers is coarse, but not profane.

FEAR FACTOR (SUSPENSE)—Some.

AGE 0–2		No.
AGE 3–4		No. The dogfight will scare them, the moral dilemmas will bore them.
AGE 5–6	★★	Yes, although you may have to offer a lap to sit on.
AGE 7–10	★★★	You bet. They'll even want to talk about the ethical issues afterward.
AGE 11–12	★★	Even jaded older kids will be caught up in this engaging tale.
AGE 13+	★	Ditto.
ADULT	★★★	You'll be surprised how much you like it.

SUGGESTED AGES—5–12

Shootist, The (PG)

1976 Western
Directed by Don Siegel
Starring John Wayne, Lauren Bacall, Ron Howard, Jimmy Stewart, Hugh O'Brian, Richard Boone

John Wayne's last role is a perfect valediction to his career. He plays a legendary but retired gunslinger—a shootist—who, when informed that he is dying from cancer, wants to put his affairs in order and die quietly and peacefully. Not surprisingly, few people in town want to let him do that: Hugh O'Brian and Richard Boone want to settle old scores, and almost everyone else in town wants to pry into the man's affairs. The film is intelligently written, well acted, and has lots of wry humor. It also deals with death in a way that many children will find approachable and understandable. A surprising treat.

SEX OR NUDITY—None.

VIOLENCE—Lots of shooting.

LANGUAGE—Some. Relatively salty.

FEAR FACTOR (SUSPENSE)—Minimal. We know from the beginning that Wayne is dying.

AGE 0–2		No way.
AGE 3–4		Still no way.
AGE 5–6		Nope, still too tough for this group.
AGE 7–10	★★★	Perfect for this group.
AGE 11–12	★★★	Ditto.
AGE 13+	★★★	They will appreciate this film more than you or they imagine.
ADULT	★★★	A surprising treat.

SUGGESTED AGES—7–99

Singin' in the Rain (No Rating)
1952 Musical
Directed by Gene Kelly, Stanley Donen
Starring Gene Kelly, Debbie Reynolds, Donald O'Connor, Jean Hagen, Cyd Charisse

We had forgotten just how terrific this movie really is. In fact, we would argue that it is the best movie musical of all time. It is truly funny, with a plot set in the early days of Hollywood during the transition from silent films to talkies, and the musical numbers are wonderful to listen to and watch. Which is a more joyous number—"Singin' in the Rain" or "Make 'Em Laugh"? Let your kids argue about that for a while. In fact, they probably will! When two of our kids finished watching it for the first time recently, the seven-year-old and the twelve-year-old agreed on something, perhaps for the first time: We had to buy this film. Enjoy!

SEX OR NUDITY—None, but the modern dance scene with Gene Kelly and Cyd Charisse is wonderfully sexy.
VIOLENCE—None.
LANGUAGE—None.
FEAR FACTOR (SUSPENSE)—None.

AGE 0–2		Too bad.
AGE 3–4	★	Maybe the music and dancing will hold their attention in spurts.
AGE 5–6	★★	They'll start to appreciate it.
AGE 7–10	★★★★	Get ready for them to dance around the house singin'.
AGE 11–12	★★★★	A delight.
AGE 13+	★★★★	Ditto.
ADULT	★★★★	You've probably forgotten just how great this film is.

SUGGESTED AGES—6–99

Snoopy Come Home (G)

1972 Animated
Directed by Bill Melendez
Starring the Peanuts Gang

In this, our all-time animated favorite, Snoopy learns that his first owner, a little girl named Laila, is pining away for him in a hospital. He and Woodstock set out to find her, but they encounter "No Dogs Allowed" signs everywhere they go. They manage to sneak into the hospital, where Laila begs Snoopy to come back to live with her. He reluctantly agrees, and the Peanuts gang stages a maudlin farewell party for its favorite canine where even Lucy submits to a good-bye kiss. Snoopy takes off, leaving poor Charlie Brown more morose than ever. But a no-dogs policy at Laila's apartment complex means Snoopy can't live there after all. He returns home and takes back all the going-away bequests he made. Wonderful, hummable songs with genuinely funny lyrics, laugh-out-loud humor, and just the right amount of poignancy.

SEX OR NUDITY—None. Good grief! This is a Charlie Brown video.

VIOLENCE—None. Charlie Brown doesn't even get the football pulled out from under him.

LANGUAGE—None. Nothing to worry about.

FEAR FACTOR (SUSPENSE)—None. There is never any danger, but don't be surprised if you or your child tear up at the good-bye party.

AGE 0–2	★★★★	They won't understand the subtleties in the story, but they'll love the Peanuts gang, the slapstick humor, and the music.
AGE 3–4	★★★★	An absolute winner.
AGE 5–6	★★★★	Ditto.
AGE 7–10	★★★	Even though they may be a little old for this one, they'll appreciate Charles Schultz's uncanny wisdom about human nature.
AGE 11–12	★★	Worth seeing for the sentimental value.
AGE 13+		Sorry, no.
ADULT	★★★★	You're never too old for Charlie Brown.

SUGGESTED AGES—2–10

Some Like It Hot (No Rating)

1959 Comedy
Directed by Billy Wilder
Starring Jack Lemmon, Tony Curtis, Marilyn Monroe, Joe. E. Brown,
George Raft

Entertainment Weekly thinks this is the number two comedy of all time.
The American Film Institute ranks it number fourteen on its list of the
top 100 films. We're in complete agreement: This film is absolutely hysterical. You'll be surprised how many kids enjoy it!

The plot is a gas: Jack Lemmon and Tony Curtis play musicians during
Prohibition who inadvertently witness a mob slaying. On the run from
gangsters intent on rubbing out all witnesses, they pretend to be women,
and join an "all-girl" band on a train trip to Florida. Don't worry: You
won't have to explain cross-dressing to your kids—it all makes perfect
sense in context. But you will have to explain Prohibition. And it's certainly worth it! You'll be laughing more than the kids. But they'll stay
with it.

SEX OR NUDITY—Some. It's all about sex and role reversal. But there
is absolutely nothing to worry about.
VIOLENCE—Some. A big shoot-out at the beginning, with a glimpse of
a bloody dead body. But nothing too graphic or disturbing.
LANGUAGE—None.
FEAR FACTOR (SUSPENSE)—Minimal.

AGE 0–2		No way.
AGE 3–4		Sorry, still no.
AGE 5–6		Nah, still pushing it.
AGE 7–10	★★	Sure, why not.
AGE 11–12	★★★	They might a bit bewildered, but will love it.
AGE 13+	★★★★	Perfect.
ADULT	★★★★	Ditto.

SUGGESTED AGES—9–99

Sound of Music, The (G)

1965 Musical
Directed by Robert Wise
Starring Julie Andrews, Christopher Plummer, Eleanor Parker, Peggy Wood

In a word, superb. The true story of Maria von Trapp, an irrepressible governess who becomes the adoptive mother of the seven talented von Trapp children and, with her husband, sees them safely out of Nazi-occupied Austria. Most kids will need your help with the historical context and with the notion of nuns in habit in a serious film. It's long, it deals with serious subject matter, and it's a musical—all seemingly good reasons for your kids to resist it. But after the first few frames, they'll be drawn in. (One option for those with short attention spans or early bedtimes: see it in two installments, like a miniseries.)

SEX OR NUDITY—None.

VIOLENCE—None.

LANGUAGE—None.

FEAR FACTOR (SUSPENSE)—Some. How could you possibly forget the graveyard scene?

AGE 0–2		No, not yet.
AGE 3–4		Ditto.
AGE 5–6	★★	They'll enjoy the kids' antics and the music, but that's about it.
AGE 7–10	★★★★	Perfect.
AGE 11–12	★★★	They'll even appreciate the historical context.
AGE 13+	★★★	They won't mind seeing it again.
ADULT	★★★	Neither will you.

SUGGESTED AGES—6–99

Sounder (G)

1972 Animal
Directed by Martin Ritt
Starring Paul Winfield, Cicely Tyson, Kevin Hooks

A beautiful if sometimes slow film set in Louisiana in the 1930s. It is the story of an African-American sharecropper's family, their survival, and the maturation of David, the oldest son (played by young Kevin Hooks). The father is imprisoned for stealing food for his hungry family, and the family proves they can do the seemingly impossible: carry on and run the farm without him. The desire of the family to maintain both their dignity and the family unity is inspiring, and the setting—the Depression era, pre–civil rights South—should provoke fascinating family conversations.

SEX OR NUDITY—None.

VIOLENCE—Some. A prison guard hits David, and a white neighbor shoots Sounder, David's dog.

LANGUAGE—"Damn."

FEAR FACTOR (SUSPENSE)—Some. Will Sounder survive? Will the father return?

AGE 0–2		Nope.
AGE 3–4	★	Barely; the dog isn't in enough scenes.
AGE 5–6	★★	They'll like it.
AGE 7–10	★★	Perfect for this group, but it is still a "like it," not a "love it."
AGE 11–12	★★	Ditto.
AGE 13+	★	Pushing it.
ADULT	★★	A better conversation starter than pure entertainment.

SUGGESTED AGES—5–13

Splash (PG)

1984 Comedy; Fantasy/Science Fiction
Directed by Ron Howard
Starring Tom Hanks, Daryl Hannah, John Candy

A very funny film about a normal guy (Tom Hanks) who falls in love with a gorgeous woman (Daryl Hannah) who is, well, strange. Strange in that when she arrives in New York at the Statue of Liberty, she is completely nude. Strange in that when she tells Hanks her name, it sounds like a high-pitched squeak and televisions tend to explode. She also likes to eat whole lobsters and learns English—quite quickly—from television and then speaks in commercial sound bites. It is all sort of understandable because she is a mermaid. Right, a mermaid. Think nothing of it; this is a fairy tale. A sweet, adult, perfectly enjoyable fairy tale. With the added pleasure of John Candy as Hanks's ne'er-do-well brother in one of his funniest roles. Don't let the nudity or language keep you or the kids away. It is a treat.

SEX OR NUDITY—Some. We see Hannah nude, mostly from the rear. Lots of kissing and implied sex.
VIOLENCE—Minimal.
LANGUAGE—Some, yeah, but not too raunchy.
FEAR FACTOR (SUSPENSE)—Minimal.

AGE 0–2		No way.
AGE 3–4		Ditto.
AGE 5–6	★★	OK for this group.
AGE 7–10	★★★★	But perfect for this one.
AGE 11–12	★★★★	Romantic without a lot of sex, which should surprise this group.
AGE 13+	★★★★	Simply captivating.
ADULT	★★★	Quite entertaining.

SUGGESTED AGES—6–99

Stand by Me (R)

1986 Drama
Directed by Rob Reiner
Starring River Phoenix, Wil Wheaton, Corey Feldman, Kiefer Sutherland

Four good friends—boys looking at puberty from the safe distance of middle school—sneak off on an overnight camping trip to find a dead body. (Sounds grim, but it's really just an excuse for an adventure.) They set off with few provisions but with high expectations for drama and excitement. They outsmart a junkyard bully, outrun a train, and outwit a band of older boys who also want to find the body. But what makes this film such a treat is seeing friendships deepen as the boys reveal their fears and dreams, and their genuine but awkward compassion for each other's quirks and shortcomings. The adolescent high jinks aren't bad either.

SEX OR NUDITY—Some raunchy talk about female anatomy.
VIOLENCE—Minimal. Some daredevil antics that will scare sensitive kids, but no real violence.
LANGUAGE—A lot. Abundant (and often inaccurate). Mainly the adolescent variety boys use to insult each other. Liberal use of the F-word.
FEAR FACTOR (SUSPENSE)—High. Be prepared for a few brief but highly memorable and potentially scary moments: a loaded gun accidentally goes off, the boys get stuck on a railroad viaduct in front of a speeding train, and they finally find the dead body. (There are two lingering shots of the corpse's face.) The film has an all-in-good-fun tone, but it *is* based on a Stephen King short story, after all. Let kids know when to cover their eyes and reassure them that the boys in the story will all be safe in the end.

AGE 0–2		Don't even consider it.
AGE 3–4		No way.
AGE 5–6		Ditto.
7–10	★★	Maybe. Older, stout-hearted (and mainly male) adventure lovers will adore it, especially

"Barf-o-Rama," a tall-tale interlude about a pie-eating contest.

AGE 11–12   ★★★★   A good choice for kids clamoring to be allowed to see R-rated fare in the theater. It will make them feel grown-up without scaring the pants off them.

AGE 13+   ★★★★   Perfect, especially for boys.

ADULT   ★★★★   This film is loaded with nostalgia value and packs a good scare.

SUGGESTED AGES—9–99

Starman (PG)

1984 Fantasy/Science Fiction
Directed by John Carpenter
Starring Jeff Bridges, Karen Allen, Charles Martin, Richard Jaeckel

A surprisingly sweet science-fiction romance. An alien visitor is shot down over Wisconsin, where he assumes the human shape of a dead house painter. The painter's widow is stunned, then angry at this intruder who looks like her husband. He forces her to drive him back to meet his spaceship and outrun a search party bent on killing him, and along the way she finds her anger turning to love. Sounds improbable, doesn't it? Sounds corny, doesn't it? Trust us, it's not.

SEX OR NUDITY—None.
VIOLENCE—Minimal.
LANGUAGE—Minimal.
FEAR FACTOR (SUSPENSE)—Minimal.

AGE 0–2		No way.
AGE 3–4		Ditto.
AGE 5–6	★	We would wait a year.
AGE 7–10	★★★	They'll think of it as *E.T.* with grown-ups.
AGE 11–12	★★★	Sure. Give it a try.
AGE 13+	★★★	Ditto.
ADULT	★★★	You'll be surprised how much you like it.

SUGGESTED AGES—6–99

Star Wars (PG)
1977 Fantasy/Science Fiction
Directed by George Lucas
Starring Mark Hamill, Harrison Ford, Carrie Fisher, Alec Guinness,
James Earl Jones

There are only two questions open for debate on this epic intergallactic
tale of good versus evil: At what age do you let your child first see it?
And, how many repetitions do you allow? We can try to answer the first:
The battle scenes, not to mention the hideous Jabba the Hut, are too
potent for most kids under six. Smaller kids will certainly be able to follow the very visual, fast-paced action, but it's probably not good for
them to be exposed to such battle-intensive drama. Besides, the film's
larger message will be lost on them. As for the question of how often you
let your children watch the film, we're at a loss, having watched it dozens
and dozens of times ourselves. Buy it, don't rent it.

SEX OR NUDITY—None.
VIOLENCE—Some. Lots of shooting, big pyrotechnics.
LANGUAGE—Minimal.
FEAR FACTOR (SUSPENSE)—Some. Can be too much to take for small
kids.

AGE 0–2		No.
AGE 3–4		Wait a year or two.
AGE 5–6	★★	OK for the older kids in this category.
AGE 7–10	★★★★	Perfect.
11–12	★★★	One of those rare films they'll watch again and again, even at this age.
13+	★★	Probably only for nostalgic value.
ADULT	★★★★	Incredibly exciting no matter how many times you've seen it.

SUGGESTED AGES—6–99

Sullivan's Travels (No Rating)

1941 Comedy; Drama
Directed by Preston Sturges
Starring Joel McCrea, Veronica Lake, William Demarest

Preston Strurges wrote and directed this Hollywood classic about a successful movie director (Joel McCrea) who goes undercover as a hobo during the Depression in order to understand poverty. It is a combination of sophisticated humor, slapstick, and pathos. At first accompanied by the studio's press retinue, and later by Veronica Lake—a broke, aspiring actress giving up on her dream and hitching home—McCrea is ready to return to his former life when events conspire against him. After he is mugged, robbed, suffers amnesia, and imprisoned, he really learns what it is like to be part of the underclass.

As a message movie, this film becomes more relevant and poignant as time goes on. As entertainment, it is timeless.

SEX OR NUDITY—Minimal. Sexy but no sex.
VIOLENCE—Some. A few fights, a mugging, some violent prison guards.
LANGUAGE—Minimal. Nothing to worry about.
FEAR FACTOR (SUSPENSE)—Some. Great drama, but nothing gratuitous.

AGE 0–2		No way.
AGE 3–4		Nope.
AGE 5–6		Ditto.
AGE 7–10	★★	They'll start to appreciate it.
AGE 11–12	★★★	They will enjoy it.
13+	★★★★	Perfect for this group.
ADULT	★★★★	A gem.

SUGGESTED AGES—7–99

Superman (G)

1978 Fantasy/Science Fiction
Directed by Richard Donner
Starring Christopher Reeve, Margot Kidder, Gene Hackman, Marlon Brando, Ned Beatty, Jackie Cooper

This was the first, and in many ways still the best, of all the superhero comic book adaptations. There is a sense of innocence and awe, and the special effects, which won an Oscar, are terrific. The story follows Superman from his birth on Krypton, to growing up in Smallville, to his emergence as—dum de dum—Superman! Gene Hackman plays arch villain Lex Luthor and Ned Beatty is his bumbling sidekick. Because the film doesn't take itself too seriously, despite Marlon Brando as the portentous Jor-El, it is enjoyable.

SEX OR NUDITY—None.

VIOLENCE—Some. Superhero stuff.

LANGUAGE—None.

FEAR FACTOR (SUSPENSE)—Minimal. The initial scenes of a trail of really bad guys and the destruction of Krypton may be disturbing for younger children.

AGE 0–2		Not quite.
AGE 3–4	★★	You bet!
AGE 5–6	★★★	Perfect for this group.
7–10	★★★	Ditto.
11–12	★★	OK for superhero nostalgia, but too many kids are spoiled by more recent, more cynical fare.
AGE 13+	★★	Ditto.
ADULT	★★	Not bad.

SUGGESTED AGES—3–14

Superman II (G)

1980 Fantasy/Science Fiction
Directed by Richard Lester
Starring Christopher Reeve, Margot Kidder, Gene Hackman, Marlon Brando, Ned Beatty, Jackie Cooper

This sequel isn't quite as good as the original, but it is still fun. This time, the earthly bad guys Gene Hackman and Ned Beatty are overshadowed by supervillains who originate from Krypton, and who have the same superpowers as the Man of Steel. First seen in the original being found guilty of treason by a tribunal headed by Jor-El, Superman's father, the supervillains come to earth to exact an intergalactic, multigenerational revenge. Plus the romance between Superman and Lois Lane heats up. A bit more sex and a bit harder edged in the violence category, but still fun.

SEX OR NUDITY—Minimal. Just talk, but a fair amount of talk.
VIOLENCE—Some, yep, of the superhero kind, but with a bit of an edge.
LANGUAGE—None.
FEAR FACTOR (SUSPENSE)—Minimal.

AGE 0–2		Not quite.
AGE 3–4	★★	You bet.
AGE 5–6	★★	Perfect.
AGE 7–10	★★	Ditto.
AGE 11–12	★★	OK, but pushing it with this group. The romance may hold them.
AGE 13+	★★	Solely for the romance.
ADULT	★★	You may get a little bored.

SUGGESTED AGES—4–13

Support Your Local Gunfighter (G)

1971 Western
Directed by Burt Kennedy
Starring James Garner, Suzanne Pleshette, Jack Elam, Harry Morgan

This is not really a sequel to *Support Your Local Sheriff*, but it does have an overlapping cast, the same director, and a similar sensibility. It is a parody without being a spoof. James Garner plays a con artist who tries to pass off Jack Elam as a notorious gunfighter. Terrific fun.

SEX OR NUDITY—Minimal.

VIOLENCE—A lot. Shoot-outs, brawls, the usual, but nothing disturbing.

LANGUAGE—Minimal. Nothing to worry about.

FEAR FACTOR (SUSPENSE)—None.

AGE 0–2		No way.
AGE 3–4	★	Barely appropriate.
AGE 5–6	★★	They'll enjoy it.
AGE 7–10	★★	Right on.
AGE 11–12	★★	Surprisingly entertaining.
AGE 13+	★	OK.
ADULT	★★	Enjoy.

SUGGESTED AGES—6–99

Support Your Local Sheriff (G)

1969 Western
Directed by Burt Kennedy
Starring James Garner, Joan Hackett, Walter Brennan, Harry Morgan, Jack Elam, Bruce Dern

A very funny near-spoof of virtually every Western cowboy movie. We say "near-spoof" because this film, made more than twenty years ago, does not go quite so over the top as many of the more recent spoofs. But no cliché is spared. Garner plays a man passing through a lawless gold-rush town on his way to Australia. He winds up becoming sheriff and uses his wits and his gun to tame the town. That's a bit of a challenge, since every other sheriff has either fled town or been killed. And the jail, well, it has no bars on the windows or doors. An amusing film with terrific actors who are clearly enjoying themselves.

SEX OR NUDITY—Minimal. There may be a kiss, but we may have missed it. But you can appreciate. "Madame Orr's House."
VIOLENCE—A lot. Tons of shoot-outs and fights, but with a cartoon sensibility.
LANGUAGE—Minimal. A "damn" here or there.
FEAR FACTOR (SUSPENSE)—None.

AGE 0–2		Nope.
AGE 3–4	★	They won't appreciate the humor, but they will enjoy the Old West action.
AGE 5–6	★★	Right on.
AGE 7–10	★★★	Perfect for this group.
AGE 11–12	★★★	Ditto.
AGE 13+	★★	The wry humor should hold them.
ADULT	★★	Not bad at all.

SUGGESTED AGES—6–99

Take the Money and Run (PG)

1969 Comedy
Directed by Woody Allen
Starring Woody Allen, Janet Margolin, Marcel Hillaire, Louise Lasser

We confess: We wanted to include at least one Woody Allen film, and this is the only one that made the cut. The rest are arguably funnier, more poignant, more polished. But they are also more consumed with sex, neurosis, and Allen's adult schtick. This film makes the cut, but only barely.

Take the Money and Run is Allen's first film as a director-writer-star. It is a pseudo-documentary about Virgil Starkwell (Allen) who is the world's most inept criminal. It is full of one-liners and sight gags, many of them quite funny. Our favorite: the famous bank robbery note where the entire staff debates whether Allen has written "gun" or "gub." A very funny film that is a perfect introduction to early Woody Allen.

SEX OR NUDITY—Minimal. A fair amount of talk, some kissing, and one scene with extreme close-ups of lovemaking, but nothing really inappropriate.

VIOLENCE—Minimal. Some gunplay in botched robberies and prison breaks.

LANGUAGE—Minimal. Nothing to worry about.

FEAR FACTOR (SUSPENSE)—None.

AGE 0–2		Nope.
AGE 3–4		Ditto.
AGE 5–6		Still not right.
AGE 7–10	★★	They'll like it.
AGE 11–12	★★★	Perfect.
AGE 13+	★★★	This group will love it, and may even start to ask about Woody Allen.
ADULT	★★★	So will you.

SUGGESTED AGES—8–99

Thief of Bagdad, The (No Rating)

1940 Action/Adventure
Directed by Ludwig Berger
Starring Sabu, Conrad Veidt, June Duprez, Max Ingram, Tim Whelan, Michael Powell

There were at least four versions, including a made-for-television film, of this classic tale of *The Arabian Nights*. This is our favorite by far. The story centers on a young boy (played by Sabu, best known from his role in the *The Jungle Book,* who is resourceful enough to escape death numerous times, defeat the arch villain, and tame a rogue genie in order to help a prince escape from prison and win the hand of the princess. Whew! There is a certain breathlessness about this film, and it not just the nonstop action. It is also is beautifully designed and photographed. A warning: The genie is anything but genial! And for kids who love the 1992 Disney hit *Aladdin*, with the madcap performance of a genie and the voice of Robin Williams, *this* genie may prove a bit disturbing. But kids should love it for its *Indiana Jones* sensibility, and you'll certainly appreciate Conrad Veidt, best known for his role as the Nazi colonel in *Casablanca*, in his performances as the evil Grand Vizier of Bagdad.

SEX OR NUDITY—None.

VIOLENCE—Some. A fair amount of sword fighting.

LANGUAGE—None.

FEAR FACTOR (SUSPENSE)—A lot. A terrifying jailer threatens to cut off the boy's hands, feet, and head. And the battle against a giant spider will be scary for younger—and maybe older—kids.

AGE 0–2		No way.
AGE 3–4		Pushing it a bit, but the color may capture their imagination.
AGE 5–6	★★★	Perfect.
AGE 7–10	★★★	Ditto.
AGE 11–12	★★	They'll enjoy it, but might consider themselves too old.
AGE 13+	★★	Ditto.

ADULT   ★★   You'll love the set design.

SUGGESTED AGES—5–12

Thin Man, The (No Rating)
1934 Comedy; Drama
Directed by W. S. Van Dyke
Starring William Powell, Myrna Loy, Maureen O'Sullivan, Cesar Romeo, Porter Hall

Nick and Nora Charles—William Powell and Myrna Loy—became the model for every detective (and romantic) team. The sophisticated dialogue may be too quick for most kids, but this comedy-mystery established the prototype not only for the five sequels that followed, but for dozens of other detective flicks. Be forewarned: Nick and Nora like their booze. Their dog Asta almost steals the show. Enjoy!

SEX OR NUDITY—Minimal. Talk, but no action.

VIOLENCE—Minimal. A shooting.

LANGUAGE—None.

FEAR FACTOR (SUSPENSE)—Minimal.

AGE 0–2		No way.
AGE 3–4		Ditto.
AGE 5–6		Still no way.
AGE 7–10	★	The dog may entertain them, but not enough.
AGE 11–12	★★	Still a stretch.
AGE 13+	★★★	They'll begin to appreciate the dialogue and the chemistry between Powell and Loy.
ADULT	★★★	Enjoy yourself!

SUGGESTED AGES—10–99

Third Man, The (No Rating)

1949 Drama
Directed by Carol Reed
Starring Orson Welles, Joseph Cotten, Trevor Howard

A moody, beautifully photographed mystery set in post—World War II Vienna. Orson Welles plays Harry Lime, who is presumed (by some) to be dead, and by others—Army intelligence—to be a dastardly criminal engaged in black market activities. Joseph Cotten, a writer of pulp Westerns, has been summoned to Vienna by his friend Welles (now dead or at least disappeared), and is determined to find out the truth. The music is haunting, the story easy to follow, and the acting first-rate. One warning: The criminal activity Welles is accused of is doctoring penicillin, and the consequences (as described by Trevor Howard, the army intelligence chief) may be disturbing to some children. Kids, he says, die because they are getting diluted medicines.

SEX OR NUDITY—None.
VIOLENCE—Minimal. A few shots fired.
LANGUAGE—None.
FEAR FACTOR (SUSPENSE)—A lot. Shadows, chases, eerie characters

AGE 0–2		Nope.
AGE 3–4		Still no way.
AGE 5–6		Ditto.
AGE 7–10	★	Maybe, and it is a big maybe, for the oldest kids.
AGE 11–12	★★	A fifty-fifty shot at engaging them.
AGE 13+	★★★	Get them to sit through the first few minutes and they'll be hooked.
ADULT	★★★★	A classic.

SUGGESTED AGES—10–99

Those Magnificent Men in Their Flying Machines (No Rating)
1965 Action/Adventure
Directed by Ken Annakin
Starring James Fox, Sarah Miles, Terry-Thomas, Stuart Whitman, Robert Morley

In 1910, a British newspaper magnate established a competition: an air race challenging pilots from all over the world to fly from London to Paris. Airplanes were then fairly new, having a history of only ten years of successful flying, including one pilot who had successfully made the London-to-Paris jaunt. The trip across the English Channel was considered quite dangerous and thus newsworthy. Kids and parents will love this story of adventure, intrigue, sabotage, and romance. The antique planes, which crash often, are a wonder to behold, and the humor sufficient to keep the film aloft.

SEX OR NUDITY—Minimal. Romance and the occasional towel-draped body, but nothing to worry about.
VIOLENCE—Minimal. Crashes and more crashes, but nothing violent.
LANGUAGE—Minimal. There may be an occasional "damn."
FEAR FACTOR (SUSPENSE)—Minimal.

AGE 0–2		Not quite.
AGE 3–4	★	If they've flown or like planes, this will hold their attention.
AGE 5–6	★★	Not a bad fit.
AGE 7–10	★★★	Perfect.
AGE 11–12	★★	May find it a bit long.
AGE 13+	★★	OK.
ADULT	★★	Not bad.

SUGGESTED AGES—6–14

Three Musketeers, The (No Rating)

1948 Action/Adventure
Directed by George Sidney
Starring Lana Turner, Gene Kelly, June Allyson, Gig Young, Van Heflin, Robert Coote, Vincent Price

There were no fewer than six versions made of the classic Alexandre Dumas tale, and we have included three of them: the 1948, 1974, and 1993 productions. *The Three Musketeers* is the tale of swashbucklers battling the evil Cardinal Richelieu for the honor of the Queen of France. The 1948 version has tremendous production values and features the wonderful athleticism of Gene Kelly in the role of D'Artagnan. It is the most traditional of the various adaptations.

SEX OR NUDITY—None.

VIOLENCE—A lot. More sword fights than you can shake a sword at.

LANGUAGE—None.

FEAR FACTOR (SUSPENSE)—Minimal.

AGE 0–2		Nope.
AGE 3–4	★	They won't understand much, but will they love the sword fights.
AGE 5–6	★★	Sure, they'll love it.
AGE 7–10	★★★	Ditto, and they'll understand it.
AGE 11–12	★★★	A treat.
AGE 13+	★★	They might find it a bit simple for their "mature" tastes.
ADULT	★★	The cast is a treat.

SUGGESTED AGES—5–12

Three Musketeers, The (PG)
1974 Action/Adventure
Directed by Richard Lester
Starring Oliver Reed, Raquel Welch, Richard Chamberlain, Michael York, Charlton Heston, Faye Dunaway

This version of the Alexandre Dumas classic is slightly less lavish than the 1948 production, but grittier, a bit more violent, and certainly more tongue-in-cheek. It is also sexier, but don't let that stop you. An interesting footnote: The director, Richard Lester filmed additional scenes that became *The Four Musketeers.*

SEX OR NUDITY—Some. Lots implied but little shown.
VIOLENCE—A lot. Sword fights aplenty, some gunfights.
LANGUAGE—Minimal.
FEAR FACTOR (SUSPENSE)—Minimal.

AGE 0–2		Nope.
AGE 3–4	★	They won't understand much, but will love the sword fights.
AGE 5–6	★★★	Perfect.
AGE 7–10	★★★	Ditto.
AGE 11–12	★★★	Better than the 1948 production.
AGE 13+	★★★	Just fine.
ADULT	★★	Not bad.

SUGGESTED AGES—5–14

Three Musketeers, The (PG)

1993 Action/Adventure
Directed by Stephen Herek
Starring Charlie Sheen, Kiefer Sutherland, Chris O'Donnell, Oliver Platt, Tim Curry, Rebecca De Mornay

We hate to admit it, but this is the version of the classic tale that kids will probably like the best. It is the least true to the original Alexandre Dumas story, but many kids will recognize the stars and the energy will keep them entertained. The cast truly seems to be enjoying themselves, and Tim Curry's portrayal of the villainous Cardinal Richelieu is terrific.

SEX OR NUDITY—Minimal. Nothing to worry about.
VIOLENCE—A lot. You bet, but it is expected.
LANGUAGE—Minimal.
FEAR FACTOR (SUSPENSE)—Minimal.

AGE 0–2		No way.
AGE 3–4	★	Barely, but no harm done.
AGE 5–6	★★	They'll like it.
AGE 7–10	★★★	They'll love it.
AGE 11–12	★★★	Ditto.
AGE 13+	★★★	The best of all the versions for this group.
ADULT	★★	Not bad.

SUGGESTED AGES—5–99

Time After Time (PG)

1979 Fantasy/Science Fiction; Drama
Directed by Nicholas Meyer
Starring Malcolm McDowell, David Warner, Mary Steenburgen

A very creative idea that is relatively well executed (if you'll excuse the pun) about Jack the Ripper escaping to 1979 America with H. G. Wells (in his time machine) in pursuit. Thus we have two men very much of their time (Victorian England) forced to deal with a very different world. But it is also both a battle of the wits and a life-or-death pursuit.

SEX OR NUDITY—Minimal. Some kissing and the suggestion that something serious is about to happen. The couple is shown together in bed the next morning.

VIOLENCE—Some. The opening scene of a prostitute being lured and killed by Jack the Ripper, though not graphic, has a disturbing, lurid quality to it. A later killing is equally disturbing.

LANGUAGE—Minimal. A bit of cursing.

FEAR FACTOR (SUSPENSE)—Some. It is moody, and except for the two killings, not particularly scary.

AGE 0–2		No way.
AGE 3–4		Ditto.
AGE 5–6		Still not right for this crowd.
AGE 7–10	★★	But only for the older kids.
AGE 11–12	★★	They'll find it quite entertaining.
AGE 13+	★★	They'll find it mildly entertaining.
ADULT	★★	So will you.

SUGGESTED AGES—9–99

To Kill a Mockingbird (No Rating)

1962 Drama
Directed by Robert Mulligan
Starring Gregory Peck, Mary Badham, Phillip Alford, Rosemary Murphy, Robert Duvall

This powerful film about a gentle Southern lawyer who defends an innocent black man accused of raping a white woman is one every family should see. In perhaps the greatest role in his career, Gregory Peck plays Atticus Finch, a dignified widower who stands up, almost single-handedly, against racial hatred in a fearful, divided Depression-era town. What makes this searing drama a family film is not only its important subject matter, but its narrator: Scout Finch, a little girl who is both wide-eyed and precocious. Not only does Scout take in the whole drama—sneaking into the segregated courtroom to watch the trial—she unknowingly stops an angry lynch mob with a few innocent hellos. If seeing this film was a formative experience for you, you'll want to share it with your adolescent and then talk about what it means to stand up for what you believe in.

SEX OR NUDITY—None.

VIOLENCE—None.

LANGUAGE—None.

FEAR FACTOR (SUSPENSE)—Some. There is one frightening scene where Scout and her brother are attacked by the mysterious Boo Radley (Robert Duvall). The real terror in this film is imagining what might have happened if not for Atticus Finch's quiet strength.

AGE 0–2		No way.
AGE 3–4		Ditto.
AGE 5–6		Ditto.
AGE 7–10		Ditto.
AGE 11–12	★★★★	Insist that your adolescent watch this one with you. You'll both be glad you did.
AGE 13+	★★★★	Perfect.
ADULT	★★★★	It's just as good as, if not better, than you remember.

SUGGESTED AGES—11–99

Tootsie (PG)

1982 Comedy
Directed by Sydney Pollack
Starring Dustin Hoffman, Jessica Lange, Bill Murray, Teri Garr, Dabney Coleman, Charles Durning

Not your usual man-in-high-heels slapstick bit, this all-star comedy is as wry as it is moving. Unable to find work because of his temperamental ways, actor Michael Dorsey goes on an audition disguised as a woman. He lands a part in a soap opera where his alter-ego, Dorothy Michaels, finds himself/herself at the center of a love triangle between his beautiful soap opera costar and her widowed father. A lot of neat social satire as well as old-fashioned quick-change humor as Dorsey struggles to keep all the balls in the air.

SEX OR NUDITY—Minimal. One quick cut-away.
VIOLENCE—None.
LANGUAGE—Minimal. Nothing really offensive.
FEAR FACTOR (SUSPENSE)—None.

AGE 0–2		No.
AGE 3–4		No.
AGE 5–6		Still no. Too slow-moving at first; they'll be gone by the time it gets funny.
AGE 7–10	★★	OK for the older kids in this group.
AGE 11–12	★★★	They'll just start to get the jokes.
AGE 13+	★★★	Perfect.
ADULT	★★★	A winner.

SUGGESTED AGES—9–99

Top Hat (No Rating)

1935 Musical
Directed by Mark Sandrich
Starring Fred Astaire, Ginger Rogers, Edward Everett Horton

Probably our favorite of the Fred Astaire—Ginger Rogers musicals. There is a plot involving mistaken identity, but it is of little consequence. The dialogue is snappy (perhaps a bit too snappy for younger children) and the art deco sets are terrific. But your kids will want to watch this classic over and over again for a very simple reason: The musical numbers are a treat. The dancing is wonderful, and the songs are among the best Irving Berlin ever did: "Cheek to Cheek," "Top Hat, White Tie and Tails," and "Isn't This a Lovely Day to Be Caught in the Rain."

SEX OR NUDITY—None.

VIOLENCE—None.

LANGUAGE—None.

FEAR FACTOR (SUSPENSE)—None.

AGE 0–2		Sorry, no.
AGE 3–4	★	If they like music and dancing, they'll sit through bits.
AGE 5–6	★★	They'll start to get hooked.
AGE 7–10	★★	Ditto.
AGE 11–12	★★★	They'll appreciate it.
AGE 13+	★★★	Elegance personified.
ADULT	★★★★	Oh, go ahead. Enjoy yourself.

SUGGESTED AGES—6–99

Topper (No Rating)

1937 Comedy
Directed by Norman McLeod
Starring Cary Grant, Constance Bennett, Roland Young, Billie Burke

Cary Grant and Constance Bennett are the life of New York society—until they die in a car crash. Concerned that they will never get into heaven unless they do one good deed, and blessed with the extraordinary ability to make themselves seen by their banker, Roland Young, they make their presence very much felt on earth. A classic and rather sophisticated comedy.

SEX OR NUDITY—Minimal. Lots implied in dialogue, but nothing seen or tacky.
VIOLENCE—Minimal. There is a car crash and bodies do fly out, but this shouldn't concern anyone except the very youngest kids.
LANGUAGE—None.
FEAR FACTOR (SUSPENSE)—Minimal.

AGE 0–2		No way.
AGE 3–4		Still no way.
AGE 5–6	★	They may get it a bit, but still too sophisticated for most.
AGE 7–10	★★	They'll enjoy it more, but it is best for older, more mature kids.
AGE 11–12	★★★	Just fine.
AGE 13+	★★★	Perfect.
ADULT	★★★★	It is so much better than the television series most of us grew up with and liked.

SUGGESTED AGES—9–99

Top Secret! (PG)

1984 Comedy
Directed by Jim Abrahams, David Zucker, Jerry Zucker
Starring Val Kilmer, Lucy Gutteridge, Omar Sharif

One of the earliest spoofs, after *Airplane!*, from the Zucker brothers–Abrahams team. Val Kilmer plays an Elvis-like rock star invited to East Germany—explain *that* to the kids—to participate in a cultural festival. There he is embroiled in spy work involving Nazis and French resistance fighters. Huh? Doesn't matter. It is inoffensive, relatively tame (and lame) spoof.

SEX OR NUDITY—Minimal. One shot of (many) entangled bodies. But nothing obvious or offensive.

VIOLENCE—Minimal. Does "skeet surfin' " count? Plus a cartoonish shoot-out.

LANGUAGE—Minimal. One "a— h—."

FEAR FACTOR (SUSPENSE)—None.

AGE 0–2		Nope.
AGE 3–4	★	Some sight gags may connect.
AGE 5–6	★★	More certainly will.
AGE 7–10	★★★	The equivalent of a Happy Meal.
AGE 11–12	★★★	Yep, they'll love it too.
AGE 13+	★★★	Ditto.
ADULT	★★	It's OK to laugh with them.

SUGGESTED AGES—8–12

Tora, Tora, Tora (PG)

1970 Action/Adventure
Directed by Richard Fleischer, Kinji Fukasuku, Toshio Masudo
Starring Martin Balsam, Jason Robards, Joseph Cotten, E. G. Marshall,
James Whitmore, Soh Yamamura,

This Japanese-American coproduction *works*. It was intended to show the events leading up to and including the attack on Pearl Harbor from two different perspectives—the Japanese and the American—and it succeeds. The behind-the-scenes disagreements, uncertainties, and personalities provide a wonderful context to extraordinary war footage and re-creations. A wonderful history lesson and surprisingly good entertainment.

SEX OR NUDITY—None.
VIOLENCE—Some. This is a war flick with plenty of dying but little on-screen gore.
LANGUAGE—Minimal. A few salty expressions.
FEAR FACTOR (SUSPENSE)—Enjoyably suspenseful, even for kids—and adults–who know the outcome.

AGE 0–2		No way.
AGE 3–4		Still no.
AGE 5–6	★★	Once they understand that the story is being told simultaneously from two perspectives, they'll be intrigued.
AGE 7–10	★★★	Ditto on the dual-perspective issue. This group should really like it.
AGE 11–12	★★★	Bull's eye.
AGE 13+	★★★	Right on.
ADULT	★★★	Surprisingly entertaining.

SUGGESTED AGES—6–99

Toy Story (G)

1995 Animated
Directed by John Lasseter
Starring the voices of Tom Hanks, Tim Allen, Annie Potts, Wallace
Shawn, John Ratzenberger, Don Rickles

A marvelously creative animated feature about toys that come to life
when their owner is not around. Andy, the young boy, favors a wind-up
cowboy named Woody (Tom Hanks) until he receives a gift of Buzz
Lightyear (Tim Allen), a heavily advertised spaceman. Jealous, Woody
causes Buzz to suffer a serious "accident." Recognizing his responsibility, Woody organizes the other toys into a rescue party. This film
received a great deal of attention when it first came out because it was
the first completely computer-generated cartoon. Yes, the animation is
terrific, but that is not what sets it apart. More importantly, it is very well
written. It is a story about friendship and the desire to be wanted,
themes kids (and adults) identify with strongly. A true treat!

SEX OR NUDITY—None.

VIOLENCE—Some. Even by cartoon standards, pretty tame.

LANGUAGE—None.

FEAR FACTOR (SUSPENSE)—Minimal.

AGE 0–2	★	Sure. They won't understand it all, but should be fascinated, and perhaps a bit confused, by recognizable toys coming alive.
AGE 3–4	★★★	They'll love it.
AGE 5–6	★★★★	Ditto.
AGE 7–10	★★★★	Same for this group.
AGE 11–12	★★★	Just fine.
AGE 13+	★★	They'll probably think themselves too old, and won't give it a fair chance.
ADULT	★★★	Wonderful.

SUGGESTED AGES—3–11

Treasure Island (No Rating)

1934 Action/Adventure
Directed by Victor Fleming
Starring Wallace Beery, Jackie Cooper, Lewis Stone, Lionel Barrymore

There are about five different productions of this classic tale by Robert Louis Stevenson involving eighteenth-century pirates. We've included two: this one, by Victor Fleming, the director of the *Wizard of Oz*, and a Disney version made in 1950. The story pits the young cabin boy, Jim Hawkins, against the one-legged and treacherous Long John Silver in search of treasure. Enjoy!

SEX OR NUDITY—None.

VIOLENCE—Lots of swordplay and the promise or threats of violence

LANGUAGE—None. Nothing offensive, but even a request for a glass of water or a bottle of rum is delivered ominously.

FEAR FACTOR (SUSPENSE)—Some. There is a general feeling of tension throughout.

AGE 0–2		No way.
AGE 3–4		Still too rough.
AGE 5–6	★★	Make sure you sit close by.
AGE 7–10	★★★	Perfect, but still stay nearby.
AGE 11–12	★★★	Treasure indeed!
AGE 13+	★★	They may think themselves too sophisticated, but they'll love it.
ADULT	★★	A good old yarn.

SUGGESTED AGES—6–99

Treasure Island (No Rating)

1950 Action/Adventure
Directed by Byron Haskin
Starring Bobby Driscoll, Robert Newton, Basil Sydney

This is the Disney version, and it is just as good as the earlier Victor Fleming production. In fact, some say Robert Newton's portrayal of Long John Silver is the definitive version. Purists beware: Disney changed the ending.

SEX OR NUDITY—None.

VIOLENCE—Lots of swordplay and the promise or threats of violence

LANGUAGE—Nothing offensive but even a request for a glass of water—or a bottle of rum—is delivered ominously

FEAR FACTOR (SUSPENSE)—Some. There is a general feeling of tension throughout.

AGE 0–2		No way.
AGE 3–4		Still too rough.
AGE 5–6	★★	Make sure you sit close by.
AGE 7–10	★★★	Perfect, but still stay nearby.
AGE 11–12	★★★	Perfect.
AGE 13+	★★	They may think themselves too sophisticated, but they'll love it.
ADULT	★★	A good old yarn.

SUGGESTED AGES—6–99

True Grit (G)

1969 Western
Directed by Henry Hathaway
Starring John Wayne, Glen Cambell, Kim Darby, Robert Duvall

John Wayne won an Oscar for his portrayal of Rooster Cogburn, a one-eyed, hard-drinking U.S. Marshall. Still, it is not our favorite John Wayne Western—*The Shootist* remains number one in that category. Wayne is a hard-boiled tough guy—would we expect otherwise?—who has a tender-enough spot in his heart to help a fourteen-year-old girl track down her father's killer. The scenery is gorgeous, and the finale rip-snortin'.

SEX OR NUDITY—None.

VIOLENCE—A lot. Many shootings, a hanging.

LANGUAGE—None.

FEAR FACTOR (SUSPENSE)—Some. When the fourteen-year-old heroine falls into a snake pit, it may be a bit much for the very young or the squeamish.

AGE 0–2		No way.
AGE 3–4		Ditto.
AGE 5–6	★	Still may be a bit too much.
AGE 7–10	★★	Just right.
AGE 11–12	★★	May find it a bit dated.
AGE 13+	★★	Ditto.
ADULT	★★	Fine for John Wayne fans, a bit tedious for others.

SUGGESTED AGES—7–99

Truman Show, The (PG)

1998 Drama
Directed by Peter Weir
Starring Jim Carrey, Laura Linney, Ed Harris, Noah Emmerich

A fascinating movie that you either love or hate. We're fans, and give it high marks. It is about a seemingly ordinary fellow named Truman Burbank (Jim Carrey) who lives in a seemingly perfect small town. What he doesn't know is that he is the star of a twenty-four-hours-a-day, seven-days-a-week television program. His every move is recorded by unseen television cameras, and the entire environment is controlled. It is a story (or, more accurately, a satire) about today's commercialism and obsession with the media, and about freedom and individual will. If you buy into the premise, it is fascinating; if you don't, it is verrry long and you'll probably bail out. Hang in there and go with the flow; it is a very interesting concept, quite well executed.

SEX OR NUDITY—Minimal. Some references to marital relations, a bit of kissing, but nothing to be concerned about.
VIOLENCE—Minimal.
LANGUAGE—Minimal. There may be a few salty expressions that we didn't notice.
FEAR FACTOR (SUSPENSE)—Some. Two critical scenes involving a boat at sea in a storm that may be disturbing for some kids.

AGE 0–2		No way.
AGE 3–4		Still no way.
AGE 5–6	★	They still won't get it.
AGE 7–10	★★★	Older kids will like it.
AGE 11–12	★★★	If they get into it, this group will love it.
AGE 13+	★★★★	Ditto.
ADULT	★★★★	Suspend your disbelief and enjoy.

SUGGESTED AGES—8–99

Twelve Angry Men (No Rating)

1957, 1997 Drama
Directed by: Sidney Lumet (1957); William Friedkin (1997)
Starring: Henry Fonda, Lee J. Cobb, Ed Begley, E. G. Marshall, Jack Klugman, Jack Warden, Martin Balsam (1957); Jack Lemmon, George C. Scott, Hume Cronyn, Ossie Davis, Edward James Olmos (1997)

A brilliant film about one man's attempt to convince the eleven other members of a jury that the defendant in a murder trial should not be convicted. This is a powerful, dramatic tour de force by a great cast. Kids may balk at first, but encourage them to stick with it for ten minutes and they'll be hooked.

The film was remade in 1997 with another terrific cast, and just a bit of updating to expand the ethnic makeup of the jury. You can't go wrong with either version. If your kids enjoy it as much as we suspect they will, try both versions.

SEX OR NUDITY—None.

VIOLENCE—None.

LANGUAGE—Some rough language, but nothing gratuitous

FEAR FACTOR (SUSPENSE)—Some. Drama and suspense, but no fear.

AGE 0–2		No way.
AGE 3–4		Ditto.
AGE 5–6		Still no way.
AGE 7–10	★★★	They'll be surprised by how much they understand and how much they like it.
AGE 11–12	★★★★	Perfect.
AGE 13+	★★★★	Ditto.
ADULT	★★★★	Ditto.

SUGGESTED AGES—7–99

Twelve O'Clock High (No Rating)

1949 Drama
Directed by Henry King
Starring Gregory Peck, Hugh Marlowe, Gary Merrill, Millard Mitchell, Dean Jagger

A classic World War II film about a squadron of American bomber pilots stationed in England. The story centers on the pressures the men live under and the difficulty experienced by their commanding officers in trying to keep a professional distance from their subordinates. This is a war flick, but one with much more focus on the human dimensions. Still, the war footage—documentary and re-created—is super. A bit talky, but Dean Jagger won an Oscar for best supporting actor, and Gregory Peck is top notch.

SEX OR NUDITY—None.

VIOLENCE—Minimal. For a war flick, there is surprisingly little.

LANGUAGE—None.

FEAR FACTOR (SUSPENSE)—Some. Tension permeates the film.

AGE 0–2		No way.
AGE 3–4		Ditto.
AGE 5–6		Still not right for this group.
AGE 7–10	★★	If they stay with it, they'll enjoy it.
AGE 11–12	★★	Ditto.
AGE 13+	★★	This group will enjoy it and begin to appreciate the human dimension of leadership.
ADULT	★★	Not our favorite war flick, but still very solid.

SUGGESTED AGES—8–99

Von Ryan's Express (No Rating)

1965 Action/Adventure
Directed by Mark Robson
Starring Frank Sinatra, Trevor Howard

An exciting, well-made film about an escape from a prisoner-of-war camp during World War II. Sinatra plays the colonel who leads the escape attempt by hijacking a train transporting prisoners. You may have to discuss prisoners of war, but this is an adventure yarn that won't raise many social or political issues. It is escapist entertainment, and not bad at that.

SEX OR NUDITY—Minimal.

VIOLENCE—Some. This is a war flick, but nothing gruesome is shown.

LANGUAGE—Minimal. Little to worry about.

FEAR FACTOR (SUSPENSE)—Some. Will they make it?

AGE 0–2		No way.
AGE 3–4		Ditto.
AGE 5–6		Still not right for this group.
AGE 7–10	★★	Just fine.
AGE 11–12	★★	Ditto.
AGE 13+	★★	For war flick fans primarily.
ADULT	★★	There are worse ways to spend an evening.

SUGGESTED AGES—7–99

"Wallace and Gromit: The Wrong Trousers," "Wallace and Gromit: A Close Shave" (No Rating)
1995 Animated
Directed by Nick Park
Starring assorted Claymation figures

These daffy animated shorts, which have reached cult status among some Generation Xers, bear absolutely no resemblance to Saturday morning cartoons. The animation is dazzling, the humor subversive, and the stories preposterous. Still, you'll find yourself—and your visually sophisticated older children—howling at the exploits of Wallace, a nutty inventor, and his faithful dog, Gromit. In "Wrong Trousers," their happy home is upset when a new lodger, an evil penguin, moves in. In "Close Shave," they solve Britain's tragic sheep-rustling mystery. Little kids will squeal with delight when Wallace's automatic porridge-dispensing invention goes awry, and teens and adults will appreciate this witty send-up of British eccentricity.

SEX OR NUDITY—None.

VIOLENCE—None.

LANGUAGE—None.

FEAR FACTOR (SUSPENSE)—None.

AGE 0–2		No.
AGE 3–4		No harm done if they watch, but they won't really get it.
AGE 5–6	★★★	They'll like the visual humor even if they don't get the wordplay and the satire.
AGE 7–10	★★★	Ditto.
AGE 11–12	★★★	Rent these animated shorts and your kids will either think you've really lost it or you're really cool.
AGE 13+	★★★★	Teenagers are way into Wallace and Gromit.
ADULT	★★★★	You'll get a big kick out of seeing what has happened to animated shorts since the last time you watched.

SUGGESTED AGES—5–99

West Side Story (No Rating)
1961 Musical; Drama
Directed by Robert Wise and Jerome Robbins
Starring Natalie Wood, Richard Beymer, George Chakiris, Rita Moreno, Russ Tamblyn

The winner of ten Academy Awards, this brilliant, captivating musical is loosely based on Shakespeare's *Romeo and Juliet*. Set in New York City in the late 1950s, it has the "native" Jets battling the recently arrived Puerto Rican Sharks for turf. In their midst, an ex-Jet leader finds love with the Shark leader's sister, Maria. This film, and the Broadway show that preceded it, probably defines the great modern American musical. What's more compelling? The extraordinary score and lyrics by Leonard Bernstein and Stephen Sondheim? Or the brilliant choreography of Jerome Robbins, where even the fist fights are extraordinary examples of ballet and modern dance? A superb film, and there won't be a dry eye in the house!

SEX OR NUDITY—Minimal. Kissing, and wonderfully suggestive dancing.
VIOLENCE—Some. Gang fights and a stabbing.
LANGUAGE—Minimal. Gee, Officer Krupke, krup you.
FEAR FACTOR (SUSPENSE)—Some. Love or war? Which will prevail?

AGE 0–2		Nope, sorry.
AGE 3–4	★	They might begin to appreciate the music and the dance.
AGE 5–6	★★	Still a bit young, but they will start to appreciate it.
AGE 7–10	★★★	This group will enjoy it enormously.
AGE 11–12	★★★★	"The best ever, Dad."
AGE 13+	★★★★	Ditto.
ADULT	★★★★	Still a classic.

SUGGESTED AGES—5–99

Willy Wonka and the Chocolate Factory (G)

1971 Fantasy/Science Fiction
Directed by Mel Stuart
Starring Gene Wilder, Jack Albertson, Peter Ostrum

Imaginative fantasy about five lucky kids turned loose in an enormous chocolate factory. One's a glutton, one's a brat, and one, our hero, is a poor but honest newspaper boy. The bad kids get their just desserts—in one case, literally falling into a vat of chocolate—but young Charlie's decency, modesty, and old-fashioned good manners carry the day. The factory itself is a wonder of imagination: fantastic, weird, a little scary . . . in short, everything kids dream of.

SEX OR NUDITY—None.

VIOLENCE—None. Some bizarre "punishments," but not nothing violent.

LANGUAGE—None.

FEAR FACTOR (SUSPENSE)—Minimal.

AGE 0–2		Not quite ready for this one.
AGE 3–4		Ditto.
AGE 5–6	★★★	Perfect.
AGE 7–10	★★★	Ditto.
AGE 11–12	★	Only for nostalgia's sake.
AGE 13+		Nah.
ADULT	★★	You may find it a tad preachy, but your kids won't.

SUGGESTED AGES—5–10

Winchester '73 (No Rating)

1950 Western
Directed by Anthony Mann
Starring Jimmy Stewart, Dan Duryea, Shelley Winters, Stephen McNally

This classic Western is credited with reviving the genre. It is an unusual and well-told story of one man in pursuit of another who has stolen his one-of-a-kind rifle. Several related stories weave in and out, all the while maintaining a growing tension. There is plenty of action (killing, drinking, cheating, and stereotypes. This film is clearly not politically correct, but it is a great old Western adventure.

SEX OR NUDITY—Minimal.
VIOLENCE—A lot. Old-fashioned shootouts, bar brawls, and a scalping.
LANGUAGE—Minimal. Just rough, not foul.
FEAR FACTOR (SUSPENSE)—Some. Bad guys who are creepy.

AGE 0–2		Nope.
AGE 3–4		Still not right.
AGE 5–6	★★	Yep, but stay nearby.
AGE 7–10	★★★	Perfect.
AGE 11–12	★★★	Ditto.
AGE 13+	★★★	They'll realize this is one of the better Westerns.
ADULT	★★★	Surprisingly good and not just nostalgic.

SUGGESTED AGES—6–99

Wizard of Oz, The (G)

1939 Fantasy/Science Fiction
Directed by Victor Fleming
Starring Judy Garland, Ray Bolger, Bert Lahr, Jack Haley, Billie Burke

Still looking good at sixty years of age, this film, virtually a cultural icon, has an unforgettable score, a deeply resonant story, and some of the most frightening scenes ever shown in a children's film. They're not scary because they're gory; it's because they are so eerily close to the stuff of real childhood nightmares. You know the film and your children well enough to know which scenes will push their buttons. Here, then, is just a quick catalogue of those scenes in case there are any you've forgotten (or repressed): the flying monkeys, those strange little munchkins, those creepy trees with branches like hands, the fireball thrown at the Scarecrow, the unstuffing and restuffing of the Scarecrow (that one scared us most), Miss Gulch stealing little Toto, and the dead, retracting stockinged feet of the Wicked Witch. Still, it's a great film. You know best when your child is ready to see it.

SEX OR NUDITY—None.

VIOLENCE—Some. See above.

LANGUAGE—None.

FEAR FACTOR (SUSPENSE)—A lot. See above.

AGE 0–2		No.
AGE 3–4		We don't recommend it.
AGE 5–6	★	Maybe. Your call.
AGE 7–10	★★★	OK.
AGE 11–12	★★	OK.
AGE 13+	★	Are they too old already?
ADULT	★★★	Still casts its spell.

SUGGESTED AGES—7–99

Yankee Doodle Dandy (No Rating)
1942 Musical
Directed by Michael Curtiz
Starring James Cagney, Joan Leslie, Walter Huston, Richard Whorf,
Irene Manning

James Cagney won a best actor Oscar for his portrayal of George M.
Cohan, and you'll have no doubt why. Told in flashbacks, it is a terrific
story well told. The songs are among the most familiar and cherished in
American musical history, and Cagney's dancing is first-rate. It is also a
terrific history of vaudeville, stage, and film. You'll smile, you'll whistle
along, you'll all cherish this classic.

SEX OR NUDITY—Minimal. A kiss or two.
VIOLENCE—Minimal. Some slapstick, local kids beating up the thirteen-
year-old Cohan, and an old-fashioned spanking.
LANGUAGE—None.
FEAR FACTOR (SUSPENSE)—None.

AGE 0–2		Not quite.
AGE 3–4	★★	Sure, why not. They'll enjoy the music and dancing.
AGE 5–6	★★★	They'll love it.
AGE 7–10	★★★	Not only will they love it, they'll start to appreciate just what makes a great musical film.
AGE 11–12	★★★★	Watch them dance around the house.
AGE 13+	★★★★	Ditto.
ADULT	★★★★	A classic to be shared.

SUGGESTED AGES—4–99

Yearling, The (G)

1946 Animal; Drama
Directed by Clarence Brown
Starring Gregory Peck, Claude Jarman, Jane Wyman

A classic tearjerker, well worth the Kleenex. But be forewarned, the climax is wrenching. Set in the Florida Everglades in 1870s, *The Yearling* is the touching coming-of-age-story of Jody Baxter, a boy who adopts a fawn after he kills its mother. The fawn provides a badly needed emotional outlet for Jody, whose parents are too preoccupied with their own grief and their desperate struggle against the harsh Everglades environment to see how much their son needs to love and be loved. The deer begins destroying the family's badly needed corn crop, and despite the family's efforts to pen it in, it escapes and reduces the second planting to nothing but useless shoots. The father, bedridden after a farming accident, tells Jody he must kill the deer; Jody can't do it, so his mother shoots the deer—wounding, but not killing it. In one of the most tragic scenes in the annals of juvenile films, Jody is forced to put the creature out of its misery. He runs away in despair, but is found days later. In the end, Jody reaches a deeper understanding of himself and his parents.

SEX OR NUDITY—None.

VIOLENCE—Minimal. A couple of menacing hillbillies raise hell, but no one is seriously hurt.

LANGUAGE—None.

FEAR FACTOR (SUSPENSE)—A lot. The climax is undeniably wrenching, and incidents leading up to it will be upsetting to sensitive children.

AGE 0–2		No way.
AGE 3–4		Ditto.
AGE 5–6		Ditto.
AGE 7–10	★★	Only for the upper end of this age group.
AGE 11–12	★★★★	Yes, but keep the Kleenex handy.
AGE 13+	★★★	Ditto.
ADULT	★★★★	Make that two boxes of Kleenex.

SUGGESTED AGES—10–99

Young Frankenstein (PG)

1974 Comedy
Directed by Mel Brooks.
Starring Gene Wilder, Teri Garr, Marty Feldman, Cloris Leachman, Madeline Kahn, Peter Boyle

In this hilarious parody of the old Frankenstein movies, Gene Wilder is the grandson of the original Baron von Frankenstein, who was obsessed with the idea of bringing the dead back to life. Shot in black and white (which adds a wonderful moodiness that may frighten younger children), the setting is a Transylvania castle that has been willed to the grandson, himself a renowned, modern-day surgeon. This is a movie with terrific performances and a very witty script. Many of the scenes are takeoffs of other classic films (this may be lost on kids, but will add to your enjoyment).

SEX OR NUDITY—Minimal. A few references, but nothing to worry about.

VIOLENCE—Minimal.

LANGUAGE—Minimal. A few inappropriate words.

FEAR FACTOR (SUSPENSE)—A lot. It is moody, with a few skeletons and dead bodies.

AGE 0–2		No way.
AGE 3–4		Still no way.
AGE 5–6		Nope, it will frighten this group too.
AGE 7–10	★★	But only for the older kids.
AGE 11–12	★★★	Perfect.
AGE 13+	★★★	Ditto.
ADULT	★★★	A very funny film.

SUGGESTED AGES—9–99

THE TEN BEST LISTS

By Category

TEN BEST ACTION/ADVENTURE FILMS
The Adventures of Robin Hood
Ben-Hur
Captains Courageous
The Dirty Dozen
Goldfinger
The Great Escape
The Mask of Zorro
Mutiny on the Bounty
North by Northwest
Raiders of the Lost Ark

TEN BEST ANIMATED FILMS
Adventures of Rocky and Bullwinkle, Vols. 1–12
Aladdin
Bugs Bunny Classics
James and the Giant Peach
The Jungle Book
Lady and the Tramp
The Lion King
Snoopy Come Home
Toy Story

*Wallace and Gromit: The Wrong Trousers, Wallace and
    Gromit: A Close Shave*

TEN BEST ANIMAL FILMS

Babe
The Black Stallion
Fly Away Home
Homeward Bound: The Incredible Journey
Lassie
Mouse Hunt
Old Yeller
Phar Lap
Shiloh
The Yearling

TEN BEST COMEDIES

Abbott and Costello Meet Frankenstein
Big
The Borrowers
Dumb and Dumber
The In-Laws
Mrs. Doubtfire
The Princess Bride
Some Like It Hot
Tootsie
Young Frankenstein

TEN BEST DRAMAS

Anne of Green Gables/Anne of Avonlea
Apollo 13
Casablanca
Driving Miss Daisy
Little Princess
Little Women

Mr. Smith Goes to Washington
The Secret Garden
To Kill a Mockingbird
Twelve Angry Men

TEN BEST FANTASY/SCIENCE-FICTION FLICKS

Close Encounters of the Third Kind
The Empire Strikes Back
E.T. The Extra-Terrestrial
Freaky Friday
The Indian in the Cupboard
Jurassic Park
Superman
Willy Wonka and the Chocolate Factory
The Wizard of Oz

TEN BEST MUSICALS

Brigadoon
Fiddler on the Roof
Grease
Mary Poppins
The Music Man
My Fair Lady
Singin' in the Rain
The Sound of Music
West Side Story
Yankee Doodle Dandy

TEN BEST SPORTS FILMS

The Bad News Bears
Brian's Song
Chariots of Fire
Hoosiers
A League of Their Own

Little Big League
The Pride of the Yankees
Rocky
Rudy
The Sandlot

TEN BEST WESTERNS

Butch Cassidy and the Sundance Kid
Destry Rides Again
High Noon
Little Big Man
Shane
The Shootist
Support Your Local Gunfighter
Support Your Local Sheriff
True Grit
Winchester '73

By Age

TEN BEST FILMS FOR TODDLERS

Film	Category
Are You My Mother?	
(And Two More P.D. Eastmann Classics)	Animated
Babe	Animal
Barney's Great Adventure	Fantasy/Science-Fiction
Bugs Bunny Classics	Animated
The Jungle Book	Animated
Lady and the Tramp	Animated
Preschool Power (Jacket Flips and Other Tips)	Comedy
Road Construction Ahead	Drama
The Robert McCloskey Library	Animated
Snoopy Come Home	Animated

TEN BEST FILMS FOR PRESCHOOLERS

Film	Category
The Adventures of Milo and Otis	*Animal*
Aladdin	*Animated*
Lady and the Tramp	*Animated*
Babe	*Animal*
The Brave Little Toaster	*Animated*
Charlotte's Web	*Animated*
The Land Before Time	*Animated*
The Mouse and the Motorcycle	*Comedy*
Preschool Power (Jacket Flips and Other Tips)	*Comedy*
Road Construction Ahead	*Drama*

TEN BEST FILMS FOR AGES 5 TO 6

Film	Category
Aladdin	*Animated*
Beethoven	*Comedy*
The Black Stallion	*Animal*
The Borrowers	*Comedy*
Bugs Bunny Classics	*Animated*
Charlotte's Web	*Animated*
Homeward Bound: The Incredible Journey	*Animal*
Mary Poppins	*Musical*
Mouse Hunt	*Animal*
Toy Story	*Animated*

TEN BEST FILMS FOR AGES 7 TO 10

Film	Category
Anne of Green Gables/Anne of Avonlea	*Drama*
The Bad News Bears	*Sports*
The Black Stallion	*Animal*
The Borrowers	*Comedy*
E.T. The Extra-Terrestrial	*Fantasy/Science-Fiction*

The Empire Strikes Back	*Fantasy/Science-Fiction*
Mrs. Doubtfire	*Comedy*
The Princess Bride	*Comedy*
Raiders of the Lost Ark	*Action/ Adventure*
Toy Story	*Animated*

TEN BEST FILMS FOR AGES 11 TO 12

Film	Category
Apollo 13	*Drama*
Austin Powers, International Man of Mystery	*Comedy*
Big	*Comedy*
E.T. The Extra-Terrestrial	*Fantasy/Science-Fiction*
Grease	*Musical*
Stand by Me	*Drama*
To Kill a Mockingbird	*Drama*
Wallace and Gromit: The Wrong Trousers, Wallace and Gromit: A Close Shave	*Animated*
West Side Story	*Musical*
The Yearling	*Animal*

TEN BEST FILMS FOR AGES 13 AND OLDER

Film	Category
Amadeus	*Drama*
American Graffiti	*Comedy*
The Breakfast Club	*Drama*
Breaking Away	*Sports*
Casablanca	*Drama*
Chariots of Fire	*Sports*
Good Morning, Vietnam	*Comedy*
A League of Their Own	*Sports*

North by Northwest

Action/
Adventure

Sullivan's Travels

Comedy

Special Categories

TEN GREAT WAR FILMS (THAT ARE OK FOR KIDS TO SEE)
The Bridge Over the River Kwai
The Dirty Dozen
Glory
Good Morning, Vietnam
The Great Escape
Lawrence of Arabia
The Longest Day
Patton
Tora, Tora, Tora!
12 O'Clock High

TEN TASTELESS MOVIES YOU CAN SAFELY SAY YES TO:
Ace Ventura: Pet Detective
Airplane!
Austin Powers, International Man of Mystery
Bean
Dirty Rotten Scoundrels
Dr. Dolittle
Dumb and Dumber
The Mask
The Producers
Top Secret

TEN SIBLING SAGAS
Addams Family Values
American Graffiti
Duck Soup
Honey, I Shrunk the Kids
A League of Their Own
Little Big Man
Little Women
Meet Me in St. Louis
On the Waterfront
Seven Brides for Seven Brothers

TEN MOVIES ALMOST AS GOOD AS THE BOOKS
Charlotte's Web
From Russia with Love
The Great Gatsby
Heidi
The Indian in the Cupboard
Jurassic Park
Little Women
The Mighty
The Secret Garden
The Yearling

TEN COMING-OF-AGE MOVIES
American Graffiti
Breaking Away
Captains Courageous
The Flamingo Kid
Fly Away Home
Little Women
My Favorite Year
Old Yeller

Stand by Me
The Yearling

TEN MOVIES SURE TO MAKE YOU SHED A TEAR (FOR YOUNGER CHILDREN)

Anne of Green Gables/Anne of Avonlea
Charlotte's Web
E.T. The Extra-Terrestrial
Heidi
Homeward Bound
Lassie
The Lion King
Little Women
The Mighty
Old Yeller

TEN SURE TO MAKE YOU SHED A TEAR (FOR OLDER CHILDREN)

Brian's Song
Captains Courageous
Casablanca
The Cure
Gone with the Wind
The Great Escape
Mr. Smith Goes to Washington
On the Waterfront
The Shootist
West Side Story

TEN MOVIES FEATURING HEROES, HEROINES, AND UNDERDOGS

The Bad News Bears
Forrest Gump

Hoosiers
A League of Their Own
The Mask of Zorro
The Mighty
Mulan
National Velvet
Rocky
Rudy

TEN MOVIES THAT TEACH A LESSON
(WITHOUT A HEAVY HAND)

Breaking Away
Crimson Tide
Driving Miss Daisy
The Flamingo Kid
Glory
Good Morning, Vietnam
On the Waterfront
Rocky
Sullivan's Travels
To Kill a Mockingbird

TEN BLACK-AND-WHITE CLASSICS
KIDS WILL SIT THROUGH

Abbott and Costello Meet Frankenstein
Captains Courageous
Casablanca
Duck Soup
Heidi
King Kong
The Maltese Falcon
Mr. Deeds Goes to Town
Mr. Smith Goes to Washington
Sullivan's Travels

MOVIES WE WISH WE COULD HAVE INCLUDED

ADULT THEMES, TOO MUCH VIOLENCE, SEX, PROFANITY—BUT STILL AWFULLY GOOD

—Please let us know what you think!

Animal House
The Buddy Holly Story
City Slickers
The Color Purple
Do the Right Thing
The Fugitive
Get Shorty
Good Will Hunting
The Imposters
Jaws
Malcolm X
*M*A*S*H*
My Left Foot
Primary Colors
Quiz Show
Rain Man
The Right Stuff
Schindler's List
Shine
Top Gun
Treasure of the Sierra Madre
The Usual Suspects
Wrongfully Accused

MOVIES WE INTENTIONALLY LEFT OFF OUR LIST

TOO WRENCHING, TOO CRUDE, TOO VIOLENT, TOO MATURE, JUST NOT GOOD ENOUGH TO MAKE THE BEST LISTS

—But here too, please let us know if you disagree.

Bambi
Batman
Dumbo
Home Alone
The Horse Whisperer
Jumanji
Pinocchio
Prince of Egypt
The Santa Clause
101 Dalmatians

MOVIES WE HOPE
TO INCLUDE NEXT TIME

Anastasia
Antz
Babe: Pig in the City
A Bug's Life
Pleasantville
Waking Ned Divine
You've Got Mail

LIST OF FILMS
BY DIRECTOR

DIRECTOR	FILM	CATEGORY
Abbott, George	*Damn Yankees*	Sports
Abrahams, Jim	*Airplane!*	Comedy
Abrahams, Jim	*Top Secret!*	Comedy
Aldrich, Robert	*Dirty Dozen, The*	Action/ Adventure
Allen, Woody	*Take the Money and Run*	Comedy
Allers, Roger	*Lion King, The*	Animated
Annakin, Ken	*Longest Day, The*	Action/ Adventure
Annakin, Ken	*Those Magnificent Men in Their Flying Machines*	Action/ Adventure
Anspaugh, David	*Hoosiers*	Sports
Anspaugh, David	*Rudy*	Sports
Avildsen, John G.	*Karate Kid, The*	Sports
Avildsen, John G.	*Rocky*	Sports
Ballard, Carroll	*Black Stallion, The*	Animal
Ballard, Carroll	*Fly Away Home*	Animal
Ballard, Carroll	*Never Cry Wolf*	Action/ Adventure
Bancroft, Tony	*Mulan*	Animated
Barton, Charles	*Abbott and Costello Meet Frankenstein*	Comedy
Benjamin, Richard	*My Favorite Year*	Comedy

Beresford, Bruce	*Driving Miss Daisy*	Drama
Berger, Ludwig	*Thief of Bagdad, The*	Action/ Adventure
Bergman, Andrew	*Freshman, The*	Comedy
Bluth, Don	*All Dogs Go to Heaven*	Animated
Bluth, Don	*Land Before Time, The*	Animated
Brooks, Mel	*Producers, The*	Comedy
Brooks, Mel	*Young Frankenstein*	Comedy
Brown, Clarence	*National Velvet*	Sports
Brown, Clarence	*Yearling, The*	Animal
Butoy, Hendel	*Rescuers Down Under, The*	Animated
Camp, Joe	*Benji*	Animal
Campbell, Martin	*Mask of Zorro, The*	Action/ Adventure
Capra, Frank	*Mr. Deeds Goes to Town*	Comedy
Capra, Frank	*Mr. Smith Goes to Washington*	Drama
Carpenter, John	*Starman*	Fantasy/ Science- Fiction
Chaplin, Charlie	*Gold Rush, The*	Comedy
Chaplin, Charlie	*Great Dictator, The*	Comedy
Chaplin, Charlie	*Kid, The*	Comedy
Chaplin, Charlie	*Modern Times*	Comedy
Clayton, Jack	*Great Gatsby, The*	Drama
Clements, Ron	*Aladdin*	Animated
Clements, Ron	*Little Mermaid, The*	Animated
Columbus, Chris	*Mrs. Doubtfire*	Comedy
Connell Sutton, Carey	*Preschool Power (Jacket Flips and Other Tips)*	Comedy
Cook, Barry	*Mulan*	Animated
Cromwell, John	*Prisoner of Zenda, The*	Action/ Adventure
Cuaron, Alfonso	*Little Princess, A*	Drama
Cukor, George	*Adam's Rib*	Comedy

Cukor, George	*My Fair Lady*	Musical
Cukor, George	*Philadelphia Story, The*	Comedy
Curtiz, Michael	*Adventures of Robin Hood, The*	Action/ Adventure
Curtiz, Michael	*Casablanca*	Drama
Curtiz, Michael	*Yankee Doodle Dandy*	Musical
Da Costa, Morton	*Music Man, The*	Musical
Donen, Stanley	*Charade*	Comedy
Donen, Stanley	*Damn Yankees*	Sports
Donen, Stanley	*On the Town*	Musical
Donen, Stanley	*Seven Brides for Seven Brothers*	Musical
Donen, Stanley	*Singin' in the Rain*	Musical
Donner, Richard	*Superman*	Fantasy/ Science- Fiction
Dragoti, Stan	*Necessary Roughness*	Sports
Dunham, Duwayne	*Homeward Bound: The Incredible Journey*	Animal
Dwan, Allan	*Heidi*	Drama
Evans, David Mickey	*Sandlot, The*	Sports
Farrelly, Peter	*Dumb and Dumber*	Comedy
Fleischer, Richard	*Tora, Tora, Tora*	Action/ Adventure
Fleming, Victor	*Captains Courageous*	Action/ Adventure
Fleming, Victor	*Gone with the Wind*	Drama
Fleming, Victor	*Treasure Island* (1934)	Action/ Adventure
Fleming, Victor	*Wizard of Oz, The*	Fantasy/ Science- Fiction
Ford, John	*Mister Roberts*	Drama
Foreman, Milos	*Amadeus*	Drama
Frank, Melvin	*Court Jester, The*	Musical

Frawley, James	*Muppet Movie, The*	Comedy
Friedkin, William	*Twelve Angry Men (1977)*	Drama
Fukasuku, Kinji	*Tora, Tora, Tora*	Action/Adventure
Gabriel, Mike	*Rescuers Down Under, The*	Animated
Gomer, Steve	*Barney's Great Adventure*	Fantasy/Science-Fiction
Hamilton, Guy	*Goldfinger*	Action/Adventure
Haskin, Byron	*Treasure Island (1950)*	Action/Adventure
Hata, Masanori	*Adventures of Milo and Otis, The*	Animal
Hathaway, Henry	*True Grit*	Western
Hawks, Howard	*Big Sleep, The*	Drama
Hawks, Howard	*Bringing Up Baby*	Comedy
Heckerling, Amy	*Clueless*	Comedy
Heckerling, Amy	*Look Who's Talking*	Comedy
Henson, Brian	*Muppet Treasure Island*	Comedy
Herek, Stephen	*Mighty Ducks*	Sports
Herek, Stephen	*Mr. Holland's Opus*	Drama
Herek, Stephen	*Three Musketeers, The (1993)*	Action/Adventure
Heston, Fraser C.	*Alaska*	Action/Adventure
Hewitt, Peter	*Adventures of Tom and Huck, The*	Action/Adventure
Hewitt, Peter	*Borrowers, The*	Comedy
Hill, George Roy	*Butch Cassidy and the Sundance Kid*	Western
Hiller, Arthur	*In-Laws, The*	Comedy
Hitchcock, Alfred	*North by Northwest*	Action/Adventure
Holland, Agnieszka	*Secret Garden, The*	Drama

Horton, Peter	*Cure, The*	Drama
Howard, Ron	*Apollo 13*	Drama
Howard, Ron	*Cocoon*	Fantasy/Science-Fiction
Howard, Ron	*Splash*	Comedy
Hudson, Hugh	*Chariots of Fire*	Sports
Hughes, John	*Breakfast Club, The*	Drama
Hughes, John	*Ferris Bueller's Day Off*	Comedy
Huston, John	*African Queen, The*	Drama
Huston, John	*Annie*	Musical
Huston, John	*Maltese Falcon, The*	Drama
Jewison, Norman	*Fiddler on the Roof*	Musical
Johnson, Patrick Read	*Baby's Day Out*	Comedy
Johnston, Joe	*Honey, I Shrunk the Kids*	Fantasy/Science-Fiction
Johnston, Joe	*Rocketeer, The*	Fantasy/Science-Fiction
Jones, Chuck	*Bugs Bunny Classics*	Animated
Kazan, Elia	*On the Waterfront*	Drama
Keaton, Buster	*General, The*	Comedy
Kelly, Gene	*On the Town*	Musical
Kelly, Gene	*Singin' in the Rain*	Musical
Kennedy, Burt	*Support Your Local Gunfighter*	Western
Kennedy, Burt	*Support Your Local Sheriff*	Western
Kershner, Irvin	*Empire Strikes Back, The*	Fantasy/Science-Fiction
King, Henry	*Twelve O'Clock High*	Drama
Kleiser, Randal	*Flight of the Navigator*	Action/Adventure
Kleiser, Randal	*Grease*	Musical

Kramer, Stanley	*It's a Mad, Mad, Mad, Mad World*	Comedy
Kulick, Buzz	*Brian's Song*	Sports
Kwapis, Ken	*Dunston Checks In*	Animal
Lasseter, John	*Toy Story*	Animated
Lean, David	*Bridge on the River Kwai, The*	Action/ Adventure
Lean, David	*Lawrence of Arabia*	Drama
LeRoy, Mervyn	*Mister Roberts*	Drama
Lester, Richard	*Four Musketeers, The*	Action/ Adventure
Lester, Richard	*Superman II*	Fantasy/ Science- Fiction
Lester, Richard	*Three Musketeers, The (1974)*	Action/ Adventure
Levant, Brian	*Beethoven*	Comedy
Levinson, Barry	*Good Morning, Vietnam*	Comedy
Lloyd, Frank	*Mutiny on the Bounty*	Action/ Adventure
Lounsbery, John	*Rescuers, The*	Animated
Lucas, George	*American Graffiti*	Comedy
Lucas, George	*Star Wars*	Fantasy/ Science- Fiction
Lumet, Sidney	*Twelve Angry Men (1957)*	Drama
Luske, Hamilton	*Lady and the Tramp*	Animated
Mankiewicz, Joseph	*Guys and Dolls*	Musical
Mann, Anthony	*Winchester '73*	Western
Marquand, Richard	*Return of the Jedi*	Fantasy/ Science- Fiction
Marshall, Garry	*Flamingo Kid, The*	Drama
Marshall, George	*Destry Rides Again*	Western
Marshall, Penny	*Big*	Comedy

Marshall, Penny	*League of Their Own, A*	Sports
Marton, Andrew	*Longest Day, The*	Action/Adventure
Masudo, Toshio	*Tora, Tora, Tora*	Action/Adventure
McCarey, Leo	*Duck Soup*	Comedy
McLeod, Norman	*Horsefeathers*	Comedy
McLeod, Norman	*Topper*	Comedy
Melendez, Bill	*Snoopy Come Home*	Animated
Meyer, Nicholas	*Time After Time*	Fantasy/Science-Fiction
Milestone, Lewis	*Red Pony, The*	Animal
Minkoff, Rob	*Lion King, The*	Animated
Minnelli, Vincente	*American in Paris, An*	Musical
Minnelli, Vincente	*Band Wagon, The*	Musical
Minnelli, Vincent	*Brigadoon*	Musical
Minnelli, Vincente	*Meet Me in St. Louis*	Musical
Moore, Robert	*Murder by Death*	Comedy
Mulligan, Robert	*Man in the Moon, The*	Drama
Mulligan, Robert	*To Kill a Mockingbird*	Drama
Musker, John	*Aladdin*	Animated
Musker, John	*Little Mermaid, The*	Animated
Neame, Ronald	*Hopscotch*	Comedy
Nelson, Gary	*Freaky Friday*	Fantasy/Science-Fiction
Nichols, Charles	*Charlotte's Web*	Animated
Noonan, Chris	*Babe*	Animal
Oedekerk, Steve	*Ace Ventura: When Nature Calls*	Comedy
Oz, Frank	*Dirty Rotten Scoundrels*	Comedy
Oz, Frank	*Indian in the Cupboard, The*	Fantasy/Science-Fiction

Oz, Frank	*Muppets Take Manhattan, The*	Comedy
Panama, Norman	*Court Jester, The*	Musical
Park, Nick	*Wallace and Gromit: The Wrong Trousers, Wallace and Gromit: A Close Shave.*	Animated
Penn, Arthur	*Little Big Man*	Western
Peterson, Wolfgang	*NeverEnding Story, The*	Fantasy/ Science-Fiction
Petrie, Daniel	*Lassie*	Animal
Pollack, Sydney	*Tootsie*	Comedy
Reed, Carol	*Third Man, The*	Drama
Reiner, Rob	*Princess Bride, The*	Comedy
Reiner, Rob	*Stand by Me*	Drama
Reitherman, Wolfgang	*Jungle Book, The*	Animated
Reitherman, Wolfgang	*Rescuers, The*	Animated
Reitman, Ivan	*Ghostbusters*	Fantasy/ Science-Fiction
Reitman, Ivan	*Junior*	Comedy
Ritchie, Michael	*Bad News Bears, The*	Sports
Ritt, Martin	*Sounder*	Animal
Roach, Jay	*Austin Powers, International Man of Mystery*	Comedy
Robbins, Jerome	*West Side Story*	Musical
Robinson, Phil Alden	*Field of Dreams*	Sports
Robson, Mark	*Von Ryan's Express*	Action/ Adventure
Rosenbloom, Dale	*Shiloh*	Animal
Russell, Charles	*Mask, The*	Comedy
Sandrich, Mark	*Top Hat*	Musical

Schaffner, Franklin	*Patton*	Drama
Scheinman, Andrew	*Little Big League*	Sports
Schepisi, Fred	*Roxanne*	Comedy
Scorsese, Martin	*Age of Innocence, The*	Drama
Scott, Tony	*Crimson Tide*	Drama
Selick, Henry	*James and the Giant Peach*	Animated
Seltzer, David	*Lucas*	Drama
Shadyac, Tom	*Ace Ventura: Pet Detective*	Comedy
Sharpsteen, Ben	*Fantasia*	Animated
Shoedsack, Ernest	*King Kong*	Fantasy/ Science- Fiction
Sidney, George	*Three Musketeers, The (1948)*	Action/ Adventure
Siegel, Don	*Shootist, The*	Western
Silberling, Brad	*Casper*	Fantasy/ Science- Fiction
Smith, Mel	*Bean*	Comedy
Sonnenfeld, Barry	*Addams Family, The*	Comedy
Sonnenfeld, Barry	*Addams Family Values*	Comedy
Spielberg, Steven	*Close Encounters of the Third Kind*	Fantasy/ Science- Fiction
Spielberg, Steven	*E.T. The Extra-Terrestrial*	Fantasy/ Science- Fiction
Spielberg, Steven	*Jurassic Park*	Fantasy/ Science- Fiction
Spielberg, Steven	*Raiders of the Lost Ark*	Action/ Adventure
Stern, Daniel	*Rookie of the Year*	Sports
Stevens, George	*Gunga Din*	Action/ Adventure

Stevens, George	*Shane*	Western
Stevenson, Robert	*Absent-Minded Professor, The*	Comedy
Stevenson, Robert	*Mary Poppins*	Musical
Stevenson, Robert	*Old Yeller*	Animal
Stuart, Mel	*Willy Wonka and the Chocolate Factory*	Fantasy/Science-Fiction
Sturges, John	*Bad Day at Black Rock*	Drama
Sturges, John	*Great Escape, The*	Action/Adventure
Sturges, Preston	*Sullivan's Travels*	Comedy
Sullivan, Kevin	*Anne of Green Gables/Anne of Avonlea*	Drama
Swift, David	*Pollyanna*	Drama
Thompson, Caroline	*Black Beauty*	Animal
Trousdale, Gerry	*Beauty and the Beast*	Animated
Turtletaub, Jon	*Cool Runnings*	Sports
Verbinski, Gore	*Mouse Hunt*	Animal
Ward, Jay	*Adventures of Rocky and Bullwinkle, Vols. 1–12*	Animated
Weir, Peter	*Truman Show, The*	Drama
Weisman, Sam	*George of the Jungle*	Comedy
Welles, Orson	*Citizen Kane*	Drama
Wicki, Bernhard	*Longest Day, The*	Action/Adventure
Wilder, Billy	*Some Like It Hot*	Comedy
Wincer, Simon	*Free Willy*	Animal
Wincer, Simon	*Phar Lap*	Animal
Wise, Robert	*Sound of Music, The*	Musical
Wise, Robert	*West Side Story*	Musical
Wood, Sam	*Night at the Opera, A*	Comedy
Wood, Sam	*Pride of the Yankees, The*	Sports
Wyler, William	*Ben-Hur*	Action/Adventure

Wyler, William	*Friendly Persuasion*	Drama
Wyler, William	*Funny Girl*	Musical
Yates, Peter	*Breaking Away*	Sports
Young, Terence	*From Russia with Love*	Action/Adventure
Zaillian, Steven	*Searching for Bobby Fischer*	Drama
Zemeckis, Robert	*Back to the Future*	Fantasy/Science-Fiction
Zemeckis, Robert	*Forrest Gump*	Drama
Zieff, Howard	*My Girl*	Comedy
Zinnemann, Fred	*High Noon*	Western
Zucker, David and Jerry	*Airplane!*	Comedy
Zucker, David and Jerry	*Top Secret!*	Comedy
Zwick, Edward	*Glory*	Drama
	Are You My Mother? (And Two More P. D. Eastmann Classics)	Animated
	Brave Little Toaster, The	Animated
	Dr. Dolittle	Comedy
	Madeline	Animated
	Marx Brothers, The	Comedy
	Mighty, The	Drama
	Mouse and the Motorcycle, The	Comedy
	Parent Trap, The	Comedy
	Road Construction Ahead	Drama
	Robert McCloskey Library, The	Animated

ACKNOWLEDGMENTS

Special thanks to our spouses, Paul and Sarah, for putting up with countless hours of screenings—good and bad.

To Deb Shiau, our unbelievably capable assistant: Thank you for a wonderfully critical eye, and for getting us through the shoals of database design. To Lydia Wills and Jonathan Russo, our agents and friends: As always, thanks for having faith.

Annie Murphy, the former Editor-in-Chief of *Parents*, "got it" from the very beginning, and provided the guidance and leadership that made this book a reality. Laura Yorke and Lara Asher, our terrific editors, made the process a particularly pleasant one. Carolyn Foley, our copy editor, did a smart, thorough, and sensitive job.

To our friends, Elizabeth Havales, Rich Langsam, Zeno Levy, Nina Lehman, Ava Seave, Nancy Segal, Bert Schachter, and David Storey: Thank you for your recommendations, and for putting up with our retort, "Maybe in the next edition!"

ABOUT THE AUTHORS

Steve Cohen is a managing director at Scholastic Inc., and serves on the White House literacy initiative, "Prescription for Reading Partnership." He was part of the start-up team of *Scholastic Parent & Child* magazine, and launched the Parent Bookshelf and the "Everything You Always Wanted to Know About Preschool, Kindergarten, First Grade" series of books. He is the author of *Learn-to-Read Treasure Hunts* and coauthored the bestselling *Getting In!* and *Getting to the Right Job*. He teaches at the Stanford Professional Publishing Course, has taught in the M.B.A. program at Fordham University, and graduated from Brown University. He lives with his wife and two children in New York City.

Patricia S. McCormick reviews books and movies for *Parents* magazine. She was a regular contributor to the "Taking the Children" feature in the Arts & Leisure section of the *New York Times*, and has written for *Town & Country, Reader's Digest, Parenting,* and *Mademoiselle*. She has received degrees from Rosemont College, Columbia University, and the New School. She teaches creative writing at a public elementary school in New York. Her first novel, a young adult book, will be published by Front Street Books. She lives with her husband and two children in New York City.